BUSINESS IN A VIRTUAL WORLD

Business in a Virtual World

Exploiting information for competitive advantage

Fiona Czerniawska

and

Gavin Potter

MACMILLAN
Business

First published 1998 by
MACMILLAN PRESS LTD
Houndmills, Basingstoke, Hampshire RG21 6XS
and London
Companies and representatives
throughout the world

ISBN 0–333–72121–7 hardcover

A catalogue record for this book is available
from the British Library.

This book is printed on paper suitable for recycling and
made from fully managed and sustained forest sources.

10 9 8 7 6 5 4 3 2 1
07 06 05 04 03 02 01 00 99 98

Editing and origination by
Aardvark Editorial, Mendham, Suffolk

Printed and bound in Great Britain by
Creative Print and Design (Wales) Ebbw Vale

For My Mother
FCz

For Jane
GSMP

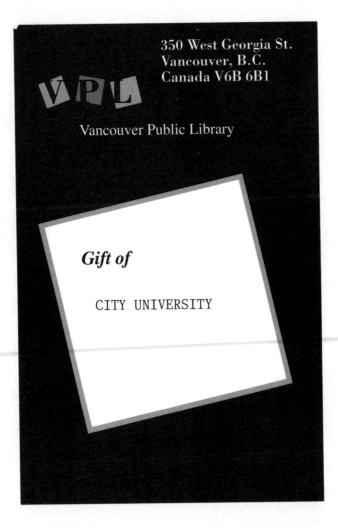

Contents

Preface

Every business consists of two types of element: the physical and the virtual. The physical elements are items such as buildings, machinery and people; the virtual elements are items such as information about customers, knowledge about how to get the best from a manufacturing process and the rights to exploit a particular invention.

The information revolution provides organisations with an unparalleled opportunity to move elements of their business from the physical domain to the virtual domain. No longer does the development of new products have to be done on paper, no longer do you have to sell to your customers within shops, no longer do you have to keep large stocks of every item that you sell. Almost every element of a business can be converted from the physical into information that is stored and manipulated within a computer.

Once that transition is made, new laws of economics take over. Information can be manipulated in ways that would be impossible with a physical object, information can be transmitted around the world at phenomenal speed, information can be duplicated and sold many times over without incurring additional costs. These attributes of information mean that organisations that embrace the virtual world can play to a different set of rules, rules that are often stacked heavily in their favour.

Yet despite the enormity of the potential changes, our management methods are still firmly rooted in the physical. We can, for example, measure, account for and depreciate physical assets, yet there is no agreed method for accounting for the information we maintain on our customers, or indeed any other information, assets that in many organisations far exceed the value of the physical goods they sell.

The work that we do with organisations has made us realise that all businesses are undergoing, or about to undergo, a fundamental revolution, a revolution so enormous that it dwarfs any changes since the Industrial Revolution took place in the 19th century. Businesses will increasingly move their assets and processes from the physical domain to the virtual domain, new laws of economics will take over, and different rules and business models will apply.

The purpose of this book is to open your eyes to the revolution that is taking place, a revolution that will affect every organisation whether large or small, national or international, manufacturing or service.

Part I – The New Economics of Information – examines why companies should move their assets from the physical domain to the virtual domain, and the new laws that will apply once their assets are transferred. Part II – The Virtual Business in Action – describes how the leading edge companies are exploiting the new laws of economics to restructure radically the industries within which they operate, and Part III – Exploiting the Virtual Potential of Your Business – describes some of the new management tools that will be required to operate successfully once the transition is made.

Acknowledgements

In writing this book, we have of course drawn heavily on our experiences and those of our colleagues and our clients. We are pleased to acknowledge the enormous debt that we owe to each and every one. The views contained within this book are, however, our own, and are not necessarily the views of the organisations for which we work. This is a book that looks to the future, and there are as many different views of the future as there are people thinking them.

As great a debt must be paid to the information revolution. This book was produced by two people using two computers and making extensive use of the facilities offered by the Internet to communicate. Without the ability to transfer the authoring process from the physical to the virtual, this book could not have been completed so quickly. Our thanks go to all the pioneers of the information revolution that made this possible.

And finally our thanks go to our partners and families for their support, patience and tolerance over the past year.

Introduction:
Information and the
Virtual Business

When Galileo first looked up at the night sky through a telescope, he saw that the universe was made of many more stars than anyone had realised:

> [I saw] other stars in myriads which have never been seen before, and which surpass the old, previously known, stars in number more than ten times.[1]

Business today is experiencing the same kind – and magnitude – of revelation. The information revolution now means that we can look at any part of our business – whether an investment decision, an office building or an individual product – and examine all the individual bits of information that make it up: we can attribute costs to a single activity or good; we can watch the shopping behaviour of individual customers in our stores; we can evaluate the return from a complex range of marketing activities. Like Galileo, we are surprised at what we see. What we thought were markets turn out to be complex, interdependent systems; what we thought was an organisation turns out to be an interactive group of individuals. There is a whole new – 'virtual' – universe out there, every bit of information a new star waiting to examined, understood and made use of. It is a universe which will challenge fundamentally (and already is challenging) many of our existing ideas about doing business. It is a universe that offers immense possibilities and massive dangers. The companies that do not explore and exploit it will fail.

Whether you work in bulk chemicals or software, the airline business or supermarket retailing, financial services or manufacturing, you and your competitors are finding new ways of using information that radically overturn the existing order. It is no longer sufficient to be the largest, to have the best products or the most efficient marketing. It is no longer sufficient to have the most established brand, the lowest costs or the best customer service. Our consulting experience suggests that, wherever you are and whoever you are, you are vulnerable to a competitor who uses information to overturn the established order in your market. Wherever we look, we see businesses that were once leaders in their fields – by virtue of their size or their low production costs – wiped out, sometimes almost overnight, by a competitor who has managed to harness information in order to secure a competitive advantage.

Take, for example, the story of People Express, the American airline company. It rose from nowhere, based on an innovative proposition of cheap, no-frills service coupled with radical methods of empowering their employees. For years, this combination looked set to succeed, and the People Express share price rose from $8.50 at start-up to $22 at the end of 1983. By 1983 People Express was one of the most profitable airlines in the business; soon it was the fifth largest carrier in the USA. However, in 1984, American Airlines launched their reservation system, called Sabre. This enabled American Airlines to collect information on a daily basis showing how full each of their flights had become. By using this information to predict sales, they were able to charge a wider range of prices and still fill their planes. If a particular flight was not selling well, they lowered their prices. If sales had exceeded expectations, they increased their prices. By using prices in this new way ('yield management'), they maximised the profit obtained from each flight. They could charge (when appropriate) lower prices than their lowest-price competitors and still generate more profits. Don Burr, the Chief Executive of People Express, and other commentators have no doubt that yield management was instrumental in putting them out of business: in 1986 People Express was taken over by Texas Air Corporation. By using information in a new way, American Airlines were able to transform an industry: competitors without such information lost out or had to change. There are few carriers left which do not practise this brand of 'yield management' today. Indeed, American Airlines have been so successful at this practice that it is now a service that they offer to other airlines. This way of doing business is spreading: hotels, car hire companies and holiday tour companies are all now beginning to practise their own versions of yield management; even one of our local restaurants charges a different price for each dish depending on the probable number of customers at a particular time in the evening.

Harnessing accurate and instantaneous information about the sales of their products enables these organisations to gain a significant competitive advantage. More often than not, it is also a sustainable strategy, as the initial competitive advantage leads to others: American Airlines can, by practising sophisticated real-time pricing of their products, gain further information about how the volume of sales varies depending on the price charged, information that can be used to develop ever more sophisticated pricing models and to establish a lead that their competitors find very difficult to match.

But this is not the only way in which organisations have used information to change fundamentally the way in which their industries operate. Sam Walton opened his first store in 1962 and, by the mid-1990s, Wal-Mart had become the world's leading retailer. The strategies that fuelled this growth are well known: putting stores into towns that were ignored by rival retailers; keeping prices down; saturating areas before moving on; empowering staff. What is less well known is how Wal-Mart has used information to revolutionise the supply chain to its stores. The insight here was to link information directly from stores to distribution centres, which enabled a new method of distribution – 'cross-docking' – to be introduced. Using this method, goods are centrally ordered, delivered to one side of a distribution centre and then transferred into cages for delivery to individual shops on the other side. As a result, one full lorry has to make fewer trips to a store than do several half empty lorries making many trips to a store; inventory has also been cut. This, of course, also means that Wal-Mart has to track several thousand parcels, cases and packages. However, capturing information on where each parcel was, and where it was supposed to go, enabled Wal-Mart to revolutionise the economics of their supply chain, providing them with a significant competitive advantage. Again, the advantage has proved sustainable: as other retailers have adopted similar principles, Wal-Mart has gone several stages further. Rather than link store requirements to central distribution centres, they are now linked directly to the computers of the firm's main suppliers, thereby reducing ordering times still further and allowing just-in-time replenishment systems to be introduced. Wal-Mart's distribution costs are estimated at 3 per cent of sales, compared with an industry average of nearer 5 per cent. In a business such as retailing, with its wafer-thin margins, these differences, as Wal-Mart so clearly demonstrates, can make all the difference between success and failure. Wal-Mart is now using sophisticated forecasting models to try to predict sales patterns so that goods can be ordered in advance of requirements, further reducing stock requirements and improving the responsiveness of their supply chain.

There are many lessons that underlie Wal-Mart's successful use of information to revolutionise its industry, but perhaps the most important to us is the sustainable nature of the advantage achieved. By identifying the information requirements required to break the industry paradigm, and by then using that information to change the way in which it does business, Wal-Mart has given itself a competitive advantage which – just like American Airlines – it has been able to sustain over a number of years. This is one of the most fundamental aspects of exploiting information. It is not a one-off exercise (like cost-reduction or business process re-engineering), but – as we will demonstrate during the course of this book – one which creates a virtuous circle that ensures a business continues to stay ahead.

In fact, information is causing an even more fundamental revolution in many sectors. Why should customers go to an insurance broker to purchase insurance when all the quotes are available to them at the cost of a local telephone call? Why should they go to a travel agent when descriptions of the holidays available, together with the lowest price quotes, are available in their own home? Why should a customer go to a local branch of a bank when they can obtain all the information that they need from the local automatic teller machine (or, even better, from the comfort of their armchair)? Once you start thinking in this way, it is difficult to think of any industry – with the possible exception of hairdressing – where it is a requirement for the customer to have face-to-face contact with the supplier. Even medicine can – and is – reducing the need for direct contact between doctor and patient by the use of telesensing equipment which can monitor the vital signs of a patient being operated upon. Disintermediation (that is, removal of the middle man) is already happening and is set to continue. Moreover, the more savvy customers have started to use information to their advantage. Why purchase a single item, for example, and pay single item rates for it when you can identify fellow consumers, club together and thereby demand a volume discount? Some users of the Internet are already banding together in this way in order to drive prices down.

In other industries, it is not so much the business processes that are changing but the fundamental structure of the industry itself, which is being reshaped by those companies which have grasped the principles of the information revolution. The Internet, for example, allows organisations to share information with their customers at close to zero cost, and one might expect that, for such an important and talked about new market, the big players of the computer industry – the IBMs, the Digitals and the AT&Ts – would dominate. However, the software industry, revolutionised by this no-cost way of distributing information and software, is now not dominated by these players but by a 25-year-old graduate who started with barely a cent to his name. In 1994, Illinios graduate Marc Andreessen literally gave away his product to millions of Internet users. Today, he runs an organisation called Netscape Communications worth $2bn dollars. As the *Wall Street Journal* put it, the day after the organisation was floated on the New York stock exchange in August 1995:

> it took General Dynamics Corp. 43 years to become a corporation worth today's $2.7 billion: it took Netscape Communications Corp. about a minute.[2]

How can organisations spring up so quickly? Again, we would argue that it is the rise in the power of information and the use to which it is put that has transformed the software industry. Andreessen's insights were two-fold: first, he realised that it is possible to distribute information over the Internet at virtually no cost; second, he realised that, in world where manufacturing and distribution costs are negligible, the most important competitive advantage is to 'own' your customers – hence the policy of literally giving away the product – and to 'own' the market – in which developing the industry standard is clearly enormously important. The money is not, he reasoned, made from the product but from the follow-on sales (in the form of support, upgrades and, in particular, sales to other organisations that wish to licence the product for their customers). Never mind more familiar strategies (sell existing products to new markets; sell new products to existing markets) – competitive advantage in this context comes from transforming the 'rules of the game' almost overnight, throwing away the old way of doing things and creating new industry paradigms.

Many of the executives whom we have interviewed argue that software is somehow different and that such radical shake-ups could not possibly happen in their industry – but why not? Although, so far, this method of distribution has had a major impact only on the software industry, there are many other businesses that trade in information:

books, magazines and newspapers, plus the less obvious ones such as the music and financial services industries. In fact, any industry that sells products that can be converted into bits and transmitted down the telephone lines faces a fundamental revolution in the way in which it gets its information to consumers. Nor, we would argue, are such changes going to be limited to these information-based industries, because even the most 'physical' industries have an information aspect to them. A ball-bearing is not just a lump of processed metal but has measurements, a weight, a track record. A hamburger consists of information about its calories and nutritional value as well as the meat and flour that make up its contents. A visit to a hairdresser consists of information about how a particular cut will look to others as much as it involves the physical styling of hair. An electrical battery consists of information about how much energy it contains and how long it will last, together with the metal and chemicals that make up its shape. Every product sold consists of information that can be sold and manipulated, along with the atoms which make up its physical structure.

The recognition of this and the exploitation of the information aspects of products are beginning to transform even the most physical of businesses. It is hard to imagine a more physical process than parcel distribution – moving packages from A to B – but is that really what a distribution company is selling? FedEx realised that its customers do not just want a parcel to be delivered safely to a specified address in a specified time: they also want to be able to find out exactly how the delivery of the parcel is progressing. FedEx is not merely a delivery service: it is selling confidence that the package has been delivered safely to its destination. As a result, the company put its parcel tracking system on to the Internet, so that any customer can find out exactly where in the world their package has reached. By providing this information to their customers, FedEx are able to give their customers the confidence that their packages have arrived. A new use of information has again led to a competitive advantage. Nor is it difficult to imagine additional services that could be provided when competitors started to provide a similar service. Once again, information does not just give a one-off gain but sustainable benefits.

FedEx's approach is not the only way in which organisations are using information to transform the production and distribution of physical products. Indeed, for many corporations, one of the big battlegrounds of the 1990s is improving their time to market. The pace of change is becoming more hectic: no sooner have you launched your product than your competitors launch similar products – the life-cycles of products are getting shorter. Companies that can launch more products more quickly than their competitors will win. Again, it is an area in which the use of information is a revolutionising force: enlightened companies have realised that the trick of winning this battle is to hold off converting their product into its physical form until the last possible moment. Information – unlike physical goods – can be transmitted round the world literally at the speed of light; it can be manipulated with computers far faster than any physical object can be changed; it can be duplicated at no cost, whereas reproducing physical goods is a slow and expensive business. It makes sense, therefore, for as many activities as possible – product development, sales, marketing and distribution – to be performed in the virtual world, thereby increasing speed and decreasing costs. Boeing is just one of the companies already doing this: instead of building complex physical models of their new aircraft to test in stress rigs and wind tunnels, the company has developed a virtual design environment. By building and testing models of their new aircraft in the virtual, rather than the physical, world, Boeing have been able to cut down substantially the time it takes to design each new component. Not only that, but the exploration of designs in a virtual environment is enabling considerably more designs to be tested under a wider range of conditions. Transforming what would normally have been a physical product into information and manipulating the information has given Boeing a competitive advantage. Again, it is easy to see that improvements to the tools they use within their virtual environment to test and manipulate their designs will lead to a long-term competitive advantage. By the time their rivals catch up with this particular approach to design, Boeing will have been able to apply the learning it has acquired in the meantime to stay ahead.

In fact, a whole new industry has grown up around this principle of keeping products in the information domain until the last possible moment. It is now possible to have machines that will take designs directly from a computer and then manufacture them in small slices by the process of laser sintering. The range of materials that can be manipulated in this way currently remains small, but, as the technology improves, it is possible to imagine all sorts of item being designed and produced in this way. Similarly, while it is likely that these types of process will initially be confined to high-value products (prototypes and small one-offs), it will be applied to cheaper and cheaper items as this method of production takes off. It may eventually be possible for individuals to order exactly what they want rather than buying what the manufacturer has already decided to produce. The age of mass-production will truly be dead; let's welcome the age of mass-customisation.

Of course, you may be thinking that all this talk of virtual design environments and laser sintering may not be particularly relevant to your business today, but we would like to argue that the underlying principles illustrated by these examples are already very real. Even the most prosaic of industries can benefit by keeping its products in the information world. It is now possible, for example, to go into a store in New York and, by typing in your physical measurements, get a pair of Levi jeans produced that exactly fit you: 'Your left leg is half an inch longer than your right leg? No problem, sir, we'll provide a pair that will fit you exactly in a few days.' Rather than having to keep every conceivable shape of jeans in stock, Levi's can now take information directly from their customer and convert it at the last possible moment into what the customer requires. Service is improved (customers get what they want) and stockholding and distribution costs are reduced, so everyone wins. Companies that are using information from their customers to design products that exactly meet their customers' needs are already gaining a significant competitive advantage.

Not surprisingly, the knowledge-based industries are also beginning to harness and exploit information. By storing information globally and providing sophisticated search and access mechanisms, they can ensure that – as consultancies are proud to claim – 'at the end of every day, every one of our consultants has access to all the knowledge of every other consultant'. But why should this advantage be confined purely to the pure knowledge-based industries? Why shouldn't all salesmen know what the most successful ways of clinching a deal with a new product are? Why shouldn't all the manufacturing plants know of the best and most successful ways of manufacturing a new product? Why isn't all knowledge shared around the organisation? Pricing, channels to market, customer service, distribution and costs of manufacturing, the development of new products, the move from mass-production to mass-customisation – these can all be transformed by sharing information. How, for example, does your organisation gather information from (or about) its customers? And what does it do with this information once it has been gathered? Many of the examples we have looked at – American Airlines, FedEx, Levi's – involve providing information to customers in a new way. At the end of the 20th century, information on customers and the best way to do business is a true source of sustainable competitive advantage: if your organisation cannot collect such information, and use it in continually more sophisticated ways, you do not have a long-term future. The economics of collecting, processing and using information are now so cheap that if you do not harness your organisation's energies to using information, your competitors surely will. If you are not first, you will find it extremely difficult to catch up. As you take the first steps to capturing and using information, your competitors will be taking the second. Tesco, the UK's leading supermarket chain, launched a loyalty card in 1995. Although its main rival, J Sainsbury, announced the launch of its card the following year, Tesco was able to use its initial advantage to announce that they were going to use their loyalty card as the base for offering banking services: the information and experience Tesco had gathered in 1 year helped the company stay ahead and has left their main competitor in the unenviable position of following their lead.

How many times a year does your board discuss new ways of using information? When they do discuss the subject, how much of the time is spent discussing the strategic importance of information? How much of the time is spent discussing the cost of information technology? Our experience suggests that the primary topic at such board meetings is about why the costs of the IT department are always going up and the results of all this expenditure seem to make so very little difference? Boards have not been brought up in the information age – where technology can make information cheaply available, where the power of their child's Nintendo game is greater than the power of the computers that took man to the moon, and where the techniques for analysing the information gathered are now infinitely more sophisticated than they were 20, 10 or even 5 years ago. Most organisations do not possess the right sorts of visionary who will identify how their information can be used to transform their business. How many of you still think that information is 'detail', of interest only to the 'bean-counters' in your organisation? How many of you still think that it is the provenance of the IT department, that information is synonymous with technology?

The aim of this book is to change your mind. If we want to do one thing, it is to make you realise that information is the single most important asset your organisation possesses, that its uses are limitless and its implications enormous, and that you are almost certainly under-exploiting its potential at the moment. This is not a theory and it is certainly not just another management fad. This is for real. Technology has revolutionised the costs of using information; processing power is now over 1000 times cheaper than it was in 1980; information can, and is, collected electronically at almost every transaction that happens both between a business and its customers and within a business; new techniques make access to this information and using this information ever more cheap and effective.

This information is there to be used. Those organisations that use it will discover an invaluable source of competitive advantage. Those that fail to exploit the opportunity – or even are slow to realise it – are destined to spiral in an ever more depressing game of catch-up. The old business paradigm is being destroyed. In the 15th century, the medieval guilds were put out of business by the advent of the first information revolution (the advent of printing, which made it impossible for them to hold on to their secrets). Likewise, the second information revolution at the end of the 20th century will put out of business those who try to ignore it, those who still try to play by the old rules.

This book, therefore, is intended to be a blueprint for a different kind of company: one based on information rather than physical assets; one which sells information as much as (or more so than) physical products; one which uses information to create new markets and find new ways of communicating with its customers. This is the virtual company, an organisation that is constructed out of the key building block of the next decade – information.

Notes

1. Galileo Galilei, *The Starry Messenger* (1610), quoted in *The Faber Book of Science*, edited by John Carey, London: Faber & Faber, 1995.
2. *Wall Street Journal*, 10 August, 1995.

Part I
The New Economics of Information

2 The Technological Foundations

This is book is about building a virtual business, not about the technology that enables you to do so. In fact, we hope we mention computers, the Internet and the other bits and pieces of technological plumbing that you need to process information rather less often than other books of this sort. However, at the same time, we have to recognise that without technology none of this would be possible. Building the virtual business, therefore, inevitably involves understanding something about the technological trends that have underpinned the information revolution, and which are now driving our ability to process and share information ever more quickly, and to see where those trends might lead in the future.

One company more than any other has dominated the information revolution, dictated its pace and enabled the enormous changes that we see around us to occur. That company is not Bill Gates' Microsoft, despite the fact that almost all of us use its software, nor is it IBM, despite its early dominance of computing and information processing. That company is Intel – the makers of the chips that reside in most of the world's computers.

To understand the birth of the information revolution, one has to go back to 1958 and the invention of the integrated circuit by Jack St Clair Kilby, a Texas Instruments engineer. Up to that point, the only way to manipulate information was to use a complex combination of capacitors, resistors and transistors, physically joined together on a printed circuit board. Anyone who remembers the 1950s and 60s will recall the size of even the most trivial information-processing devices such as record players: they were so big that they used to dominate our living rooms. The integrated circuit did away with the need to create such large and cumbersome physical devices for the handling of information by placing many thousands of components on to a single silicon chip. Integrated circuits can be created to perform virtually any information-processing function and, by combining these integrated circuits, information-processing devices of incredible complexity (like the computer) can be quickly and cheaply created. It is this invention which has driven the pace of the information revolution and has enabled the unprecedented changes that have occurred to take place.

And what a pace it has been. In 1965, just 7 years after the invention of the integrated circuit, Gordon Moore, one of the co-founders of Intel, formulated what has since come to be known as Moore's law: that the number of transistors (the main electronic building block) contained within an integrated circuit would double every 18 months. He based this observation on the fact that it took approximately 18 months to 2 years to develop a new fabricating plant for integrated circuits and that the level of improvement in the ability to pack components on to an integrated circuit from one generation of fabricating plant to another was approximately double. History has proved Moore to be correct: when the 4004 chip was launched in 1971, it contained 2,300 transistors, but by 1996 (which saw the launch of the Pentium Pro P6 chip), microprocessors of approximately 5.5 million transistors could be crowded into the same space (Figure 2.1).

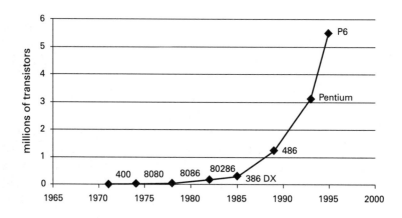

Figure 2.1   Since the 1970s, the number of transistors in an integrated circuit has doubled every 18 months

As US Vice-President Al Gore pointed out in a recent speech, if Rolls Royce cars had improved at the same speed, they would now be able to travel at millions of miles an hour; and as one wag in the audience retorted, they would also be only 0.1 mm long. This comparison illustrates one of the fundamental and most important facets of the information revolution: if we can divorce information from the physical substrate on which it has traditionally resided – in other words, if we can work in the virtual rather than the physical world – we can start to imagine and achieve quantum leaps in improvement in performance. Nothing exemplifies better the significance of this shift from the physical to the virtual than Moore's law itself. Making improvements solely in the physical domain cannot and will not yield improvements of anything like the same order of magnitude.

Sceptics among you may be wondering whether this level of achievement will continue: in fact, despite the physical problems of working at this tiny level (where measurements are made in tens of atoms), the level of progress shows no sign of abating. The next two jumps in performance are already achievable under laboratory conditions, and considerable effort is currently being expended to replicate them in commercial terms. Intel invested some $2.4bn in 1994, yet, despite increasing investment to produce the next generation of chip, still continues to show a healthy return on its investments. As the company's CEO, Andy Grove, has published a book entitled *Only the Paranoid Survive*, it seems unlikely that we are going to see any cessation of the frenetic pace of improvement in the integrated circuit industry.

It is worth considering exactly what this means to the average business. As we have already noted, the power of the computer sitting on your desktop today is probably greater than that of a supercomputer 20 years ago. A Sega games machine is considerably more powerful than the computer that helped to land the first man on the moon in 1969. Such comparisons may be familiar, but they still illustrate the immensity of the change that has occurred in the last three decades of the 20th century. What is less well recognised is that we have also seen a transformation in the power available to perform analysis. Personal computers started to take hold in the early 1980s – a mere 15 or so years ago – but is there a desk in your office today that doesn't have one on it? The first PCs could analyse approximately one page of calculations; in the late 1980s and early 1990s, they were used to manage the departmental budgets – the equivalent of perhaps 10–20 pages of calculations. By the mid-1990s, there had been a complete revolution: it is now possible for virtually any organisation to download all its management information and manipulate it in seconds. A large retailer might have 500 stores and sell a total of 20,000 different lines. It is now possible to download and manipulate the weekly sales by product and outlet on to a PC costing no more than $3,000. In a few years' time, it will be possible to analyse, on a daily basis, individual transaction data from an Electronic Point of Sale (EPOS) system, on a similarly priced computer. This computing power is revolutionising the way in which businesses analyse themselves. Why select the best options for your business through a combination of trial and error (and gut-feel), when you can use this computing power to evaluate each scenario exhaustively? Leading edge organisations are using such power to develop and test not only complex scenarios, but also – through using sophisticated mathematical techniques (such as genetic algorithms – programs that literally breed with each other to produce stronger and better solutions) in order to identify new ways of solving long-standing business problems. Doing this may take a lot of computing power, but if it is so cheap anyway, who cares?

However, while the growth of computing power has been apparently smooth and unrelenting, the evolution of the way in which we exploit the information held on a computer has been less predictable. Since the introduction of the first business computers in the 1950s, there have been three dramatic and fundamental shifts in the way in which information has been managed. The first period – from the 1950s to the 1980s – focused on centralised computing power: it was the era of the big mainframe, guarded by the acolytes and high priests of the data-processing department. Although substantial but comparatively simple transactions (such as billing and invoicing customers) were automated, few people – even the technical pundits – foresaw the potential advantages that moving from the physical to the information world would bring. One pundit famously predicted that the world would only need three computers.

Developments in technology meant that, by the beginning of the 1980s, it was possible to produce computers small enough and cheap enough to sit on an individual's desk. And, because the amount of power that can be purchased for the same price doubles roughly every 18 months (in line with Moore's law), the personal computing paradigm quickly became the dominant way of working both in the office and at home. Once again, key industry players – as well as myriad other organisations – failed to spot this shift from large mainframes to small personal computers. IBM, dominant throughout the previous decades, ceded control to two smaller organisations, Microsoft (from whom it licensed its operating system for its range of personal computers) and Intel (from whom it purchased the integrated circuits required to produce the machines). It was a loss of control that almost cost the company its business, and IBM is only now beginning to recover from the massive losses (both financial and in terms of reputation) that it suffered at the end of the 1980s. This was the era when swathes of the population were inducted in the use of computers and the information revolution. Small businesses could start to compete with large ones, as the physical trappings of business were automated – typing pools and secretaries became word-processing programs; telephonists became automated switchboards; and schools started introducing computers and computer training into the classroom. Information became cheaply available: encyclopaedias (such as Microsoft's Encarta) could be bought for around $75 whereas previously conventional encyclopaedias in book form, which contained about the same amount of information, cost many thousands of dollars.

Now it seems we have crossed the threshold into the third phase of the information revolution: networking of these individual computers together. What this means is that not only will you have massive processing power sitting on your desk in the office, or in your study at home, but you will also be able to receive and transmit vast volumes of information. This development threatens to be just as much of a paradigm shift as the first two stages in computer evolution. As before, those organisations which do not take advantage of the opportunities it brings, or which ignore the threats that it poses, are likely to fail, and those which can foresee and exploit the changes are becoming leaders in their markets.

It is important to be specific about what we mean by networking. Every day we are being subjected to an immense amount of hype about the Internet and its ability to revolutionise the world. However, we should not forget that the Internet started out as, what many of those who used it perceived it to be, a 'free plaything' for the military and the academics trying to build a robust network in case the Cold War between the Soviet Union and America ever heated up into atomic conflagration. Nobody – yet – has worked out how to convert what is essentially a free model of networking into something that pays. As a consequence, the Internet is becoming over-used and is already starting to break down. Investments are being made, with many of the large telephone companies investing huge amounts of money to strengthen the backbone of the network, but these companies will undoubtedly expect to be paid and to achieve a return on this investment. How exactly this will be achieved, no one quite seems to know. There are suggestions that there should be more than one sort of net, with perhaps a 'first-class' net for businesses (for which they will have to pay), and a 'second-class' net for the ordinary person using such facilities from home. Others have proposed that advertisers might be prepared to pay, and this could be used to fund the expansion of the net. At the moment, that proposition looks of dubious value, as there is little evidence that such advertising pays. New wave digerati economists are desperately seeking to release the true power of this medium by identifying fresh ways to translate old physical media (print, paper and television) into new forms that can exploit both the interactivity of the Internet and its ability to address individuals rather than mass-markets. The first attempts seem interesting: type a word into one of the major search engines (which assist you to find information on the Internet), and targeted advertising will be flashed on to your screen. Thus, when you type in the name of a holiday resort, advertisements for cheap fares are flashed up. Whether an economic model will be found which makes the Internet a commercial proposition remains to be seen, but attempts are clearly being made in the right direction.

More fundamentally, however, what this technological plumbing does show is that there is an interesting and new method of communication. It would be a brave person who would attempt to predict exactly what form the technology will take to support communications between individuals and organisations, but it would be an even braver organisation that ignored this phase of the information revolution. Companies are investing many billions of dollars in replacing existing copper wires with optical fibres capable of carrying many millions of times as much traffic. In addition, the introduction of an agreed standard for the transmission of digital information, asynchronous transmission mode (ATM), has meant that companies can afford to make huge investments in building the silicon switches and routers that can manage the gigabytes of information that will need to be transmitted to enable this communication to take place. AT&T, Fujitsu, IBM and all the other manufacturers of telecommunications equipment are making precisely that investment. Changes are happening. Even if we cannot predict exactly how they will occur, we are confident that occur they will.

So far, we have concentrated on the cutting edge of the information revolution, the vast changes in the processing power available and our ability to communicate with each other in the virtual realm. However, it is as important to remember that, as the price/performance ratio improves, it is not only leading edge technology that becomes cheaper – so do technologies that were expensive some years ago, and this means that these can now also be exploited in new ways. It was not perhaps surprising that the market for slide rules (two pieces of wood that used together could perform multiplications and divisions, for those of you too young to remember) collapsed with the introduction of the pocket calculator. Less predictable – especially to the Swiss – was the fact that the bottom could drop out of the physical (cogs and mechanical gears) watch market when the Japanese realised that they could convert the information contained within a conventional timepiece into digital bits: not only were digital watches more accurate, but they were also cheaper to produce (they are so cheap now, that they are often given away in Christmas crackers). It took the reinvention of the watch as a fashion accessory by Swatch to restore Swiss pride and something approaching their original place in the industry.

History is currently repeating itself with the introduction of digital cameras. They are not currently of such high quality as conventional cameras, and they still cost two to three times as much, but prices halved in 1997 alone and, already, companies are bringing out printers to produce prints of a high quality direct from these cameras. Which consumers are going to choose to send their films away to the processing laboratory when they can see the results immediately on a computer and produce similar quality prints at home? Why spend time making marginal improvements to the quality of films in the physical domain when moving the process to the virtual domain offers orders of magnitude improvement in cost, quality and consumer convenience? What price Kodak shares when faced with such an onslaught?

It is always tempting to think of the high-end technology when considering the information revolution, but industries are being transformed just as much – if not more so – by low-end technologies. The competitive threats facing your business will not come just from competitors using more sophisticated analytical techniques or from better methods of communicating with customers, or even from their exploitation of the latest, most expensive technologies. Your business is just as much under threat from organisations that steal a march by introducing cheap low-end technology that shifts a process or product from the physical domain to the virtual domain. We have already talked about how Moore's law has accurately predicted for the past 25 years the development of the high-end personal computer, but we also need to consider the implications of Moore's law on the low-end integrated circuit.

As well as seeing the ever-increasing power of personal computers, we have also seen the introduction of integrated circuits into many different goods. The pocket calculator and digital watch were early examples of this and, in both cases, the aim was to convert physical methods into virtual-based methods of performing the same task (the watch tells the time; the calculator gives the results of arithmetic calculations). Here and in other similar devices, the introduction of a new way of processing information adds value; all (or virtually all) of the old product is replaced by the new. In the 1990s these integrated circuits are now so cheap that they can replace many physical products. BMWs now contain chips that enable the engine to be tuned thousands of times every second; other cars contain chips that mean that the car's 'personality' can be changed from a souped-up sports car to a sedate family saloon at the press of a button. Washing machines and other similar value goods all now contain chips that claim to make them better in some way – safer, more efficient, faster. The battleground of the information revolution is thus moving further and further down the price chain, and organisations are now grappling with how to apply the opportunities of the information revolution to even the lowest price goods.

Once again, it is the rapid fall in processing costs that is making all this possible. A smart card the size of a conventional credit card can be produced for about $7, but contains the same processing power as the Apple II computer that launched the personal computing revolution in the early 1980s at a cost of several thousand dollars. Give everyone a smart card in their wallet, and what are the implications? Current thinking revolves around their use as payment systems (smart cards are hard to fake and transactions made with them are very cheap to process, especially in comparison with physical cash), but there will be other applications – medical records, social security details and so on. And if the cost of a smart card falls to just a few cents – and this is not far off – what might the applications then be? People are already looking at the next generation of technology. What about radio transmitters that cost a few cents to produce? Every product, from an expensive car to the humble lettuce, could have such a transmitter incorporated within its label, enabling the manufacturer, retailer or whoever to track its progress. Such technology could revolutionise the supply chain of virtually any business. Just-in-time delivery systems could be refined so that the arrival of goods could be predicted within seconds, checkouts at supermarkets could count the price of goods simply by passing them under a radio-receiving device. Lettuces could even be monitored for freshness, or a history of their delivery could be printed out for sceptical consumers. Known as radio frequency identification devices, these are already being used to track animals, tag convicted criminals and lock cars. If you do not start thinking through the implications of this technology, you can be sure that someone else will.

However, it is not just the technology itself or the products that we incorporate into it which have changed remarkably, even since the beginning of the 1990s. What has also been revolutionised is the ability of organisations to collect, store and exploit information about each and everyone of us. From the 1950s to 80s, information was collected and stored on large mainframes. Systems focused around the transactions they had to perform (billing systems being concentrated around billing, bank account systems being based around each bank account and so on). As a result, most organisations could not link different items of information together, even those about the same customer. The 1980s saw a change: companies wanted to combine all the information they had collected about individuals in order to analyse spending patterns and cross-sell products. This was a major task, but by the mid-1990s most organisations could collect information by customer and store it in a database. (It is worth pausing to consider how many databases contain your personal information – we counted literally hundreds that hold our details, and those are just the ones that we know about.)

The 1990s have seen another revolution. The networking of devices has enabled organisations to start to collect information at a much more detailed level, starting at the point where the transaction occurs. Electronic data input devices are used to collect information, which is then transmitted back to a central computer so that one's actions can be monitored, the most common system in use being the EPOS device used by retailers. Information collected from the bar code reader is used not only for stock control, but also, by using a technique called market basket analysis, to build up profiles of the individuals shopping in a store. The introduction of loyalty cards means that this information can now be linked directly to the individual and be used to target you with marketing materials specifically aimed at encouraging you to spend more. Similarly, when you shop for insurance and other financial products, your details are automatically entered on to a computer. Yes, the computer will quickly work out your premiums, but it will also store that information so that it can be analysed and sold to other organisations that might wish to make use of it. Networking makes collecting and distributing information both easy and cheap.

Given this digital abundance – a world where the cost of information halves and computing power doubles every 18 months and where the availability of information is ever increasing – what is stopping a faster uptake of digital technology?

We see two major obstacles to this. The first is a lack of imagination. Look at the press today (1998); some 90 per cent of its reporting on the information revolution revolves around the Internet and the World Wide Web. Look at where today's talent is going. It is flooding like lemmings into the sexy subjects of multimedia, developing web browsers and so on. In short, it is moving into the technological plumbing as if this were the next gold rush. Changes to people's lives are not made by changes to technology but by the application and exploitation of that technology. We do not see the training, the university courses, the enthusiasm for understanding how this technology can be exploited.

The second is the software industry. Whereas factories and machines are the building blocks of economic life in the physical world, the building blocks of the virtual world are software programs. And the problem with software is that its development is essentially an art: people redesign and reinvent with alarming regularity. The industry is new. It has yet to develop specialist roles such as architects, structural engineers and quantity surveyors; it has yet to develop the concept (although people are trying) of reusable parts. As an industry of such fundamental importance to the future, it rests on remarkably shaky foundations. Nowhere is this better exemplified than in the millennium problem. Most of you reading this book will probably be aware that, come the year 2000, much of the software on which your business depends may fail to continue working. Much early and even comparatively recent software used only two digits to store the year part of a date. Come 2000, these dates will probably read 00 and cause untold and unknowable problems. We already have computer programs reporting that cans of baked beans have been on the shelf for 97 years because, when the life of a can of baked beans was added to today's date, it went past 99. There really is a problem here; if something is not done about it, many, many systems will fail. Imagine if these were buildings. It is not just the occasional building that will fail; it would be as if whole towns suddenly collapsed all round the world. Imagine how we would feel about the building industry if that occurred. Imagine the blame that we would pour over the architects of this disaster – and the software industry is just as important if not more so to modern day living.

However, despite this shaky foundation, the information revolution looks set to continue. The number of transistors on a chip will continue to double every 18 months; the cost of integrated circuits will continue to fall; it will become easier to communicate information; the amount of information collected on individuals will continue to increase. No one needs to be clairvoyant to make these predictions. What is much less certain is how business will exploit the opportunities that the information revolution brings, and respond to its threats. If you think you are at the cutting edge by putting the most powerful PCs on all your staff's desks, think again. If you think you have re-engineered the way you communicate with customers by setting up a website, think again. As we show in subsequent chapters, the information revolution is changing radically the way in which businesses are managed and the markets in which they compete. However much you have done to exploit technology and information so far, one thing we can guarantee is that it is nothing compared to what you will need to do in the future.

Summary

In this chapter, we have looked at how changes in technology have prepared the ground for both the virtual economy and the virtual company. There have been three main components to this:

❑ the continuous and continuing reduction in the cost of computing power, which now means that it is possible for companies to analyse easily volumes of data that only a handful of years ago would have required massive supercomputers;

❑ alongside this, a growth in the amount of data that are available to be analysed, a trend that started with the advent of PCs, has continued as information resources have been transferred to CDs, and is now making ever-increasing volumes of information available across networks such as the Internet;

❏ paradigm shifts in technology and the information that can be gathered by and stored on it not being confined to high-end technologies: even basic technology is becoming cheaper and smarter, changing some of the most mundane everyday goods.

Obstacles remain to making full use of the opportunities that these trends offer. Many companies lack the imagination to identify ways of exploiting this technology; the software that we need to exploit it is still comparatively immature and fragile; the economic models by which we earn profits from it are still uncertain. However, as computing power goes on becoming cheaper and information more available, technology is going to continue revolutionising the way in which we do business.

3 The Competitive Advantage of Information

In the James Bond film *Goldeneye,* a familiar scene takes an unfamiliar twist. The villain is preparing to destroy London: 'What's the game?,' asks Bond, assuming that it is the gold in the Bank of England vaults that is at stake. 'Oh no,' counters the bad guy, 'we're going to take all the information off all the computers across London': bank account details, share accounts, credit card numbers – it is information, not gold, which he is after. Of course, on this occasion the good guy wins, but it probably won't be long until someone tries something like this for real.

What the bad guy realised – and much of business is starting to catch up with his thinking – is that information is the most important asset of our society today. Whereas computers have provided individual companies with the opportunity to gain an edge over their immediate rivals, it is information which is starting to revolutionise the much wider competitive landscape. It is information which will be the single most important battlefield of business as we go into the next century. Whatever sector we are in, whatever markets, whatever products or services, information is starting to change radically the way in which we do business:

- A gas company loses half its hundreds of thousands of customers to a start-up with a small workforce but sophisticated customer management software.
- A group of manufacturers get together to pool their information on customers, with the aim of running joint marketing campaigns across their different industries.
- Airport outlets restock their shelves every hour, based on the destination of outgoing flights.

We could go on; information is changing the basic premises on which we manage all our businesses. One by one, established rules are falling, assumptions are being questioned and theories are being disproved:

> The command-and-control organization that first emerged in the 1870s might be compared to an organism held together by its shell. The corporation that is now emerging is being designed around a skeleton: *information*.[1]

In this chapter we will demonstrate just how widespread and fundamental these changes are by looking in detail at how they are affecting some of the lynchpins of our economic environment.

Breaking down the barriers to entry

Michael Porter's *Competitive Strategy* first appeared in 1980; it rapidly became one of the influential business books of recent years, establishing the framework for innumerable corporate strategies and influencing a generation of executives. In it, Porter identified six key barriers to entry that prevented competition and enabled the players in a particular sector to maintain their profits:

- economies of scale,
- capital requirements;
- product differentiation;
- access to distribution channels;
- government policy;
- switching costs.

Taking each one of these points in turn, it is instructive to see just how much has changed in the 18 years since the book was published.

From economies of scale to different scope

One of key principles of the competitive landscape throughout the 1970s and 80s was that the cost of production would decline as the volume of production increased. It therefore made sense to merge factories and companies together: the bigger you were, the more efficient you could be. However, the massive losses of a company such as IBM were just one of the more memorable nails in this particular coffin. Being big meant that you could not always respond to market changes sufficiently quickly (in this case, switching from producing expensive mainframe computers to cheap PCs). Rather than produce goods ever more cheaply, being big meant that you acquired an onerous management structure and a bureaucratic culture. Merging companies often created more barriers between functions than it dismantled.

History has shown that economies of scale are relevant only in markets where all the participants are playing by the same set of rules: as soon as someone invents a new – better – set of rules, it does not matter how efficient you are, you are still going to be out-manoeuvred. Bookshops are a good recent example of this. Up until very recently in the UK, the price of books was governed by what was known as the Net Book Agreement (NBA) – a quasi-voluntary agreement between all the companies (large and small) to sell books at the same price. The NBA meant that small bookshops in isolated areas could offer the same value to customers as the largest (and enjoy the same margins); the basis for competition was range rather than price. By the summer of 1996, a group of retailers had succeeded in breaking the agreement by discounting the most popular titles in an effort to tempt people into their stores. At this point, traditional economies of scale came into effect: the largest booksellers could afford to make the largest reductions because their sales per square metre were high enough to absorb the reduced margin on the discounted lines. Meanwhile, publishers, to protect their margins, significantly increased the recommended price of books – clearly to the detriment of the book-buying consumer. It would be a sorry state of affairs if it were not for the coincidental appearance of Internet-based booksellers, notably Amazon. Here was a company that was not obeying any of the implicit 'rules' of the industry. It had no shops, no sales staff in the traditional sense, but what it did have was a phenomenal range and costs so low that it could easily undercut the discounts offered by even the largest conventional bookshop, even though the number of volumes it processed might be significantly fewer. Economies of scale count for nothing in this new virtual environment where physical processes are replaced by information. Not suprisingly, other booksellers have had to respond in kind (playing by Amazon's rules rather than their own), by setting up their own Web-based outlets.

From capital requirements to knowledge requirements

The only resource that Porter considered, in developing his ideas on barriers to entry, was money. Finance was a scarce commodity which meant that those who had access to it had an immense competitive advantage. But today, raising finance is perhaps the least difficult of the tasks facing an organisation. With supply outstripping demand in the world's financial markets, it has become comparatively easy for an entrepreneur to find the capital he or she needs. As Ann Winbald, a partner in Hummer Winbald Venture Partners (who specialise in lending to high-tech companies) recently commented, 'These days, monetary capital is easy to come by – finding the intellectual capital is the hard part.'[2]

You only have to consider the number of new biotechnology stocks or the amount of money being poured into Internet start-up organisations to realise that chasing the next holy grail has effectively become the latest approach to investment. Many of the companies in which these investments are made trade at enormous price/earnings ratios even though they have never sold a thing. What these investments represent is the recognition that an organisation's key asset is not its economies of scale, its track record, its brand – or any of the other trump cards traditionally held by the incumbents in a market. What the investors are betting on is the organisation's knowledge – often pure, unadulterated knowledge, untouched by conventional commercial realities – which will potentially stand the accepted way of doing things on its head. It is the ability of an organisation to gather information (from itself, from its customers, from the market as a whole) and exploit the knowledge it can distil from this which is the new scarce resource. Financial muscle, a large labour force or a major manufacturing plant is much less valuable; in fact, as many companies with large quantities of physical assets are finding, these things are often a hindrance, an impediment to change.

All over the world, large organisations are recognising the importance of information. Take the case of Jose Ignacio Lopez, the former head of purchasing for General Motors who subsequently defected to Volkswagen. In the ensuing lawsuit, German prosecutors alleged that, when he and his team left their former employer, they took with them over 4,000 pages of computer print-out giving details of every part that Opel was purchasing from its suppliers. While the case has yet to be completed, Volkswagen agreed, early in 1997, to pay $100m in damages to General Motors and buy over $1bn of General Motors parts over the next 7 years. Take the case of Northwest Airlines versus American Airlines. In the first chapter of this book, we discussed how American Airlines' yield management system – the software that allows an airline to set prices according to the level of take-up for a particular flight – had given the company a winning edge over its competitors in the late 1980s. In 1989–90, Northwest Airlines began revamping its yield management system. Between 1990 and 1992, the company hired a total of 17 former American Airlines employees. American Airlines responded by taking Northwest to court, claiming that the information that these people had allegedly transferred to their new employer was worth more than a new jumbo jet and had been responsible for increasing American's revenues by more than $100m per year.

What these cases demonstrate is the enormous economic value of information. Without access to information, companies cannot compete effectively. The acquisition and protection of these assets has therefore become one of the key competitive battlegrounds of the 1990s and will, we believe, continue to be so well into the next millennium.

From product differentiation to mass-customisation

The 1970s and 80s were a period that saw a heavy emphasis on the development of brands as a means of differentiating products and allowing manufacturers to create and nurture consumer loyalty. Brands such as Coca-Cola, IKEA, Nike and Bennetton have all been revered by marketeers as powerful examples of how brands can add value to organisations. As a result, many millions have been spent on brand development and support.

We would, however, argue that this attitude is beginning to seem anachronistic. The purpose of a brand – as exemplified by, say, soft drinks – is to generate loyalty for a product that is essentially undifferentiated, in this case, flavoured sugar and water. Attempts to change their traditional formulae have led to customer resistance despite the fact that the companies' tasting panels showed that people actually prefer the new formulation. Brands and information do not mix well: if we knew exactly what all the ingredients in Coca-Cola were, mixed in their exact proportions, the drink would probably have less of a fashionable mystique as we would also be able to make it ourselves if we chose to. The same is true for many of the brands on the market today: how many of us know how washing powder works? We buy on brand (and perhaps price) rather than information. When we start to think about it, it is very rare that we make *informed* purchases.

This is going to change – in fact, there is evidence that it is already changing as we write. Some companies are trying to link their brands to information. IKEA promotes the fact that you can call an automated telephone service to check whether an item is available in a particular store. In this instance, the company is building on its 'self-help' image, in which customers load furniture on to their trolleys to take home themselves, by providing extra information that further empowers its customers. In addition, unlike a conventional brand, it is easier to lock in one's customers with this type of 'virtual' brand. Boots the Chemists, the UK's leading pharmacy, has launched a customer smart card; rather than using this card simply to keep track of an individual's purchases, the company eventually intends the card to carry medical information and details of previous or repeat prescriptions. What incentive is there for a cardholder to switch to an alternative pharmacist when all the relevant information is contained in his card, making transactions much simpler?

Moreover, more and more brand-based companies are being forced to provide information because this is what their consumers expect. Technology and the Internet have both meant that the amount of information available to individuals is increasing exponentially: if you are not sure what you are buying from one manufacturer, you can check out the rival products quickly and cheaply. Information – as IKEA has realised – is empowering consumers. In the future, they will need to rely far less on the high-level image created by a brand but will be able to make far more informed purchase decisions. Already on the Internet, there are companies acting as 'infomediaries' who help potential purchasers find the best deal around, whether this applies to used cars or airline tickets.

Giving consumers information changes the balance of power from the corporate manufacturer to the individual purchaser. It means that consumers will be able to specify what they want more precisely rather than accept what the supplier or retailer offers. As home shopping for groceries takes off, we predict that the existing supermarket chains, whose brands at the moment are linked to choice, quality, freshness and so on, will develop information-based brands that will emphasise different qualities – the amount of information they have on a customer's previous purchases, being able to recommend recipes based on an individual's preferences and so on. In other words, the supermarket's brand will be orientated around being able to deliver to an individual the items which that individual wants. This is a trend that will not be confined to retailers: given not only escalating consumer expectations, but also the highly automated production lines and just-in-time supply chains of most manufacturers, the days of mass-production must be severely limited.

From access to distribution channels to access to customers

One of the key areas of competition in the 1980s and early 1990s was over access to distribution channels to ensure that products could be brought to market. Financial service companies invested millions in building up their branch networks; companies vied for the rights to new television channels or wavelengths; retailers built massive distribution hubs and spent millions in identifying and then purchasing the best sites for outlets. Power lay in the hands of those who could take a product and deliver it to a customer – hence the increasing strength of retailers over the last decade. However, with telephones, computers and the Internet, the obstacles that meant that manufacturers could rarely contact their consumers directly have largely disappeared: it is as easy now to buy a ticket direct from an airline as it is to go through a travel agent; it is simpler – and much more convenient – to arrange for a direct debit from your bank account via your telephone banking service than it is to visit a branch in person. Intermediaries – whether they take the form of people (such as insurance brokers) who sell on to us the products or services of others, or are simply a processing function (a teller in a bank) – are becoming rapidly redundant.

This trend of 'disintermediation' will undoubtedly continue as the growing ease of access to technology enables a wider customer base to be reached. The introduction of computer-based shopping via the Internet provides manufacturers with a cheap and effective way of reaching their customers directly. As the technical problems are overcome, and the issues about the security of transactions and money transfer are resolved, it seems likely that direct selling from the manufacturer will grow exponentially.

In this new battleground, the fight is therefore not about *how* to access your customers but about *who* your customers are. The better you can identify your customers (and the more you know about them), the less dependent you will be on traditional channels to market and intermediaries.

From government policy to unregulated markets

For much of this century – as Porter noted in 1980 – one of the most significant barriers to entry has been government policy. It was government policy that meant that electricity companies were monopolies, that telecommunications companies could only offer telephony-related services, that retailers could not sell financial services. However, in the course of just a few years, many of these 'rules' have been overturned. In the UK and parts of the USA, for example, the domestic electricity market is being completely opened up to competition – electricity companies that have enjoyed a monopoly since the end of the Second World War are having to fight off a host of new entrants – among them retailers and banks – who are exploiting the opportunity to sell discounted electricity as a means of nurturing loyalty across their existing customer base.

There are clearly a host of political, macro-economic and social factors that account for this radical shift, not least the idea that the state should pull back out of areas in which it has traditionally intervened. However, one of the strongest factors has to be the shift of balance that appears to be taking place from national governments to international companies. Multinationals such as General Electric have revenues that are larger than the GDP of small (or even medium-sized) states; every minute, millions of dollars wash through the international money markets. And we would argue that one of the major factors that has brought about the existence of these massive organisations is information.

If we look back to the 17th and 18th centuries, world trade could only be carried out at the speed at which a ship could travel from country to country. Of necessity, therefore, the individual operations in each country had to operate autonomously – you simply could not afford to wait for a management decision that could take several weeks or months to arrive. The advent of the telegraph in the 19th century changed this. For the first time, it was possible to transmit information – about, for example, a new gold find – rather than wait for physical proof of the event to arrive (either in the form of a messenger or the gold itself). It was business's first step into the virtual world. Today, it does not matter where your operations or your executives are based, you can communicate with them by telephone, fax, e-mail or video-conferencing. To make this possible, you have translated much of what you do into information. Your inspired salesman making *ad hoc* deals with customers has been codified into a sales management and appointment scheduling system; your customer care help-line now has to report statistics on its effectiveness; your culture has become the company mission statement. If you had not done this, how could you be part of an international company?

But, precisely because you have done this, your industry is becoming harder to regulate. The decline of regulation is not just a result of the relative size of many international organisations, but also a reflection of the fact that – being information based – international companies can move and adapt very quickly. If one government increases its corporate tax rate, it is now comparatively easy to switch an operation to an alternative country where the tax rate has remained low. Similarly, how do you tax the Internet? Many companies are already discovering that the law affecting Web-based transactions is still far from clear. If you can sell all your goods via a series of computer servers across Europe but keep your sales staff in the USA, who should you pay tax to – the European country where the transaction takes place, or the USA where your physical assets are located? Thus, as companies rely more and more on information – as they operate increasingly in the virtual world – we should expect to see the state's role in terms of regulation reduce still further. If we think our physical world is becoming deregulated, this is nothing compared with the free-for-all the virtual world seems likely to become.

From switching costs to universal standards

Looking back over the past 20 years, one of the most common routes to competitive advantage has been to establish a set of proprietary standards, which you keep from your suppliers and competitors, but which you use to tie in your customers to you because of the cost involved in switching to another standard. However, it is clear that this is an approach that is much less likely to succeed today. Today, what customers are looking for is the assurance that the products they buy will continue to be supported and not become obsolete – too many of them were hit by the video wars between the rival VHS and Betamax standards. VHS may have won that particular battle, but many consumers who had invested in Betamax video recorders suffered in the process. An equally infamous example is in the computer industry. The Apple range of computers was generally acknowledged to be technically superior to the PC based around the Intel microprocessor and Microsoft operating system. However, by publishing an open standard and encouraging third parties to develop products to support the PC, it was the latter which rapidly became the dominant product while Apple languished as the also-ran of the computer industry. Netscape has clearly taken this approach yet a stage further by offering their product for free as a means of establishing a standard.

These are examples of how the competitive issues, highlighted by Porter, have been reversed. The questions now are: How do I develop a sufficient number of robust alliances with other firms so that my product will be supported and sustained in the marketplace? How do I convince consumers that my product is the one that will succeed and, therefore, that when they buy it, they are buying something that will remain useful and not become obsolete overnight? How do I ensure that third parties will develop supporting products?

The birth of the virtual economy

If the rules by which the game of business has conventionally been played are disappearing, what will the rules of the future be? What will the 'virtual economy' look like? We believe it will have four principal characteristics.

1. In the absence of accepted barriers to entry and government regulation, industries will converge (some are already doing so)

Information does not recognise national boundaries but walks unquestioned through accepted check-points and customs halls. Similarly, it crosses the traditional divide between industries without a backward glance, just as it can flow around an organisation without regard to the niceties of departmental responsibilities. It is therefore inevitable that, the more that companies and economies become virtual, the less will they be able to maintain the internal distinctions to which they are accustomed. A supermarket can become a bank because it does not need to invest in a physical network of branches or cash machines to do so; it just needs to have a licence and a means to process customer transactions. A hospital can set up a mail-order company for young mothers because it has access to a customer base of pregnant women. Information is a currency that is accepted everywhere.

Indeed, it is this very transferability of information which virtually guarantees the demise of traditional industry boundaries. Companies are increasingly finding that, if they combine their information assets with those of other companies, the combined information resource is considerably more useful to all sides: two and two, in this instance, can make a lot more than four. Put together a social security or tax database with another database of people who owe debts and you have a means of tracking individual debtors over long periods of time and collecting the debt from them when they finally have the money to repay it (a process known as debt surveillance and already being offered by some companies). This is the virtual equivalent of the synergies that merging companies have traditionally sought, and its compelling economics mean that companies in the future are more probably going to be looking for ways to combine their information with others than looking to maintain the conventional barriers between industries.

2. Many smaller companies will emerge that use information and sophisticated technology to sell tailored products directly to their customers at very low cost

It is not so very long ago that the small company seemed to be on the verge of extinction. How could a handful of people, working out of one small office on a remote industrial estate, even imagine that they could compete with the juggernauts of multinational business. They could not develop the range of products, enjoy the economies of scale, access markets in a cost-efficient manner or build up a sustainable customer base.

But the virtual economy is a great leveller: the costs of setting up a website are so low that there is nothing to stop an individual having a larger, more impressive site than a large corporation (indeed, this is often the case, as the latter find it difficult to reconfigure their conventional approach to marketing to the more interactive environment of the Internet). Of course, this can be bad as well as good for consumers;

although they have much more choice, they no longer have access to familiar benchmarks of whether the company they are dealing with is reliable (an office, real people and so on). However, for the start-up it is an ideal situation: it takes just days to be able to promote an image on a par with a company that has existed for decades.

Moreover, in this new environment, small companies may have advantages that larger ones lack. First, because their contact with customers will mostly be channelled through the telephone, or increasingly e-mail, they will be able to record and keep track of their customer's preferences and needs much more effectively than a company that communicates through mass-media. Second, they will be able to offer added value services, for example by personalising products that they sell based on the information gathered and manipulated through these new media.

3. Rather than being independent, organisations will increasingly form mutually supportive networks that share information and knowledge

The conventional language of strategy makes us think of wars and battlefields, but these analogies may not always be the most appropriate in an economic environment in which there is as much to be gained from working together as from competing against each other. American consultant James Moore announced the 'death of competition' in 1996, arguing that the business environment of the future would be made up of 'ecosystems' in which groups of companies would come together to provide solutions for the complex problems that cross traditional market boundaries (electronic commerce, which involves banks, telephone companies, Internet-based firms and hardware suppliers to name but a few, being a good example):

> In the old world, [such] companies... would primarily see themselves as competing with similar businesses within their respective boxes. In the new world, companies compete to unite disparate contributors to create powerful total solutions or experiences – and then to establish thriving business ecosystems dedicated to providing these solutions to customers.[3]

Another example would be via World Network, an Andersen Consulting Enterprise, founded in 1995. Growing out of an outsourcing contract in which Andersen handles the ticket processing for a major American airline, the new company offers direct connections to the reservation systems of major American airlines.

Such networks will only be logistically possible through the exchange of information, and they will only flourish with the exploitation of shared knowledge. Providing electronic commerce solutions is an activity that is quintessentially information based. The Andersen joint venture does not rely on shared office accommodation, or even on achieving traditional economies of scale, but on being able to share the skills and experience of the participants.

4. Competition will shift from focusing on physical entities (products, geographies) to intellectual capital – information and knowledge

While the number of alliances between companies – both formal and informal – grows, while information and knowledge shared – at least within the same 'ecosystem' – increase, we believe that intellectual assets will become the most prized capital in the business world. It also seems likely that the single most important of these assets will be information on customers. Knowing who our customers are will allow us to bypass traditional middle men and distribution channels; knowing what they want – potentially on an individual basis – will enable us to develop new products and market them effectively; knowing how they behave will allow us to link up to other organisations so that our joint offering is that much more persuasive. In other words, information about customers will be at the centre of those ecosystems of the future.

This trend will be self-reinforcing. The more important intellectual capital becomes, the more systems will be built and methodologies developed that allow companies to value – and trade – their intellectual property. And in this environment, it is the information-based business – the virtual company – that will succeed.

Summary

Although we are all familiar with the term 'the information economy', few business people have given much thought until very recently to what it will actually mean for them. Yet information is changing some of the most basic rules by which our businesses, markets and economies all operate:

❑ Larger companies no longer have an inherent advantage, based on the economies of scale they can achieve; information enables much smaller companies to seize the advantage and set a new agenda.

- ❑ To compete effectively, organisations need knowledge more than they need financial capital.

- ❑ The notion of differentiating your products becomes meaningless where companies can customise goods for individual consumers.

- ❑ Having access to customers is much more important than having access to conventional distribution channels, many of which are now being bypassed.

- ❑ Information-based companies are more difficult to regulate than traditional, physically based ones.

- ❑ Information enables customers to switch between suppliers at almost no cost.

The virtual economy will, instead, be dominated by four key trends:

- ❑ Realising the advantages to be had from sharing information, industries and companies will converge.

- ❑ Many new, smaller companies will emerge that use information to compete on equal terms with large-scale multinationals.

- ❑ Organisations will increasingly form networks and alliances in order to exploit the potential of information-based synergy.

- ❑ Competition will revolve around information and knowledge rather than products or geographical markets.

Notes

1. Peter Drucker, 'The Information Executives Truly Need', *Havard Business Review*, January–February, 1995.
2. 'Start-Ups Pay Up', *Wired*, May, 1997.
3. James Moore, *The Death of Competition: Leadership and Strategy in the Age of Business Ecosystems*, Chichester: John Wiley, 1996.

4 The Raw Material of the Future

Information: the missing link in the information revolution

The implications of the information revolution have been and will continue to be vast. However, they have also – at least so far – been primarily technological. It is true that our lives have changed considerably since the widespread introduction of computers, but there has been little that has been really revolutionary in the true sense of the word. We have used computer hardware and software to automate what we already do – to speed up processes, reduce error rates and minimise costs – but not to change our lives in a profound sense. Our cars may have on-board computers, but we still use them to get around; our fridges have circuit boards, but they still keep food cold; our factories may have robots, but they still weld metal. We should, perhaps, be less amazed at what we have achieved than what we have not even begun to attempt.

The reasons for this are numerous and, until very recently, the technology itself had been difficult and expensive to exploit. But this is only a small part of the problem. Far more serious has been the scant attention that we have paid to how the information stored in this technology can be exploited. Yet – as we argue throughout this book – it is this information, and what we can with it, that will make the information revolution truly revolutionary. As two American commentators, Alan Rowe and Sue Ann Davis, have put it:

We are in the beginning of the 'real' digital revolution now. This is one of those historic points that changes the way that all society is going to work forever. It is as dramatic a change as the Industrial Revolution was to farmers. It is not about quality, flexibility, or time, but is a revolution about the availability and use of information and expertise. That is where the revolutionaries and visionaries are looking.[1]

Information has always been the poor relation of information technology. As organisations, we have been happy to give it away, lose it or even ignore it while paying vast sums of money for the hardware and software that can process it. This is because, until very recently, information has always been seen as a mere representation of something else – it was recycled information *about* something. Thus the information in your electricity bill represents how many units have been used and how much you have had to pay for it. In itself, the information has always been considered of a lesser value than the item itself. Information about the electricity consumed was considered to be of less value than the electricity that was actually used. But, and it is a crucial but, information about an object can now be separated from the object itself, and this gives it a value in its own right.

One of the first ways in which information, a representation of an object, was separated from the object itself was with the invention of the telegraph. The invention of the telegraph and telephone meant that, for the first time, information could be transmitted more quickly than physical goods. With this came the ability to take a position in the markets. If, for example, it had been a good harvest and there was likely to be a glut, it made sense to try and sell in advance of the harvest arriving. By separating the information from the object itself, the information gained a value in its own right.

Over time, the amount of information available has increased. This is true both of the increasingly complex information we hold about simple entities (a cable television company knows not just where it has laid its cables, but also details about the type of cable) and of our ability to convert more complex entities into information. When Frederick Taylor translated the way in which factory workers shovelled into a 'science of shovelling' in the 1920s, he was converting what he observed into a series of abstract principles – information. We do the same today when we represent the activities of an organisation in a series of process maps or a business model. The development of performance measurement techniques and a 'balanced scorecard' that can monitor an organisation against a combination of financial and non-financial standards are part of the same trend.

The advent of computers, and with them the ability to manipulate information, has led to a further change in the value of and definition of information. During the 1960s and 70s, information was seen very much as organised data: where data were random and unaggregated, information was 'the result of modelling, formatting, organising or converting data'.[2] More recently, information has been perceived to be something which 'adds to human knowledge',[3] that is, something that can be manipulated in its own right to provide added value and insights. This definition represents a significant departure; information is not just a 'representation' of reality. In other words, information is no longer about something – it *is* 'something'. That 'something' has a value, and the fact that the value can be exploited is one of the under-lying themes of this book.

More than a substitute

This is perhaps the most important insight today in thinking about information, but it is one that is only just being accepted and is even more rarely exploited. Information can be manipulated in ways that are impossible with physical objects, giving it enormous value. A simple example is the use of the computer-aided design techniques that now form a fundamental part of the manufacturing process. Information about a potential new product is developed within a computer system so that a virtual replica of the product can be tested, altered and sent around the world without the expense and time involved in building a physical mock-up. Of course, physical prototypes still play an important role, but their part is much reduced in the overall process. This is a quintessential example of how information has been used as a substitute for something else – the new product – in this case to reduce development costs and time to market. The value of the information comes about not just because it is a representation of the physical object, but also because it can be manipulated in ways that cannot occur in the physical world. Information is substituted for the physical object, to the benefit of all concerned.

Other methods of exploiting information are now emerging that increase the value of information still further. In 1993, for example, Stephan Haeckel (from IBM's Advanced Business Institute) and Richard Nolan (of Nolan, Norton and Company) published an article in the *Harvard Business Review* headed 'Managing by Wire'. Their argument was that companies, like aeroplanes, could be run on autopilot, the autopilot in this context being a sophisticated computer model of the business that was capable of managing a company's day-to-day performance and which needed to be flown 'manually' only through periods of turbulence. Mrs Fields Cookies was a good example, in which a model of the business had been developed to provide hour-by-hour instructions to store managers on what type of biscuit to bake, based on location, weather and many other variables. Although, in the main, Haeckel and Norton saw information like this as a substitute for reality, they also recognised that bringing a wide range of information about a company's behaviour together in a single computer model also created a whole new set of opportunities:

> When information from previously unrelated sources is structured in a meaningful way, human beings become capable of thinking thoughts that were previously unthinkable.[4]

However, the value generated by the information is not the only conclusion we should draw from this example. The other key lesson is that computer models were needed in order to bring it together and make sense of it. The information that is of value here is not information that can be handled by human beings alone: it requires a computer to analyse and then act on the huge amount of information available. For example, the tracking funds now prevalent on all the major stock exchanges require vast amounts of information on the movements of shares and financial derivatives in order to mimic the behaviour required. A subset of such information would be meaningless: it only becomes valuable when all of it can be evaluated simultaneously, something which is beyond the ability of an unaided human being. The computer model of the dealer outperforms its human rivals at least in part because it can monitor movements in prices at a more detailed level, allowing it to exploit opportunities that would, quite simply, be invisible to its human equivalent. If we summarised this information to a point at which we could analyse it, its value would be lost.

Wherever we look, this conclusion seems inevitable, as Haeckel and Norton put it:

> large organisations have become too complex for any individual, even the most brilliant executive to keep complete models of the business in mind.[4]

But many organisations still ignore the full power of information. Imagine flying in an aeroplane when you only had information on its speed, altitude and location. The thought is terrifying. There is no way that we would want to board such a flight, but every day we invest our money in companies that are being 'flown' in this fashion. They have information about their current and previous positions, but have not exploited this information in any consistent way to decide what to do in the future.

A few of you might regard this is as a little unfair. Some successful organisations do use sophisticated techniques to analyse information that enables them to exploit future opportunities. The fact remains, however, that decisions are usually taken on information that is summarised to an aggregate level – that is, the level at which the human brain can function most effectively – and this is not necessarily the optimum level at which such decisions should be made.

The detail myth

When we think of information, we tend to believe that we have to aggregate it. To make it truly valuable, we need to be able to make use of that information in our businesses or daily lives. We need to convert it into knowledge, where 'knowledge' can be defined as the ability to act upon the information. The only way in which we can extract such knowledge, being humans with only limited capacity, is to aggregate and then to look for patterns. However, there is a problems with this, which lies not so much in this model but in the assumption that almost all of us are guilty of making – that the process by which we move from information to knowledge is essentially one of distillation, that knowledge can only be obtained by winowing meaning from the information chaff.

People implicitly believe that information, like Darwinian nature, has to be 'red in tooth and claw'. Only the best information survives the evolutionary struggle: knowledge is the survival of the fittest information. It is a view evident from the way in which many organisations think about their existing data resources. 'Data-mining', for example, is a commonly promoted technique which, its proponents suggest, enables you to plunge into a mass of data and let the data – using neural networks and other sophisticated tools – tell their own 'story'. The important messages will always surface, so the theory goes.

Or is it simply that, if something surfaces, we think that it is important? Do we retrospectively justify the cut-down version of information that we habitually call knowledge? Perhaps what emerges is the result of a series of accidents and coincidences, as Stephen Jay Gould writes on the development of life itself:

> Any replay of [life's] tape would lead evolution down a pathway radically different from the road actually taken... . Each step proceeds for cause, but no finale can be specified at the start, and none would ever occur a second time in the same way, because any pathway proceeds through thousands of improbable stages.[5]

Just as our accepted ideas on evolution are now being challenged, so should this whole approach to the relationship between information and knowledge be open to question. The money your organisation spends on marketing is a good example. Imagine that you are the chief executive of a soap powder manufacturer. Your marketing budget will run into millions and will be distributed across a range of promotional and advertising activities, using a variety of media and other channels to market. The basis on which you apportion your budget between these areas will be a complex one, involving analysis of the return on previous campaigns, future trends, market research, the prices offered by your suppliers and – ultimately – gut-feel. You probably employ a small team of people who can weigh up the different options and take an informed judgement based on years of experience in the field. And you probably get what you feel to be a pretty reasonable rate of return from the expenditure overall. Yet this model has a serious flaw. If you could manage your marketing budget at a lower level of detail, you would undoubtedly increase the returns that you would achieve. More precise targeting could be made of individual consumers (a topic we cover in depth later on in the book), leading to higher returns. The question is not *whether* the marketing budget is apportioned inefficiently, but *how* inefficiently. Yet we assume that because the information has been distilled into knowledge – because the market research has become an executive report – the most important information has been preserved.

To take another example. One of us attended a conference in the early 1990s on executive information systems. While most of the speakers were taking the opportunity to extol the virtues of their reporting systems, one company – a computer supplier – stood up and said that what *worried* them about their system was that it had not helped them anticipate the 1990–91 recession in the UK. What they had thought of as the central knowledge of the organisation – effectively, the order book – only painted part of the picture: if the company had incorporated indicators about – for example – its customers' performance, it might have been better informed. Information had effectively been aggregated to too high and too simplistic a level and had been assumed, on this basis, to be the information the company needed. In fact, this 'knowledge', because the picture it gave was rosy right up to the moment when the full force of the recession struck, prevented the company from taking corrective action (discounting to stay ahead of its competitors, for example) until it was almost too late. We would argue that it is therefore not suprising that so many organisations have problems realising effectively the apparent advantages of information. Instead, we would suggest that these problems result from the fact that they are still dealing with distilled information. Just because it has been distilled does not make it any more valuable than other information.

Moreover, because the process by which information is distilled means that valuable information is lost (an inevitable part of distillation), our aggregation model is one in which value is potentially reduced rather than added. If something is lost in the process of translating information into knowledge, it is because the human brain can handle only a limited amount of information at any one time. In other words, by converting information into something with which the human brain can deal, we lose something.

Of course, this does not mean that the human being has no part to play. The analogy with flying an aeroplane is an apposite one. It simply does not make sense for pilots to interfere with the autopilot under normal flying conditions – they could do, but it would not achieve much (in fact, theoretically, assuming that the autopilot has identified the optimum flight path, it could only introduce the possibility of human error). However, what the autopilot cannot do is decide whether the criteria on which its route is optimised are the correct criteria (it might, for example, choose to fly directly through an area of turbulence that the passengers might find uncomfortable because it is the most direct route). Equally, it – unlike the pilots – is not equipped to cope with 'non-standard' (for example very turbulent) environments.

However, even with these exceptions, it remains the case that, where we use technology effectively, we need to keep information as detail for as long as possible. In the USA, a computer model has been designed which mimics the judgement of one of the best traders in the New York Stock Exchange – analysts sat with the trader over a long period, translating her instinctive actions into a set of rules that could then be used to instruct the computer model. What started off as an exercise in substitution ('Can we build a model that behaves like a dealer?') has since gone much further – the model is now capable of out-performing most traders. In this example, our assumption that knowledge, information that has been aggregated to a sufficient level for a human to take action upon it, is of the most value is not justified. The dealer model loses its value the moment its information is converted into something on which its human handlers can take decisions.

If we carry this argument further, we have to start asking why we invest so many millions of dollars in installing reporting systems that simply aggregate information in the misplaced hope that this automatically results in benefits. Taking the definition of knowledge that we used earlier – that it is the conversion of information into action – we should be asking whether these reporting systems actually ever initiated any action, or if they initiated some action, whether it was the right kind of action. If we only have a limited amount of information, the actions we can take are similarly circumscribed.

If we have problems making use of the collective knowledge of our organisations, it is usually blamed on the fact that we do not get hold of knowledge soon enough, or that the process of capturing knowledge is fraught with difficulties, the cultural barriers to knowledge-sharing for example. The argument should, however, also be considered in reverse: perhaps the problem is that we get hold of what we think of as 'knowledge' too early on. We always want to move things out of the virtual world of information into the actionable world of knowledge as soon as possible. Given the volumes of information and levels of computing power now available, we should be giving much more thought to what we do with information and not just assume that we should be aggregating it and discarding the detail. Of course, at the end of the day, we still need to do something – we still need to convert the information we have into actionable knowledge – but this point in the process is not always as early as we imagine it should be. After all, many more things are possible in the virtual world than in the physical world.

The myth of the physical

The development of robots is an apt illustration of this myth. Since the turn of the century, creating a robot that can perform even basic human tasks has been one of our dreams, a close second, perhaps, to putting a man on the moon. Indeed, the human being has always been the standard against which we judge our technological process. When Alan Turing devised the first test for artificial intelligence in the 1940s, he suggested that a computer and a human should be put on one side of a screen and another human being should be on the other; the latter was to be asked to distinguish, based on a series of responses, which – on the other side of the screen – was the human and which the computer. Progress in robotics has been both enormous and very slow. We may be able to build a machine that can help to dismantle bombs, but we still have major problems making it go up stairs. We certainly cannot make a robot capable of fooling a human being with its responses.

But why are we bothering? Rather than try to get a computer to enter the physical world of the human, why don't we try to enter the world of the computer? Virtual reality turns this way of thinking on its head: instead of trying to get the computer to enter the human world (walk, talk), we should enter the world of the computer. And this is potentially a much more fascinating world than the one we live in. It is not constrained by gravity or three dimensions, and solid objects can change shape in ways which defy physical laws. We should not be suprised if it has become our preferred film set: why watch the phys-ical world we live in every day when we could watch an entirely imaginary one designed to satisfy our wildest desires and fantasies?

We are constantly trying to fit information around our decision-making processes and our knowledge bases, whereas what we should be doing is using the information as information. If we want to make effective use of the rapidly growing volume of information 'out there', in the physical world, we need to think of it as information and not automatically try to make sense of it before we are prepared to look at it. Does it really make sense to produce marketing plans based on high-level statistics about, for example, the probable take-up of a new product? In an ideal world, wouldn't we want to know a great deal more than this? For example, rather than knowing that the market is worth $xm, we might want to know whether individual A is more likely to buy the new product than individual B and why. We might want to know how many people A and B will talk to if they like the new product, and we might want to know how many people their friends tell. In effect, we would want to be able to understand the behaviour of individuals and link this to the total value of a market, and this answer could be very different from the one calculated at a high level only. Thus, if our marketing plans are based on high-level information only, the kinds of action we take will be pretty predictable – and probably the same as our competitors. However, if we leave information as information for longer, and find new ways to understand and analyse it, we may reach a very different (and differentiated) position. To use the words of the science writer, Carl Sagan:

> If you know a thing only qualitatively, you know it no more than vaguely. If you know it quantitatively – grasping some numerical measure that distinguishes it from an infinite number of other possibilities – you are beginning to know it deeply. You comprehend some of its beauty and you gain access to its power and the understanding it provides. Being afraid of quantification is tantamount to disenfranchising yourself.[6]

A practical example of this would be shoplifting in stores. Studies have shown that up to 50 per cent of goods stolen are taken by staff; of the remainder taken by shoppers, much of it is focused on a comparatively small number of lines. Either way, we would expect there to be some pattern to the shrinkage which occurs across, for example, a department store chain. We would expect stores where a number of staff were pilfering to have higher than average shrinkage rates; in other stores, we might expect to see it concentrated in a small number of departments. Although most retailers recognise and look out for these patterns, most of them are looking at a comparatively high level: they look for entire stores or departments where shrinkage is unexpectedly high. As a result, they may be missing the much more detailed patterns of shrinkage that lie below this artificial surface. By matching the inputs and outputs to their EPOS systems by product, a different picture may emerge that shows that certain stores are prone to pilferage for a short period only (the perpetrator has exploited his or her opportunity and moved on) or that it is very specific lines within a department which are at risk. Moreover, if these variances in inputs and outputs were monitored as they happened, rather than registering in a stock-take some months later, a retailer might be able to identify problems as they occur – and thus have some chance to fix them. The kind of understanding a retailer would gain from this exercise could not have been gained by carrying out a physical stock-take. However, by exploiting information, the company can spot problems it would not otherwise have known about and – most importantly – take action in a way that it could not previously have found possible.

Another example from retailing would be defective products. Many retailers monitor the products that customers return to stores (because of some fault) at a very high level only – a single total for the entire chain would not be untypical. Returns may be tracked at product level within a store, but this detailed information does not get passed on to the head office. Thus, if 100 customers each return the same product to 100 different stores, the retailer will not be aware that there is clearly a problem with this item; only if a significant number of customers return the same product to the same store will someone start to notice. Even then, the realisation that there is a problem is often dependent on a few individuals who – often informally – pass this information back to their head offices. If the retailers were to change the way they monitor returns, to track which individual products have been returned, the chances of being able to spot a problem with a line before it occurs (and thus avoid damaging recalls) rises immeasurably. Again, much more is possible by using information at a detailed level.

Another illustration would be to compare two newspaper providers. One produces a traditional broadsheet, while the other offers a tailored on-line service in which readers are allowed to flag up the areas that they are interested in and receive digital newspapers that have been customised for their specific needs. The second company clearly has an advantage: its news is created to order, so there is little danger of wasting time on articles with no appeal to its virtual readership, and customers can make up their own 'newspapers' rather than effectively having to read someone else's. Undoubtedly, the second company will, over time, win more customers and have higher sales, which it does by holding off converting its news into actual print for as long as possible. Aggregated information – what we conventionally think of as knowledge – plays a crucial role, but only at the very end of the process.

Using information – often at a detailed level – to drive our actions and create new possibilities is quite different from our usual way of thinking about systems and information. A typical executive or enterprise information system (popular in the late 1980s but now falling rather from favour) was based around up-to-date but essentially very summarised data. Exceptions would be highlighted, allowing managers to 'drill down' to identify the exact nature of the problem. However, all that this achieved was to fit information into predetermined structures – we never learnt anything new, because the systems were designed on the basis of what we knew already.

There are lots of good arguments (and we focus on several of them in the next section) for keeping your corporate information as information – keeping your business virtual – for as long as possible. The information domain allows you to do things that the physical world does not. The moment you convert your information into action or physical reality, the deal is done: it is more difficult to change, more expensive, more subject to the conventional limitations of our everyday world.

Information is important – as we will go on to explain in the next chapter – because:

- although it is often expensive to gather, it is cheap to distribute and reproduce;
- it links organisations and individual together, rather than forcing them to compete;
- it can be used to tie your customers to you.

Ultimately, however, it is important not because of these attributes but because of what these attributes make possible – something which is the theme not just of the next chapter but of the whole book.

Summary

- ❏ To date, only a fraction of the amount of thought that has been applied to how to use computer technology has been given to how to exploit the information which that technology holds.

- ❏ We have, instead, always tended to see information as a poor substitute for physical reality. With the volumes of information available growing exponentially, and the cost of the computing power required to manipulate them falling rapidly, it is information on which we now need to focus.

❑ Only by looking at information in much more detail – and by discarding our conventional distinction between what is detailed (unimportant) and what is strategic (important) – are we going to be able to develop genuinely differentiated strategies.

❑ Organisations are usually in a hurry to go beyond information into knowledge, but, by stopping to exploit our information resources more effectively, the knowledge that we ultimately create is likely to generate new opportunities.

Notes

1.   Alan J Rowe and Sue Anne Davis, *Intelligent Information Systems: Meeting the Challenge of the Knowledge Era*, Westport, CO: Quorum, 1996.
2. John G Burch, *Information Systems: Theory and Practice*, Santa Barbara: Hamilton, 1974.
3. Eric Deeson, *Collins Dictionary of Information Technology*, Glasgow: Harper-Collins, 1991.
4. Stephan H Haeckel and Richard L Norton, 'Managing by Wire', *Harvard Business Review*, September–October, 1993.
5. Stephen Jay Gould, *Wonderful Life: The Burgess Shale and the Nature of History*, London: Penguin, 1989.
6. Carl Sagan, *Billions and Billions: Thoughts on Life and Death on the Brink of the Millennium*, New York: Random House, 1997.

The Law of Increasing Returns

We will be examining in subsequent chapters how you can exploit information to give you a competitive advantage – using information to exploit the complexity of your business; making best use of the infosphere of your products or knowledge capital; moving away from the physical aspects of your business. Each of these approaches is capable of improving business performance significantly in isolation; applied together, the benefits they can generate are even greater. However, before going on to look in detail at these, it is important that we understand the basis on which these benefits are produced, and that we understand how and why the virtual business is capable of out-performing conventional physical businesses. We need to look at the 'law of increasing returns'.

What is the law of increasing returns?

To say that something will be subject to the law of diminishing returns is accepted business wisdom. New products that initially sell well lose their competitive advantage as rival producers replicate them; costs that were once kept low through efficient processes rise as the raw material required is depleted. As the economist David Begg rather caustically puts it, 'the ninth worker's role in production is to get coffee for the others operating the machines'.[1] But what if it didn't have to be like this? Imagine what it would be like to run a business where the more you produced, the lower your costs, or where you sold products at a faster and faster rate over time. Welcome to the world of *increasing returns* – and the good news is that you are already living in it. The key question is to what extent you have a systematic approach to exploiting it.

The original law of diminishing returns was developed in the 19th century, when it was observed that if you added more inputs to a process, you would not increase the outputs by the same amount. Thus, doubling the number of coal-miners will increase coal production but not double it. Simple in itself, the law of diminishing returns continues to underpin much economic thinking. It is diminishing returns that are responsible for prices that balance out over time and for competition; without them we would have no equilibrium of free-market forces. Almost all business strategies are still based upon this basic assumption.

Most of us, if we were asked to run a light bulb factory, would, for example, assume that there is a finite minimum cost for each light bulb that is determined by the scale of our operation; we can only decrease unit costs by a given amount in order to produce more light bulbs more cheaply. Yet this theory is contradicted by, among other things, the learning curve that we encounter in practice. The idea of a learning curve is not new. Its discovery has been credited to Theodore P Wright, an engineer, who in 1922 as the assistant factory manger of Curtiss Aeroplane, calculated that the labour required to assemble a plane declined by 20 per cent with each doubling of production experience. In other words, if it took 10.0 people to build the first plane, it would take 8.0 to build the second, 6.4 to build the fourth and so on. At the time, this realisation was a source of competitive advantage in bidding for manufacturing contracts. During the Second World War, it became an accepted rule for the aircraft industry as a whole, allowing American factories to produce 230,000 planes between Pearl Harbour in early 1943 and the end of the war.[2] However, the learning curve only gained widespread acceptance in business in the mid-1960s when it was applied by the Boston Consulting Group to a wide range of very different businesses, but always with the same results – costs fell as experience rose.

Yet the existence of the learning curve means that – in contradiction to conventional economic theory – it is possible for a manufacturer to continue to reduce costs over time. Returns do not have to diminish: they can also increase. The key to understanding why this works is to appreciate what is being exploited. The reason the learning curve works is because organisations learn how to exploit the information content (in this case their knowledge of the production process) more effectively. This gives us a clue to the mechanisms behind the law of increasing returns. The mechanism is not about greater and greater economies of scale or physical domination of a market; the mechanisms that exist behind the law of increasing returns are all about exploiting the virtual, information aspects of your business – precisely the topics of this book.

'Increasing returns,' the economist W Brian Arthur has written, 'are the tendency for that which is ahead to get further ahead, for that which loses advantage to lose further advantage.'[3] Arthur, at the time of writing Virginia Morrison Professor of Economics and Population Studies at Standford University, USA, has been the foremost proponent of increasing returns, often in the face of considerable scepticism from other economists and academics. Much simplified, his argument is that in sectors where there are no constraints on resources (notably high-tech and knowledge-based industries), there is no reason for returns to diminish over time. Pharmaceutical and software companies may invest massively in the initial development of their products, but they can produce additional units (medication or software) at very low cost. Rather than experiencing negative feedback – where a company that mines diamonds, for example, so efficiently that it soon runs out of diamonds – such companies are characterised by positive feedback. Thus, Arthur argues, the success of the Japanese car industry in selling small cars into the USA market in the 1970s, when there was little real competition from domestic manufacturers, allowed the Japanese manufacturers to build up experience in this field, and this in turn allowed them to cut their costs and improve their products, making their position even more dominant. The density of high-tech firms in Silicon Valley is another example. Although the first few firms arrived here through a series of historical accidents, later firms were drawn by the highly trained workforce and the proximity of component suppliers. In this way an initial advantage has increased rather than decreased over the course of time.

Crucial to the identification of how best the law of increasing returns can be exploited is, in our view, the appreciation that all businesses consist of both the virtual and the physical. The physical may be subject to constraints, the virtual is not. All businesses have resources that are not subject to constraints, so there is no business which cannot, itself, at least in part, be subject to the law of increasing returns.

The example most often cited, and perhaps the purest example of a major company that successfully exploits the law of increasing returns is Microsoft, which used its 1980 deal with IBM to supply what became the standard PC operating system. As the PC took off, other software providers wrote systems for DOS, which in turn strengthened Microsoft's advantage; the same is now true of Windows. Conventional economic theory would hold that such an advantage would in fact be eroded over time (diminishing returns), but the opposite is true. The majority of Microsoft's expenditure is in initial development rather than in producing additional units of software; as the company's hegemony has been established it has 'locked' hardware manufacturers and other software producers into its standard. What Bill Gates has realised is that there are many ways in which the law of increasing returns can be used. The number of times they are cited as an example of the high levels of performance possible in the virtual domain provides testament to the effectiveness with which the law of increasing returns continues to be exploited within Microsoft. Its dominant position was, and is, not a matter of luck – although some luck undoubtedly helped – but will be defended and strengthened by the company's deep understanding of how best to make use of the information content of its products and markets.

Because economists and others have failed, at least until recently, to consider the exploitation of the virtual, information aspects of a business with the same attention as the physical trilogy of capital, labour and resources, many of the developments of the latter half of the 20th century appear exceedingly mysterious. Silicon Valley in the USA is an example of how a series of apparently insignificant events (the founding of the first high-tech companies in the region) had massive implications (the economic importance of Silicon Valley inside and outside the USA, and the contribution it has made to the development of computer technology). Where positive feedback occurs, small events snowball:

> In the real world, if several similar-size firms entered a market at the same time, small fortuitous events – unexpected orders, change meetings with buyers, managerial whims – would help determine which ones achieved early sales and, over time, which firm dominated. Economic activity is quantized by individual transactions that are too small to observe.[4]

Positive feedback has two further implications that are particularly relevant in this context. First, precisely because apparently minor physical events can have significant implications, the development of a business or an economy does not necessarily follow a course of continuous positive development: the fact that you have the best product does not mean that you will beat your competitors. Second, positive feedback creates a volatile environment. While conventional economics is based around stable physical equilibria – the negative feedback of diminishing returns offsets positive trends over time – an environment in which increasing returns operate accentuates small changes.

Case Study

THE ECONOMICS OF SOFTWARE COMPANIES

Microsoft is the archetypal example of a company that has enjoyed increasing returns, ever since it established its deal with IBM to supply the operating system for the latter's PC. However, the economics of software companies is such that the majority of them are exploiting similar opportunities.

Software costs a lot to develop but very little to mass-produce; it also requires virtually no inventory. Thus the ability to earn super-profits is determined by the volume of units sold (as each one is virtually all profit). Philip Elmer-Dewitt in *Time* recently illustrated this extremely clearly by comparing two theoretical companies, both of which have invested $250m in a software package that retails at $325 a copy; after variable costs are taken into account, each company makes $275 profit a copy. But if one company sells 9m units while the other sells only 1m, the difference in total profit is huge ($2.2bn compared with just $25m). Moreover, the volume leader can afford to reduce costs in order to increase the overall market size, a move that quickly plunges its competitor into loss. 'Now that is market power,' he concluded.[5]

Where does information fit in?

The law of increasing returns was intially developed to explain high-tech and knowledge-based industries in which, although the initial investment in a product was high, its marginal cost of production was very low. However, as is increasingly becoming apparent, increasing and diminishing returns co-exist in all industries. Service industries, in particular, are a hybrid of the two economic models: from day to day, they act like bulk-processing industries, but over the long term, as the more successful are able to exploit their knowledge ever more effectively, increasing returns will dominate.

We would argue that this can be taken further: the likelihood that a business will experience increasing returns is determined by the extent to which its operations are based on information rather than physical reality. Furthermore, all industries can be placed somewhere on this particular scale, and, therefore, all businesses can be subject to the law of increasing returns. This is because information fulfils the criteria that W Brian Arthur himself sets out for an increasing return environment:

- *A high up-front cost.* Companies have invested billions of dollars over the past decade in computer systems that track and store information on their operations, products, sales, costs and customers; making use of this information is relatively cheap.
- *Network effects.* Forming links with other companies (or even, dare we say it, effective links within companies), rather like creating the business of an ecosystem, can create an environment in which all sides win. By supplementing one company's core strengths with those of others, you can not only reduce costs (because you are not wasting time trying to be all things to all people), but also keep your competitors out (by allying with the key players in a market before they can).
- *Customer 'lock-in'.* Increasing returns is not simply a matter of gaining new customers but of keeping them tied into your company in the future, either by establishing standards to which other companies – and therefore your customers as well – must subscribe (as software companies do) or by establishing a critical mass on which your customers become dependent (the highly trained skills base in Silicon Valley, for example).

To these three criteria, we would add a fourth: information allows a company to redefine itself – at all levels, from strategy to the operation of individual processes. A company that is comparatively unconstrained by physical geography (a seller of services across the Internet, for example) can reconfigure its distribution to take advantage of the variances in domestic tax regimes at virtually no cost: it does not have any physical assets of any consequence that need to be relocated. Information therefore brings flexibility – in W Brian Arthur's words – adaptability:

We can begin to see that the new type of management is not a fad. The knowledge-based part of the economy demands flat hierarchies, mission orientation, above all a sense of direction. Not five year plans... . In short, it needs to adapt. And adapting never stops. In fact, in the increasing returns environment I've just sketched, standard optimisation makes little sense.[6]

Information offers a world in which the physical constraints of traditional industries (and economics) have no relevance. It follows that a company that relies on its information environment (as opposed to its traditional physical one) is more adaptable, and it is more probable that this company will experience increasing returns. All companies rely on a combination of the physical and information environments, although the exact combination – what we call the physical/virtual ratio – will vary between sectors and between individual companies.

A heavy engineering company, with massive investment in plant and machinery, is bound to find it less easy to adapt to a changing market than, for example, a publisher, most of whose production process is computer based. A bank can launch a new savings plan more easily than a car manufacturer can develop a new model. It is for this reason that manufacturing companies such as the Ford Motor Company are investing in the ability to design a prototype assembly line in virtual terms before they test it out in reality. It is estimated that this move, announced by Ford in 1996, will save the company more than £100m per annum. More importantly than anything else, the virtual world of information is not subject to the constraints and limitations of its physical equivalent. Unlike conventional raw materials – metals, minerals, chemicals, fuels – you cannot run out of information. In fact, information increases exponentially as you create it. For example, you have two sources of information: a list of families with very young children in a certain area and a list of school places. Join these two sets of information together and you have a third – a list of filled and unfilled places in schools. Add a third source of information, the textbooks used in each school and the number of sets of information increases further. By linking the lists together, you will know how many of each textbook each school will buy and which children will be reading which book. Every time you add a new source of information and link it to existing sources, you are creating innumerable new bits of information. It follows that, for every dollar you invest, you obtain in return far more than one dollar's worth of information. Information itself has an increasing return.

THE CONSULTING INDUSTRY

The 1990s have been a boom time for the consulting industry. Companies worth billions of dollars have managed, year in and year out, to demonstrate double digit growth figures. Why is this? Conventional economic thinking suggests that as companies get larger they find it harder and harder to grow. How is it that consultancies have managed to buck this trend.

The answer lies in the law of increasing returns. The consulting industry is a prime candidate to benefit from the law: it trades in knowledge, and therefore, its raw materials, once created, can be infinitely replicated and distributed at little cost; the more connections that it can make, the greater the benefits; and the knowledge it uses is hard and expensive to create, thereby providing opportunities to lock out other organisations.

The key question is whether this will continue into the future? Much will depend on the consultancy industry's willingness to embrace these concepts still further. If they continue to recognise that what drives their business is not the number of people that they employ, but the knowledge that they successfully deploy; if they recognise that what is required is new ways of leveraging the information (the virtual) within their organisations then they will continue to gain market share not only at the expense of their competitors but also from traditional physically based businesses. There are clear signs that this is set to continue.

The move of the big six accountancy based consultancies into outsourcing is a good example. Most of these consultancies will now offer to run whole departments on your behalf. 'We're based around accountancy firms', they will say, 'why don't we run your finance functions for you. We can bring far more knowledge of how to manage it effectively than you can.' And who can deny it: by collecting knowledge, by effectively exploiting the virtual in their businesses, they can run these departments more effectively. As the underlying rationale of the law of increasing returns states, 'Them that has gets'. They have successfully exploited their knowledge of IT and finance functions. Which function will they tackle next? What, in the end, will be left for the original companies to do?

But why do increasing returns matter for business?

What the idea of increasing returns offers to business is a new way of thinking about strategy. No business is either wholly physical or wholly virtual. In every business, diminishing and increasing returns co-exist. The key issue is to distinguish between them and to manage them so that you minimise your diminishing returns while maximising your increasing returns. A physical business clearly comprises, among other things, buildings, people and raw materials; a virtual business, information, even reports such as the management accounts.

Let us take an example. Up and Down Inc is a fictious elevator manufacturer. Since the 1920s, it has been making elevators, primarily for big office blocks. The company's patented 'Extra-Fast' elevator is designed as an express elevator to the uppermost floors of skyscrapers. The latter's pioneering technical design ensured that Up and Down had the biggest share of the elevator market in its locality. However, in the early 1990s, two new entrants developed similar (although not quite as fast) express elevators at much lower production costs. Hampered by old-fashioned working practices and rising costs, Up and Down's market share is being serious eroded as a result – all in all, a typical example of a company subject to diminishing returns. While this is certainly true at a superficial level, it does not mean that the company could not find areas of its business that would have an increasing return.

In looking for opportunities for increasing returns, Up and Down needs to start with its external market. What its customers really want – the company discovers – is not simply an express elevator; what they want is to know that they have moved their staff between the top and bottom floors of their offices as efficiently as possible. What they want to be sure of, when they are standing by the elevator wondering why it is taking so long, is that there is absolutely no way that the elevator could get to them any more quickly than it does. Slow, poorly programmed elevators are interpreted by the people who use them as a symptom of a slow, poorly managed employer. Conversely, a company that can prove to its employees that it takes their efficiency seriously (by installing the quickest lifts) sends out an important message about the level of efficient working they expect back. When customers purchase an 'Extra-Fast' elevator, they are going as far as they can in promoting this idea, but the elevator itself does not answer their needs because it does not explicitly demonstrate that it is moving people as efficiently as possible. What Up and Down needs to be selling, therefore, is the guarantee of maximum efficiency, backed up by the information that proves it. It needs to be able to give its customers reports of its operation against the theoretical optimum during any given period. It needs to install loudspeakers in its elevator lobbies, which tell people the time of the next elevator. In other words, what it needs to provide its customers with is information rather than just the product itself. Ideally, Up and Down wants to build a strategy that is not based on exploiting a one-off 'windfall' of information, but on using that information to create a sustainable competitive advantage, even one which will strengthen over time – an increasing return.

As noted above, four criteria are associated with increasing returns: high up-front costs to deter potential new entrants; network effects to lock potential competitors into synergistic relationships; locking customers into a product or service; and, finally, adaptability to changing markets. The next step for Up and Down, therefore, is to see how it can incorporate these factors into its idea of providing information on the efficiency of its elevators.

- *High up-front costs/low production costs.* Investing in the information aspects of the 'Extra-Fast' elevator will not come cheap and nor – if Up and Down is to deter would-be entrants – should it. The more money the company puts into creating this information now, the higher the entry barriers will be in the future. Moreover, once created, the information itself is cheap to update and disseminate. The company may be able to strengthen the advantage this gives it by making use of the one asset its competitors do not have – the length of time it has been in existence. If the company can distil the knowledge it has accumulated over time about elevator efficiency and sell this on to its customers in the form of extra reassurance that its elevators are the quickest, it will be doing something that its rivals cannot emulate.
- *Network effects.* If providing information on elevator efficiency is the key to enhancing its existing product in its customers' eyes, Up and Down should also consider linking itself to other companies that could provide related information. An engineering consultancy, for example, might be able to offer benchmarking information on building efficiency; HR specialists might be able to provide information on the costs of employee inefficiency, which Up and Down could use to bolster its case to the market.

Like the initial investment, this strategy would have the added advantage of preventing Up and Down's competitors from making similar moves – the obvious companies with whom to forge an alliance will have already been linked to Up and Down.

■ *Customer lock-in.* As we have noted above, locking out your competitors is only one aspect of creating increasing returns: you also need to lock in your customers. Particularly for a manufacturer like Up and Down, this represents the greatest challenge, although it is thus – if successful – the most effective way of creating increasing returns. A software supplier might be able to establish a set of standards to which its suppliers and customers (once critical mass had been reached) would comply, but the options are more complex for less virtual businesses. So far as this example is concerned, Up and Down would need to lock people into the information it provides. This could take several forms, a key one being for the company to widen its remit and use the experience it has on the way in which buildings help or hinder the people who work in them to become more efficient, taking information from its clients' systems and analysing it, in order to identify general bottlenecks within the building other than just frustrations with lift operation. From the cash registers in the staff restaurant, it could tell how many meals are sold per minute over lunch time; compare that with the length of time a telephone rings on average during this same period and you start to build up a picture of the way in which catering inefficiencies could be costing a company business (some of the 'smart' buildings being developed today are capable of just this kind of comparison). Having established its ability to analyse this kind of information for its customers, the incentive for them to switch to an alterntive supplier would be significantly reduced.

Up and Down Inc does not actually exist, but there are plenty of examples of real companies that are – consciously or unconsciously – already developing strategies that take advantage of this kind of environment, as our earlier case study of the consulting industry illustrates.

More than anything else, the notion of increasing returns involves a change in the way we think about how we run our businesses. The dramatic improvements in performance envisaged provide a compelling argument for looking at our organisations from a fresh perspective, distinguishing their physical and virtual attributes, and developing strategies that maximise their virtual aspects. These are the subjects of the following sections of this book.

Summary

As the name suggests, the law of increasing returns argues that it is possible for a business to enjoy continuously increasing profits from its business. There are three essential ingredients:

- high up-front costs;
- networks of alliances with other organisations;
- locked-in customers.

A virtual business is more likely to have these attributes than a conventional, physically based one because information:

- is expensive to gather but cheap to use;
- is not a finite resource;
- provides a means of linking companies and customers together;
- ensures that a company can reinvent itself almost instantly.

However, all businesses have both physical and virtual parts to them. Any organisation can take the virtual apsects of its business and potentially use them to benefit from the law of increasing returns.

Notes

1. David Begg, Stanley Fisher and Rudiger Dornbusch, *Economics*, Maidenhead: McGraw-Hill, 1991.
2. Michael L Rothschild, *Bionomics: The Inevitability of Capitalism*, London: Future, 1992.
3. W Brian Arthur, 'Increasing Returns and the New World of Business', *Harvard Business Review*, July–August, 1996.
4. W Brian Arthur, 'Positive Feedbacks in the Economy', *Scientific American*, February, 1990.
5. Philip Elmer-Dewitt, *Time*, June 5, 1995.
6. W Brian Arthur, 'Increasing Returns and the New World of Business', *Harvard Business Review*, July–August, 1996.

Part II
The Virtual Business in Action

6 The Virtual Value Chain

There cannot be a business in the developed world that is not familiar with the idea of a value chain. Whether you are a massive retailer concerned, like Wal-Mart, to distribute goods to your outlets as efficiently as possible, or a specialist supplier negotiating delivery through a third party to a small number of customer, you are managing your value chain. And your attention has almost certainly paid off: distribution costs in your business have probably fallen, delivery times have almost certainly shrunk, just as the value that you add to your customers has risen. But is this where you should focus all your attention? Is this the only way in which your organisation can add value?

In December 1995, an article by two assistant professors at Harvard Business School, Jeffrey F Rayport and John J Sviokla, appeared in the *Harvard Business Review*, which argued that the physical value chain was only one side of the equation; in every business where there is a physical value chain, there is also a 'virtual value chain':

> Every business today competes in two worlds: a physical world of resources that managers can see and touch and a virtual world made of information... Senior managers must evalutate their business – its strengths and weaknesses, its opportunities and risks – along with the value chain of both worlds, virtual and physical. Today events in either can make or break a business.[1]

Where the traditional value chain is effectively a series of interrelated functions within any organisation that link its inputs (raw materials to a factory, in-bound logistics to a retail outlet) to its outputs (outbound logistics, the sale of goods to customers), the virtual value chain refers to the value that can be generated by exploiting the information generated by any stage of this process. In this way, information, which in a physical value chain is merely one part of the supporting infrastructure, becomes, in a virtual value chain, an end in itself and one which has commercial value (Figure 6.1). Like the traditional value chain, the virtual value chain needs to be managed if its full potential is to be realised. The processes by which this value is extracted are themselves virtual (bringing together disparate pieces of data, analysing, sorting and distributing that data), as are its customers (companies that need information for their own processes).

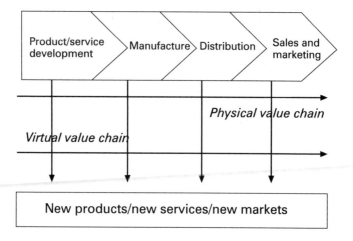

Figure 6.1   The virtual value chain

As always, it is easier to talk about this in practice than in theoretical terms. A school, for example, has just as much of a physical value chain as a parcel distribution company, although it is dealing with children rather than packages. Its essential inputs are children (to be educated), trained teaching staff, teaching materials, the school itself and something which we can loosely term knowledge (that is, the subjects in which the children are to be educated). Using these basic raw materials, the school performs a series of functions. The most important of these is clearly the task of using the teaching staff and materials to pass knowledge on to the schoolchildren, but there are also a series of supporting tasks – ensuring that children attend regularly; scheduling lessons, staff and classrooms; managing budgets. If we think about the value chain of a typical school, we would almost certainly see it in its physical terms – people, books and material – which is ironic given that one of its most significant inputs and outputs is very 'unphysical' knowledge. If we were to think about the virtual value chain of the same school, we would see things very differently.

To start with, we would probably want to translate the physical world with which we are familiar into information terms: not just numbers of pupils and staff, but the educational levels of each child and their particular strengths and weaknesses, and the skills and experience of individual teachers. Rather than think of a class as being about, for example, history, we would want to know what the levels of knowledge of history the children had before the class started, how these had changed by its end and whether particular types of pupil had gained more than others, all of which might help the school to tailor its teaching both to the class as a whole, and to the individual children within it, more effectively. Gather this information across all classes and we would soon start to build up a picture of the overall effectiveness of the school, which could then be benchmarked against other, similar schools.

In fact, this stage of the process is already underway in many countries. In the UK at least, league tables are produced that compare schools' results, even taking into account their relative catchment areas. To this extent, what we are suggesting is no different from something which many companies have already gone through; after all, a central part of the idea of a physical value chain is that information about performance is picked up *en route* so that the overall chain can be managed with increasing efficiency.

The next step in moving from a physical to a virtual value chain is to go beyond simply monitoring the physical processes, changing the way in which operations are managed by looking for areas where information can *replace* a process rather than just record it. In the example of our school, this might range from the comparatively familiar ideas of giving pupils computer-aided lessons (rather than relying on the teacher alone) or multiple-choice examinations (which can be machine read) to the more radical – providing students in remote areas with video-conferencing and e-mail rather than expecting them to spend hours travelling every day.

Once again, the number of companies that have already taken advantage of opportunities such as these, either to improve their service or cut their costs, is growing rapidly: banks are moving away from high-street branches to electronic banking across the Internet; manufacturers are cutting expensive physical processes out of their production lines. (Ford recently announced that it was expecting to save more than £100m a year by using computer simulation models to prototype future assembly lines.)

In many cases, however, the biggest prize of all has yet to be won: the information we can generate as part of the first two shifts from the physical to the virtual outlined above can have a value in its own right, and not because it is a substitute for the physical world. Rather than simply helping us understand or change the physical world, this information can take us beyond it. Rather than facilitating our ability to produce our existing products, deliver our existing services or market our existing markets, the virtual value chain provides an opportunity to create new products or services and to target new markets.

Let us go back to our school to look at how this could happen in practice. We have already seen how assembling information on input and output learning allows us to benchmark one school against another, but if the school is really to make the best use of its information capital, it needs to define new services it could provide or new markets to target. At first sight, the possibilities may seem limited, but they are in fact numerous:

- The school could sell information to their manufacturers on how effective particular teaching aids are, which the latter could then use to price their goods based on value added rather than conventional cost-plus. It could sell similar information on the effectiveness of teachers from different training centres to those training centres for them to use to promote the quality of the graduates from their programmes.
- This same information could be sold to educational companies to help them to identify gaps in the market for particular kinds of teaching aid or out-of-school service, or to help them position and target their existing products more effectively.
- The school could build up a detailed learning profile for each pupil, which could be used to develop out-of-class programmes that are tailored to the individual but which can be followed by the child itself, with or without the help of its parents; with such a

programme in place, there would be little incentive for parents to move to a different school.

- By identifying its specific strengths and weaknesses, the school might be able to launch 'open' programmes on particular subjects, much in the same way that hospitals are increasingly specialising in certain fields rather than trying to offer all services to all patients. In other words, the information would allow the school to differentiate itself and secure its longer-term funding and quality of pupils by positioning itself as a 'centre of excellence' in certain areas.

Think about it. If these are (probably just some of the) ideas for exploiting the virtual value chain in an institution as comparatively simple as a school, how many more ideas would there be in your business? Or in your competitor's business?

We have already looked at the macro-economic conditions that are changing – at the most strategic level – how we run our businesses. In this second part of the book, we want to look at the opportunities from the perspective of individual companies operating in this new environment. Where are the major opportunities – the new markets, the new services or products? Where are the greatest threats? What are the virtual businesses of the present already doing? What are they likely to be doing in the future? To answer these questions, we will take each of the major parts of the virtual value chain – product development, manufacture, distribution and, finally, sales and marketing – in turn in order to identify what we see to be the most critical building blocks of the virtual business.

Notes

1. Jeffrey F Rayport and John J Sviokla, 'Exploiting the Virtual Value Chain', *Harvard Business Review*, November–December, 1995.

The Virtual Research and Development Department

In most organisations, the research and development (R&D) function is leading the way in exploiting the information revolution. Traditional, physical ways of working are being replaced by new methods of creating products – literally straight from the researcher's mind. Out are going the physical methods of creating new drugs, to be replaced by a whole new science of bio-informatics (where drugs are created, examined and tested all within the confines of the virtual world of the computer). Out are going paper-based methods of engineering, to be replaced not just by computer-aided design, but also by new methods of working (concurrent engineering, for example) in which all the design documents are accessible to everyone via their computers, making the concept of a virtual R&D team a reality. Out are going painstaking methods for calculating the optimum design for physical components, to be replaced by programs called genetic algorithms, which employ Darwinian principles of evolution literally to breed better designs within the computer. These changes are radically improving the profitability of the companies that embrace them. Not only do they reduce costs, but – and in most cases, much more importantly – they are also dramatically reducing the time it takes to develop new products for market.

The time taken for R&D in every industry eats into the time available for the exploitation of the product or asset developed. The pharmaceutical industry quotes $1.5m per day as the average revenue that can be generated from a successful drug before the expiry of its patent. For a drug like Zantec (Glaxo–Wellcome's anti-gastro-intestinal ulcer drug), the value of the revenues generated per day before the expiry of the patent can be several times that. The oil industry quotes a similar average for the costs of failing to exploit a new resevoir. In the fast-moving consumer electronics industry, the impact of delay can be even more dramatic: you can miss out on an opportunity altogether, losing the total value of your R&D effort.

Given both the absolute and opportunity costs involved, it is not surprising that, when companies look to shift more of their processes into the virtual world, it is with the R&D department that they often start. Where else in a business can more money be saved (or made) than by shortening the time it takes to get a product to market? However, it is not just rational economics that drive this selection: it helps that R&D departments tend to be staffed by highly trained people with an interest in new technologies, people who have been selected to embrace and develop new ideas. Of all the functions in an organisation, this is the one that should show the most natural inclination to embrace the new ideas of working within the virtual world. It doesn't matter whether you are a big company with a large, formal R&D department, or a small company which can afford to invest in new product development on only a relatively small scale. However big or small you are, your R&D can be improved by making it more virtual.

R&D is, therefore, a natural place to start to explore how the new concepts of the virtual business can be exploited within organisations. The methods and underlying philosophies of the virtual economy are likely to be of direct interest to the R&D community, but understanding how these concepts can be applied in the R&D environment also tells a lot about how these same concepts can be exploited in other functions within an organisation.

■ QUESTIONS TO CONSIDER ■

Throughout this section of the book, you will find a series of questions for you to consider about your own organisation.

The purpose of these questions is to assist you in understanding how well your own organisation is equipped to use information in new ways in order to create a virtual and more profitable future.

1. Which function within your organisation has most radically changed the way in which it works as a result of the information revolution?

2. What lessons can be learnt from its successes and failures?

3. How are these lessons being assimilated and communicated to the rest of the organisation?

A generic model of the research and development activity

The actual methods used for R&D vary considerably by industry: the mechanics of R&D for a new food product, for example, are considerably different from the mechanics of researching and developing a new passenger aircraft. To help us draw parallels between such different industries, we propose to use a generic model of the R&D process, which we can use to illustrate some of the basic concepts of the virtual organisation within R&D function. This model will clearly not fit all R&D processes exactly, but it is capable, we hope, of being stretched enough so that you can fit your own R&D process within it (Figure 7.1).

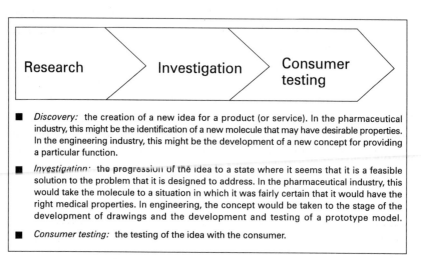

Research   Investigation   Consumer testing

- *Discovery:* the creation of a new idea for a product (or service). In the pharmaceutical industry, this might be the identification of a new molecule that may have desirable properties. In the engineering industry, this might be the development of a new concept for providing a particular function.
- *Investigation:* the progression of the idea to a state where it seems that it is a feasible solution to the problem that it is designed to address. In the pharmaceutical industry, this would take the molecule to a situation in which it was fairly certain that it would have the right medical properties. In engineering, the concept would be taken to the stage of the development of drawings and the development and testing of a prototype model.
- *Consumer testing:* the testing of the idea with the consumer.

Figure 7.1   A generic model for the R&D process

Discovery

How do new ideas come into existence? They do not generally appear out of thin air. They tend to arrive through a synthesis and examination of our own and others' experience. We may, for example, take an existing approach and modify it for a new situation; we may take an idea that has been applied in one context and apply it in another completely different context; or we may perform an experiment to generate some new experiences in order to understand what can be learnt and potentially exploited.

The traditional methods of discovery are exceedingly resource intensive. They require researchers to remain abreast with the current developments in their own fields and preferably several other fields as well. They require attendance at conferences, the reading of papers and discussions with colleagues in order that new developments can be identified, assimilated and transferred to the researcher's own particular opportunities and projects.

The use of computers and computing technology, where information is processed and handled within a virtual world, will not change this requirement. The process of discovery still needs an individual to identify the opportunity, to have the idea, to develop the concept. What moving to the virtual world will do is vastly increase the productivity that can be achieved by an individual. The model that we have used for exploring this concept is:

$$New\ discovery = Experience \times Insight$$

In other words, the more experiences to which people are subjected, the more likely they are to be able to make a discovery. Equally, the more insightful they are, the more likely they are to generate a discovery from that experience. The virtual world can, as we shall see, certainly increase the level of experiences that a person can assimilate. However, it is beginning also to help to increase the level of insight that can be extracted from that experience.

We inevitably refer to the Internet throughout this book because the Internet represents a very real and very accessible attempt to introduce the concept of a virtual world alongside the physical world. The Internet is beginning to touch all aspects of an organisation, however, it should be remembered that it was the R&D community that originally developed the concept, and it is the R&D community that, probably, continues to make best use of it today.

The Internet – then called Arpanet and sponsored by the Pentagon – was originally developed as an experimental in building a fail-safe computer network in case of nuclear war. In 1983 it consisted of fewer than 500 host computers, most of which were in academic and military research laboratories. Other academics soon, however, realised the potential, and by 1987 there were 28,000 different computers connected from research laboratories and universities. The academic and research communities had already recognised the immense value of being able to pass information easily and instantly between one other.

The Internet might have remained a simple (but difficult to use) messaging system for the research community. However, one of these academics – Tim Berners-Lee – who was then working for CERN (the European particle accelerator project), developed the World Wide Web, a multimedia method for displaying information and links from one site to another. The rest is, as they say, history, and it is estimated (although estimates vary considerably) that in 1997 over 30 million people used the Internet.

Why is this important to the R&D community? In the first instance, they were the first people to start to use the Internet. Initially, they used it to accelerate the transmission of ideas and experiences from one to another, and being able to transmit ideas quickly has already led to big savings in R&D costs. Imagine pharmaceutical researchers who, instead of relying on paper mail, receive notification of a new finding by electronic mail over the Internet: they can quickly change the direction of their work to accommodate the new findings. If the same finding had been communicated by paper, it would had to have been typed, printed and distributed around the world. Not only might our pharmaceutical researchers have had to wait several days – more probably weeks – but they might, in the interim, have been wasting time pursuing a fruitless avenue, research that would subsequently be wasted. Furthermore, because transmitting information by post is comparatively expensive, it is unlikely that researchers would send their ideas to more than a few colleagues. This leads on to the Internet's second and most powerful advantage. Until the Internet, the people who received information were chosen by the person who had that information. While information was still transmitted by post, telephone or fax, it was the person sending the information who chose who would receive it. Someone might have a burning need for a particular piece of information, but if that person is not known to the person who owns the information, he or she is clearly not going to receive it. It is true that if the information was – eventually – judged to be of general importance, it might get discussed at a conference or find its way into an academic journal, but this information could, at best, have been a year old (for many academic journals it could have been over 2 years old).

The Internet changes all this. You can choose where you want to look. The information that you take in, and the information that you choose to ignore, depends on your interests rather than on the views of the person who has placed that information. A whole new way of doing things is suddenly open to researchers: information can be obtained as soon as it is produced, and not 2 years later.

In fact, the idea of using information that is 2 years old seems almost alien today. How could any organisation work effectively if its assumptions were effectively 2 years out of date? It is, therefore, not surprising that the research community embraced the Internet – even in its early, formative days – as a way of radically reducing the time to communicate ideas.

This is not the only advantage that the Internet provides for the discovery process. It also vastly expands the number and range of experiences or ideas that can be scanned. Researchers can 'surf' the Internet by typing keywords into one of the many search engines available. Typing 'genetic algorithms', for example, into an Internet search engine (such as Yahoo or Altavista) will bring up several thousand references to the subject. These search engines constantly index the material available on the Internet by word so that it can instantly be retrieved. If the search produces too many hits to be worth investigating, the search can be refined.

Furthermore, a considerable number of research tools are now linked directly to the Internet. IBM, for example, provides details of all the patents that are available from the American patent office. If you want to search the latest patents to see what has been developed in your field, you simply have to type in 'www.patents.ibm.com/ibm.html', and within a few seconds all the relevant patents will be displayed, together with the patents that it cites and those which cite it. Researchers can do in minutes what would have taken days or weeks before, so the impetus to new discovery is further enhanced.

It is worth stressing the order of magnitude of the improvements that are being achieved. Information is being received in days rather than the 2 years it might previously have taken; researchers are examining patents in minutes rather than days or weeks. These are gains not of the 'few per cent here, a few per cent there' type: what we are talking about is a genuine revolution in the speed and scope with which we are able to access information, with research activities being performed orders of magnitude more quickly than before. This is one of the dominant themes of this book: by keeping information in the virtual domain, rather than committing it to the physical domain in the form of the printed word, revolutionary changes – not evolutionary changes – can be achieved.

We have talked so far about how the number and speed of the experiences that a researcher can absorb has dramatically increased, and about how this can enhance the discovery process. Organisations are now investigating how the insight of individual researchers can be improved. One example of this is a product called the Invention Machine Lab. This is based on an analysis of over 2.5 million patents from which, it is claimed, the salient principles for the solution of engineering problems have been extracted. Over 1,400 different physical and geometrical effects are stored. By typing in the characteristics of your problem, you can search the database to see which solutions might benefit your particular problem. We have not tried the product so have no idea how well it works. However, the underlying principle of attempting to extract useful meaning from the vast quantities of information that are now available is certainly sound. Over the next few years, we expect to see a proliferation of new techniques that enable individuals to search this virtual space of information in order to extract the most relevant ideas even more quickly and efficiently than at present.

▓ QUESTIONS TO CONSIDER ▓

4. How does your R&D department access information? How long does it take?

5. Do you have a systematic method for identifying and accessing the most useful sources of information?

6. Is information readily available to your researchers?

7. Does information have to pass through a 'gate-keeper', such as a librarian, before being accessed by your researchers?

8. How accessible is information generated from within the company?

9. What proportion of information is now transmitted in the virtual domain? What proportion of information is still transmitted physically? Why?

Investigation

If the discovery of ideas can be improved so much by keeping information in the virtual domain, it seems reasonable to ask whether we have to use the physical domain at all. If we can generate our ideas via the computer, wouldn't it also be useful to be manipulate and experiment these ideas on the computer as well? A number of companies have asked themselves this question and concluded that this must be the most effective way to go.

Let us start by examining the pharmaceutical industry. The traditional rule of thumb used by the industry is that it takes 'one chemist one week to produce one molecule'. Each molecule created is a candidate for a potential drug. Every molecule then has to be tested against a disease to see whether it has any impact, a process which, as you can imagine, is long, laborious, slow and expensive. It is not surprising that, on average, around 30 per cent of a pharmaceutical company's revenues go into new research and that a new drug costs approximately $350m to develop and takes 15 years to go from the laboratory to the patient.

The science of bio-informatics aims to change all that. Why, it asks, do you have to do all this experimentation in the physical world when you can perform at least some of the work many hundreds of times more quickly in the virtual world of the computer?

One good example of this new science is rational drug design. Many drugs consist of small protein molecules that fit into receptor sites of the invading disease and inhibit its effects. The trick is to find a molecule that fits the physical and electrostatic characteristics of the invading target. It is like trying to find two three-dimensional jigsaw pieces (of immense complexity) that fit together. The science of rational drug design performs this task inside the computer. Instead of physically creating molecules to test at the rate of one a week, a mathematical model is developed. This model can then be compared against a database of all known molecular shapes at a phenomenal rate; if the computer finds one that fits, a physical version can be produced and tested against the disease. Even if the search does not find a molecule that fits precisely, it might point to classes of molecule that almost fit, and this would, in turn, provide clues to the best direction for future research.

The science is not yet perfect. It is very difficult to develop the mathematical models of the different diseases to be investigated.

However, the first drugs to be produced using these methods are now entering the market, and many major pharmaceutical companies (such as SmithKline Beecham and Merck) are pouring millions of dollars into this type of research.

Again, underlying this approach is an important principle that underpins the virtual business. Once information is in the virtual domain, it can be manipulated many times, essentially for free. If a description of a drug or candidate molecule is produced for one particular experiment, that description can be placed on a database and used again and again. The second time you search the database, that drug will be included 'for free'. The more drugs that are contained, the more likely it is that you will find a successful match. The law of increasing returns comes into play, and, over time, drug discovery will become more and more successful at no additional cost.

If the law of increasing returns can be exploited in the pharmaceutical industry, why not in other industries as well? Other major industries are also catching on. The car industry, for example, has similar issues. Cars take a long time and considerable cost to develop. Take Ford's Mondeo: it cost over $6bn dollars and almost 6 years to bring to market. Investments of that magnitude and with that kind of lead time can be extremely difficult to recoup.

The problem with car design is the sequential nature of the process. A designer produces a design; a scale model is made; management gives approval; a prototype is built; the car is tested. At any stage, the concept can fail, and then it is back to the drawing board. No wonder the process is long and expensive, and no wonder that failures are often so high profile (like the technical difficulties identified in early versions of Mercedez's new A class car in November 1997).

Keeping the process in the virtual domain brings with it enormous advantages. Perhaps most fundamentally, designers and engineers can work together. Everyone can see the design at the same time, and everyone has an opportunity to comment on what will and what will not work. The savings from this one change alone are considerable. Car designs no longer have to cycle round long iterative loops that could take weeks or months to complete. Instead, engineers can react to designers' ideas as they are being placed on the drawing boards.

Car companies also tend to be global companies these days, and without the ability to share information across the globe, it would be almost impossible to develop and design a new vehicle. In addition, the time difference between continents can be exploited. A design that is started in Europe can be further developed by someone in the USA and then finished by someone in the Far East – three shifts within 24 hours and without any antisocial working hours. Such processes are already being put in place in industries as varied as architecture, software and engineering, further reducing the time for a new design to reach market.

Perhaps even more importantly, virtual car design, just like rational drug design, enables experiments to take place quickly and effectively. The process of testing a car on a crash-bed, for example, takes weeks to complete. Ford, on the other hand, have developed a digital crash-bed running on a Cray computer. A virtual design can be subject to a virtual experiment. In less than half an hour, the results, virtually identical to the real thing, can be produced. If a design fails, it can be quickly altered and subjected to a further round of testing.

The Boeing 777 is possibly the most famous example of an object being developed in this way. The designers used a product called CATIA (Computer-Aided Three-dimensional Interactive Application), developed by Dassault systems of France, to bring together 1,700 Boeing workstations together with 500 suppliers in countries around the world. Perhaps most importantly, the use of the virtual space enabled people to start to work together. Developments could be discussed by cross-functional teams, ideas could be considered and rejected long before a physical model was developed, and mistakes and errors could be pointed out early in the process.

The advantages are huge. Experiments can be completed in minutes; processes that once took weeks to complete now take hours or less; orders of magnitude improvements are being achieved; and any refinements to the virtual models can be stored and used again and again. It is no wonder that so much money is being invested to develop these technologies.

■ QUESTIONS TO CONSIDER ■

---

10. What experiments or R&D processes could you convert to a digital form? What savings might be achieved?

11. What learning from your current processes can be captured and reused so that you can start to exploit the law of increasing returns?

12. Have you considered working three shifts in three continents? What might the savings be? Would it benefit your clients?

Of course, life would be even easier if the computer could do all the work, and companies are working on that too. Take Human Genome Sciences, a US-based biotechnology company. They have a collection of computers analysing DNA samples. Once a gene sequence is extracted, it is sent to a powerful supercomputer that compares each gene sequence against its existing database and others on the Internet. Simultaneously, an automated literature search is triggered off, and any related articles and research papers are instantly downloaded for the scientist to review. The process of research and development is speeded up, with the minimal involvement of humans. It is not surprising that Human Genome Sciences might end up with patents on half a human being's 100,000 genes. How can an organisation that does not work in the virtual domain compete?

Taking the process one step further, why not give the computer the role of designer? As well as performing the experiments, there is no reason why the computer should not suggest possible modifications and improvements. A new development in computer science, called genetic algorithms, has already opened up this possibility. Genetic algorithms depend on Darwinian principles of evolution to produce their results. The principle is simple. The engineer tells the computer the characteristics of the object it wants; it must not weigh too much, it must have a low drag coefficient, and so on. The computer then generates many hundreds of random objects and sees how closely each of the random objects meets the criteria required. Of course, the objects will at first be nowhere near the requirements. What the computer then does, using the principles of evolution, is to kill off those objects that are furthest away from the criteria and then breed from the fittest of the remaining objects by combining their parameters. This generates a new population of objects. Some of these will be worse than their parents and will be discarded. Some, however, will be better. The process repeats itself, and an object that meets the original criteria laid down is gradually evolved.

This may sound like science fiction, but the approach has been tried successfully in a wide variety of different contexts ranging from tax optimisation through pipeline control, to the development of new wings for airplanes and the design of turbines. For example, General Electric of the USA used the approach to develop a new turbine for its largest commercial engine. The resulting design outperformed anything that anyone else had produced, and this approach is now being developed further to solve other engineering problems.

---

13. How much effort do you expend trying to automate the processes by which you carry out R&D? Have you calculated how much you might be able to save by introducing new automated technology?

14. How up to date is your organisation on the latest computer science techniques that can be applied to the R&D process?

Consumer testing

At the end of the day, once all this research, design and development has been completed, how can we be sure that the consumer is going to like our new product enough to buy it? This last part of the process can be the most difficult of all. However good the science and engineering that has gone before it, if the consumer does not like the product it will not sell, or at least it will not sell well enough to recoup the R&D costs that have been incurred.

The solution, once stated, is obvious. Involve the consumer earlier in the development process. If better and earlier consumer research can take place, it is more likely that the final product will meet consumers' needs.

Famously, the developers of the Boeing 777 did just that. Rather than start with a blank sheet of paper, they invited airlines in to make suggestions about what they would like. Not only that, but they involved advisors from four of the airlines buying the 777 (United, Cathy Pacific, Japan Airlines and All Nippon Airlines) throughout the design process. These advisors made over 1,000 suggestions ranging from overhead baggage lockers to toilet seats. This process – for which Don Tapscott in *The Digital Economy* has coined the phrase 'prosumption' – looks set to revolutionise the way in which R&D is performed. Why go to the trouble of developing a product without the involvement of the consumer? If the consumer is involved, the chances of achieving significant sales are considerably enhanced.

The Internet makes this possibility a reality. It provides a mechanism by which consumers can be linked into the R&D process. Take Microsoft, for example. They develop products, but before releasing the final version, they make available a 'Beta' (unfinished and unguaranteed) copy on the Internet. This copy is downloaded by thousands of consumers who try out the product and make suggestions for its improvement. Rather than just a few, possibly atypical, consumers suggesting how the product should be developed, there are now thousands of very different people trying out the product in all sorts of different circumstances. Which process is going to lead to a better product? The answer is obvious.

Taking this process to its logical extreme – something we will look at in more detail later in this book – is the design of an individual product for an individual consumer. Ski manufacturers, for example, are already providing systems that enable you to design your own skis on the Internet. Press a button, and a few days later they will automatically be delivered to your door. Newspapers can be designed to provide just the news that you want to read. Thousands of applications are springing up, which because the R&D process can be performed in the virtual domain, means that items can now be developed to an individual's exact requirements.

The R&D function is changing rapidly, with more and more of the processes being performed in the virtual domain. Wherever possible, the leading organisations in industries as diverse as pharmaceuticals and car manufacture are looking to exploit the information revolution to put the whole of their R&D activity into the virtual domain. The physical domain is being used only to provide a final test at the end.

■ QUESTIONS TO CONSIDER ■

15. How and when are consumers brought into your R&D process? Would there be any advantage if they were brought in earlier?

16. Could your working designs be provided to your consumers any earlier if they were provided electronically?

17. Which organisation has most developed a virtual R&D function in your industry? What competitive advantages do you perceive that they achieve from this?

18. How far are you from the leader in the industry? How long would it take you to catch up?

19. What similar industries might your industry learn from? What could be adapted from their experience?

20. What plans do you have to move your R&D function from the physical to the virtual domain?

21. How are you planning to exploit the learning from the R&D function throughout your organisation?

The gains that are being achieved by these organisations are spectacular. Tests and processes that would once have taken days or weeks are being completed in hours or minutes, leading to a major reduction in the time to market for their products. The learning and experience from one product development can be captured and used again and again on future product developments, providing organisations with an ever-increasing return on their information investments. The ability to share information means that processes can be performed concurrently, leading to further reductions in the time taken to complete the product development process.

Organisations that move in this direction will, therefore, have an ever-increasing advantage over those which remain in the physical domain, with shorter product development times and cheaper development costs. The inescapable conclusion is that this competitive advantage will lead R&D functions in all industries to seek to exploit the virtual domain. Organisations that are sensible will ensure that they are at the vanguard of this revolution in their industry. Those which will be the winners will ensure not only that they are at the vanguard of their industry, but also that they seek to exploit the learning from developments in R&D for the rest of their organisation.

Summary

Both in absolute terms and opportunity costs, R&D is an expensive process. Using information – in other words, shifting more R&D into the virtual world – offers significant advantages by:

❑ enabling researchers to exchange information much more quickly and systematically than before, thus reducing overall research time and minimising the amount of unproductive research;

❑ making much more information available to any single individual: researchers can choose what they look at rather than having to wait to be shown it;

❑ ensuring that the information available is much more up to date than used to be the case;

❑ providing the means to investigate issues using computer models and virtual reality rather than cumbersome physical tests;

❑ enabling customers to be involved in the design process from the outset, thus ensuring that the finished product will meet market needs.

Virtual Manufacturing – Exploiting the Virtual in Your Product

8

Information is changing not only the processes by which we design and manufacture, but also the products themselves. This chapter focuses on how we can add information to products to increase their value.

Organisations at the leading edge of the information revolution are already exploiting the information associated with their products or services to enhance their offering to the consumer. Products ranging from cars to books, from furniture to parcel-carrying, from cameras to drugs, have all been transformed by such a use of information, giving a competitive edge to the organisations involved. Furthermore, because information can often be distributed for close to nothing, the additional costs of enhancing the product in this way can be minimal. Thus it is not only a company's competitive edge that improves, but also its bottom line. We call this process the 'exploitation of the infosphere'.

Each and every product or service has associated with it an 'infosphere' that contains all the information associated with the product or service. An apple, for example, has associated with it information about its size, weight, type, freshness, availability, source, method of growing, price and nutritional value, recipes it can be used in, stores that sell it and so on. A piece of furniture has associated with it, for example, its size, colour, suitability for various room designs, popularity and desirability, price, functionality, stockists, availability and safety features. Every product has at least 40 or 50 different pieces of information within its infosphere. Some of the ones that we have identified as part of our work on different products include:

- weight
- author
- strength
- distribution
- height
- volume
- maker
- associated risks
- related products
- colour
- other purchasers
- mean time
  between failures
- location
- length
- producer
- acceleration
- availability
- price
- freshness
- purpose
- state of item
  (on/off, and so on)
- popularity
- quality
- where produced
- speed
- stockists
- width
- provenance
- comfort
- artists
- carrying capacity
- relative price
- sell-by date
- benefits
- nutritional value
- target consumer
  group

Some of this information will already be collected as part of the manufacture or distribution of the product, some of the information could easily be collected, and some might require radical changes to the manufacture, marketing or physical make-up of the product. Whatever the extent of available information, it will – in most organisations – be under-exploited.

So far, this is probably sounding like an executive's fantasy: how can we seriously be talking about enhancing your products or services, by using information – which costs next to nothing – while still improving your organisation's competitive edge? The secret lies in having a clear understanding of the reasons why your customers buy your goods or services. Most consumers purchase not because they want to own your product or even experience your physical service as such, but because of the benefits, or perceived benefits, that they believe the purchase will provide. They buy Coca-Cola not because they want to own the bottle but because of the physical taste sensation that Coca-Cola provides (refreshment) or the image it projects (young, healthy, energetic and so on). They buy cameras not because they want to own a camera, but because the camera allows them to take good pictures: Kodak is selling memories rather than photographic equipment. They buy drugs not because they want to own the drug concerned, but because they believe that the drug will improve their well-being.

Exploiting existing information to enhance your product/service offering

The first step to enhancing your product offering through the exploitation of the infosphere is to consider what information you already have that will be of benefit to your customers. Because you already have this information, the costs of making it available are likely to be low, the benefits – as you will see in the following case study – are potentially immense.

Case Study

THE PARCEL DISTRIBUTION INDUSTRY

Why do customers purchase the services of parcel distribution companies? Until the late 1980s, it had been assumed that the key reason was the quality of service, that is, the speed and reliability of delivery. However, the insight of FedEx in the early 1990s was to realise that the reason why customers purchase the services of parcel distribution companies was not primarily to deliver parcels to one destination or another, but to ensure that they themselves had satisfied customers.

Until this point, the battle between the parcel distribution companies had been based on these physical characteristics (speed and reliability), and they had made great progress in speeding up delivery, extending the range of locations to which they would deliver and ensuring the quality of the services that they provided. FedEx, for example, now runs a massive distribution network with over 500 flights a night of its own fleet of aeroplanes, monitoring parcels at every stage of the way to ensure the quality of service and extending the range of locations all over the world to which it can deliver.

Further improvements, therefore, to the physical qualities of its service are likely to be minimal. Reducing the delivery time by another hour is likely to prove extremely expensive and, in most cases, to be of marginal benefit to the consumer. Increasing the range of locations is, again, equally likely to be of marginal benefit. Instead, a revolution has been achieved by realising that successful parcel distribution not only involves the physical aspects of the service, but also making sure that the person who receives the parcel is satisfied, and that this satisfaction can be enhanced by the provision of information. As the Chief Information Officer of FedEx, Dennis Jones, put it:

> You create value by cutting costs, but you also create value by making your customers more capable to their customers. You make customers look good to their customers.[1]

As a result, FedEx realised that it could increase recipient satisfaction by providing information on the progress of the parcel and its probable time of delivery.

Furthermore, the company realised that this information was sitting unexploited (for these purposes) within the organisation. Operational systems contained information about the whereabouts of every parcel at any time; all that was needed was a method of distributing that information to FedEx's customers.

In this particular case, the Internet provided an ideal solution. Most customers sending a parcel (primarily businesses) have access to the Internet. FedEx simply provided access to the information within their systems across the Internet. All a customer has to do is type in the consignment number of their parcel into the FedEx website and the current location of the parcel will be displayed. Such has been the success of this move that other parcel distribution organisations, such as DHL and UPS, have followed suit – and have indeed taken the battle further. UPS's latest advertising booklet hardly mentions parcel distribution; instead its headlines say:

> Your boss wants budget information, your clients want inventory information, your customers' customers want distribution information.

Opening the booklet, it describes in detail how you can use tracking information not only to monitor a parcel, but also to assist your finance department in speeding up invoicing in situations where the invoice cannot be issued without proof of delivery; to assist your marketing department to predict demand using the history of parcels delivery; and to assist your sales department to clear parcels through customs before they have even been landed, via the use of customs papers transmitted electronically in advance.

The battleground has clearly shifted in parcel distribution. Which customers will now remain with a traditional parcel distributor that does not provide these services? The reduction in debtor days through quicker invoicing alone would, in many situations, pay for the cost of the distribution service.

Further enhancing the physical quality of FedEx's service was likely to be expensive and of only marginal value to their consumers. In other words, the battle for product dominance could not go much further within the physical domain. Benefits could, however, be obtained by exploiting the existing information that existed within their organisations. The information that would be of interest to their customers was already available as the byproduct of their administrative processes. This information could also be made available to the consumer at low cost. Furthermore, once their competitors began to emulate their offering, the offering could be further enhanced by providing information about the service itself.

So what has the result been? In 1996 UPS increased its worldwide business by more than 9.5 per cent, to $22bn, and FedEx raised its revenues by 9 per cent, to $10.3bn. Not only that, but, as Rick Goldhoff (responsible for FedEx's electronic connections) points out:

> In April over 3m callers from 117 countries accessed the FedEx web site. Of those more than 1m were tracking packages. That means there were 1m telephone enquiries that our customer staff didn't have to deal with.[2]

Thus not only does the provision of additional information assist in generating new sales and revenues, but, migrating your customers to use automated services, it can reduce costs as well.

How equipped are you to react when a competitor of yours starts to exploit the infosphere? Do you even know what your competitors are doing in this area? How are you ensuring that your business will remain competitive?

Perhaps, at least with the benefit of hindsight, it is easy to say that parcel distribution is an information-intensive activity, and, as such, it was obvious that the market would develop in this way. What about furniture retailing, for example? Few executives to whom we have spoken regard furniture retailing as a particularly information-intensive industry. Few regard it as an industry that is likely to fight its marketing battles over the information contents of its products. But even in such an unlikely industry, you can observe developments. We have, for example, already mentioned IKEA and how they provide additional information about availability. To take another example, try ringing your electricity company with a meter reading. You may be answered not by a human operator but by a computer asking you to punch in your reading using a few keys on your touch telephone. Again, making a physical process virtual enhances the image of the company and makes contacting them an efficient process (when it can be a very frustrating experience trying to get through to a company whose telephones are continually engaged); ultimately, it increases customer loyalty.

From encouraging customers to provide their own meter readings without the intervention of a human operator, it is only a small step to persuading them to order goods automatically as well. This next step has already been taken by a number of retailers. Take Action Computer Supplies, the UK's largest computer supplies retailer. Not only do they provide software so that you can examine the availability of products before ordering, but they have also made it possible to order at the same time. Providing this sort of service, especially by providing this sort of service first, businesses are likely to be able to lock in customers and shut out other organisations that are slow to respond. This strategy is clearly being undertaken by Action: they provide on-line ordering and also offer quite substantial discounts to those customers using the service. Once these customers are locked in, we predict that these discounts will be reduced, but by then the damage will have been done: other organisations, slower to respond, will find it difficult to persuade customers to switch to an alternative on-line ordering system – and Action's dominance in this field will be further enhanced.

▨ QUESTIONS TO CONSIDER ▨

1. Why do customers really buy our goods and services?

2. What information have you got that might be of interest to our customers?

3. How could you make that information available?

Eli Lilly, the drugs company that makes Humalog (a form of insulin for use by diabetics), takes a different approach – it has created a website complete with an 'education centre' that aims to answer questions about diabetes. Advertising on the site is well signposted and unobtrusive, but it would still be difficult to access the site and not realise that Eli Lilly produces specific treatments for diabetics. The provision of the information is certainly a public service, but it is also an effective tool in raising brand awareness. There are few organisations that do not have some information on their products that their customers would be interested in receiving. Remember, if you view this as too difficult to provide, you leave yourself open to a competitor who might get in first.

Exploiting information from your customers to enhance your product/service offering

So far, we have considered only those organisations which have utilised existing information to enhance their product offering, but it is also important to look at what additional information could be collected to increase the value of a product to a consumer still further.

Consider the case of Barnes & Noble, the world's largest bookseller. They, like many other booksellers, have an Internet site, make book reviews and recommendations available, and draw up bestseller lists so that particular books are brought to the consumer's attention, books that they may not have read but which might be of interest to them. While all these approaches have their merits, they suffer from a common problem: book reviews and bestseller lists provide information about the general popularity of a book, but they do not tell you if a specific book will appeal to you. Of course, what a customer wants is not information about the general appeal of a book but to know that they personally will enjoy the book in question. If a bookseller could get this latter information right, his sales would be assured. Barnes and Noble have taken the enterprising step of trying to meet this need. They offer to collect information on your preferences for particular books and authors and then to match them to their total population of customers. By identifying the customers on their database who have the most similar tastes, they are then able to offer suggestions about other authors and books you might enjoy. Not only that, but they then couple this to an e-mail messaging system that informs you when a new book has been published by an author whom you like. In this case, they are clearly adding a new opportunity to the existing shopping experience, enabling you to access the views of people with similar tastes and interests. They are, in effect, automating the word-of-mouth experiences that so many of us rely on when we buy something. They are supplementing their existing promotions with perhaps the most powerful sales message of all – the opinions of people who think in a similar fashion.

The technology to do this is available today and is not particularly complex. It has already been employed to sell CDs, and we will no doubt soon see it extended to other consumer purchases that are based on preference. There are already products into which you can type your preferences for films, music or a host of other goods or services, the program then comparing your list of choices with those of all the other customers who have typed in similar sets of preferences, and making recommendations about the items that you have not mentioned. The sales potential of this type of product is enormous: as a company, you save on the reams of market research and segmentation you would normally have to perform in order to get this degree of detail on individual preferences (which would in any case be based on imperfect information) by getting individuals themselves to type in the information you need to identify the products they are likely to buy. Consumers win too, by obtaining informed suggestions about the products they might like to purchase; they can also be alerted when new books or CDs are produced by their preferred artists or authors.

Again, the added value comes from using information as the means by which a company interacts with its customers; it also has the incidental benefit of being cheap to use as the customer performs all the work by voluntarily giving up the information.

In fact, the real question is, what is stopping the introduction of such ideas? The cost of collecting this information, processing it and returning these specific, targeted suggestions is only a few tens of thousands of dollars – less than the cost of taking on a new employee. Moreover, those who are first with the technology will have the opportunity of capturing and locking in an enlarged customer base; those who follow will never catch up. Banks are already trying to lock their customers in to their services by offering software for on-line banking. In 1996 over 1,000 banks offered on-line services in Europe alone, and many more are scheduled to make similar offerings in the near future. (We will be discussing the ease and convenience that this brings to the consumer – and the massive reduction in costs that this brings to the banks – in the following chapter.)

However, this ease itself is potential threat. If it is so easy for customers to gather information about different accounts, and then transfer their money to a different banking organisation, how are banks going to prevent customers chasing the best deal? We would argue that the answer again lies in adding information to their products. One approach the banks are taking is to persuade their customers to use standard accounting software. Once they have been successful in effecting this change, it is a relatively simple matter to link the software directly to information in their accounts. Imagine, you could then have a bank that not only presented statements about the amount of money in your account, but also directly updated your accounts when invoices had been paid and started to perform some of the basic, and very time-consuming, accounting functions on your behalf. Access to your accounts might also enable the bank to offer you more appropriate products. Imagine again: a bank could analyse your accounts, provide an on-line accounting 'health check', identify your bad debts or poor payers and then make recommendations about transferring them to a service the bank offered that would collect these debts on your behalf (for a fee, of course).

Some people might regard very targeted selling such as this as rather sinister, but it seems to us vastly preferable to receive useful mailshots – about products which are of genuine value to us in our particular circumstances – than the barrage of unsolicited mail and e-mail that we currently receive. It is a marketing battle that has barely begun. We have seen Microsoft's attempt to take over Intuit (the makers of the world's leading personal accounts software) fail because of regulatory pressures. What we assume Microsoft was after was not the market for personal accounts software – which is relatively small – but control of the on-line banking market. By controlling the world's most popular accounting software, Microsoft would potentially have been able to exert control over the way in which banks interacted with their customers. The battle for dominance in adding this intelligence – the ability to provide information on your bank account as an added value service – is still being fought in the USA. In the UK, the battle has just been joined. In 1997 the Midland Bank (one of the UK's four largest clearing banks and owned by the Hong Kong Shanghai Bank) was offering the UK's most popular small business software, Sage, at a much reduced rate to their new small business customers. It might appear to their competitors that they were simply running a loss-leading campaign to attract more business, but we predict that if they achieve a sufficiently large customer base, they will be able to link their bank accounts directly into the accounting software, thereby adding considerable value to their customer offering. It is a strategy that has the additional advantage of locking the bank's customers in, as the changes to the accounting procedures that they might have to adopt if they changed banks could be prohibitive.

The same battle can be observed even in the relatively staid and conservative world of accounting. The major professional service firms are gearing themselves up to change the way in which they audit their clients' accounts. Most of the big six accountancy firms have announced that they are developing the concept of continuous audit. Rather than providing a single end-of-year audit – primarily for statutory reasons, which many analysts believe to be of little value other than for regulatory purposes – they are all beginning to offer the concept of continuous monitoring. If customers provide a link into their systems and enable the auditors to monitor what is going on, then, they argue, they will be able to spot problems as they arise and warn companies as errors are occurring rather than some time after the event, when it may be too late to do anything about them. Although this is a more recent battle, the marketing logic is just the same as it is for the banks. If clients provide more information to the accounting firm (or bank), it should be possible to provide them with new added value services, and these in turn will attract new customers. Equally, if clients have gone to the trouble of providing that information (or changing their systems to provide that information), they are less likely to want to switch suppliers.

■ QUESTIONS TO CONSIDER ■

The second, and potentially even more powerful, way to exploit information is to engage with the customer. Customers will provide information if they perceive a real benefit in return: the book-reader will expect some new and interesting suggestions of books to read; the small business better, quicker information into its accounts; the client a cheaper and more effective audit. However, customers are unlikely to want to repeat the effort, and being first to market is therefore an opportunity to lock your customers in (by exchanging mutually valuable information) and lock your competitors out (by making sure that your customers are unwilling to give out the same information a second time around).

4. How could you help your customers if you had better information?

5. How could you increase sales if the customer had provided the information?

6. What mechanisms exist by which that information might be obtained?

Then and only then, think through the technical issues that might be involved.

We have just described three very different, and relatively novel, approaches that show how products or services can be enhanced when information is added to them. If booksellers, bankers and accountants can all radically change their business models by collecting information, it is unlikely that your business – whatever it is – will remain immune.

Changing your product/service by offering to enhance its value

The third way we have identified to exploit the infosphere is to change your product or service in order to increase its value. The technology to build intelligence into products is becoming commonplace: computing power that cost several thousand dollars in the early 1980s can now be obtained for about $5; the size of computers and their chips has become smaller.

Changing products to increase both the information they provide and their functionality is fast becoming *the* way of differentiating and improving product offerings. Take this headline from the *Sunday Times* for an illustration of the way in which cars are developing:

Cars are here to stay, for a while at least, but safety and intelligence are overtaking size and speed.[3]

BMW, for example, have already announced, and are advertising widely, the concept of on-board navigation systems. By linking an on-board computer to a satellite tracking system, it is possible to provide the car's driver with information on the car's exact location. By keying in your destination, the on-board computer can tell you exactly what turnings you should be taking in order to arrive as quickly as possible. Again, the cost of providing this facility is not outrageously expensive – such a system should cost no more than a few hundred dollars per car.

But the cost of the technology is not the main issue when making changes to your products or services. What is important is to ensure that, whatever you do to change your product, it is in the best interests of your customers. Most effort should be spent in ensuring that the right changes – those which will provide maximum benefit to the consumer – are introduced. Only then should the difficulty of implementation be considered.

As well as cars, other high-value goods are receiving the same treatment. The makers of top-end and mid-range cameras have also been considering why customers buy their products. They concluded that (most) customers do not buy cameras simply for the sake of owning a camera but because they wish to take a limited range of good-quality photographs, such as portraits of their families and friends, landscape photographs and sports scenes. By combining information about lighting conditions and focusing with professional photographers' knowledge of how best to produce these different types of photograph – all within a computer chip – they have been able to enhance their cameras to ensure that people with them can take better photographs.

The same approach can be seen with software. Microsoft's latest graphics package – Powerpoint 97 – has moved away from adding new graphics and drawing features to adding more intelligence. Rather than repackaging the tools within the product, Microsoft have fundamentally reconsidered what it is that a customer wants from a drawing package. They have realised that what customers want is the ability to produce persuasive presentations, and, on this basis, they have included examples and templates of how to produce different types of presentation. The sales presentation template, for example, takes you through how to introduce the benefits of the product to a prospective customer, whereas the strategy presentation focuses on the aspects of your markets and environment that you should be considering. As consultants, we were sceptical when we first saw this, but, having examined the templates in some detail, we have to admit that they do add value.

◼ QUESTIONS TO CONSIDER ◼

---

7. Why do your customers buy your product?

8. What is it that they really want to achieve with your product?

9. What information would enable them best to achieve their ambitions?

10. What would be the most effective way of changing your products in order to incorporate the information into them that your customers want?

11. Is it cost-effective to incorporate the information? (Do not forget to factor in increased sales from its introduction. If it is still too expensive, ensure that a mechanism is put in place to watch technology developments, as technology prices fall rapidly.)

We have seen in this section how companies are now moving away from competing on the traditional aspects of a product, such as the speed and comfort of cars, the quality of the lens and range of focal lengths of cameras, or the number of different drawing tools within a graphics package, and are moving to compete in the virtual world – the ability to provide directions to get to your destination, to get the right settings for the perfect portrait, to produce a persuasive presentation. The rapid march of technology makes adding this information cheap and of high benefit to the consumer.

Again, it is important to stress that the spoils exploiting the infosphere of a product will fall to the first company to market. In this, as in the other areas described in this book, playing catch-up is rapidly becoming an almost impossible way in which to operate.

Summary

Many of the easy improvements in the physical design of products have been achieved; further improvements are likely to be of only marginal benefit. One area that is still open for considerable improvement, however, is the exploitation of the infosphere of the product. We predict that most of the major product developments will be centred around better exploitation of the infosphere.

There are three strategies that are commonly being used to exploit the infosphere:

❏ making information that already exists within an organisation available to customers;

❏ obtaining information from customers that can then be used to add value to their use of the product or service;

❏ changing products/services to incorporate more information.

Whatever the product, exploiting its information content can add value. In some cases, that exploitation can change the market completely, but the key to this exploitation is to understand why your customers are purchasing your products – what do they really want them for? If you understand that, you are well on the way to understanding how best to exploit the infosphere of your products.

Those who get in first have a significant advantage. Not only do they reap the rewards of publicity and new customers, but they also can continue to evolve their exploitation. As soon as the companies who are following manage to catch up, they can add a new variant to keep them in the position of market leader.

Do not let technological difficulties put you off. If the costs seem large now, remember that they will fall quickly. If you do not do it, someone else will.

Notes

1. Quoted in Don Tapscott, *The Digital Economy: Promise and Peril in the Age of Networked Intelligence,* New York: McGraw-Hill, 1996.
2. *Financial Times,* 13 June, 1997.
3. *Sunday Times,* 15 June, 1997.

Virtual Distribution

9

Who talks to your customers? Does your company, or is there an intermediary between you? Is this the same for all your customers, or do you talk to some while somebody else talks to the rest? If you talk to them, how do you exploit this relationship – and if you do not, how are you planning to get round the obstacles between you?

▒ QUESTIONS TO CONSIDER ▒

1. What proportion of your customers do you communicate with directly?

2. How often do you communicate with them?

3. What information do you give them?

4. What information do you get from them?

5. What do you do with the information you receive?

6. If you could communicate directly more often, how would it help?

Talking to your customers depends on being able to access them in order to tell them about your product or service offering. Throughout most of the 20th century, a standard model of the sales and distribution of goods has been in existence. Manufacturers, whether of baked beans, cars or petrol, have developed products that have been sold through a geographically dispersed set of intermediaries such as wholesalers, retailers and distributorships. Service industries, such as insurance and travel, have followed the same model, with their services being sold through insurance brokers and travel agents. Manufacturers communicate their value/price offering to the consumer through advertising and promotion that may or may not be linked to a particular distribution channel. In a slight variation of the standard model, some industries (retail banks, for example) might own or manage their own outlets.

The focus of this chapter is very simple: selling products to customers no longer depends on this standard model. Why? Because:

- you no longer need a geographic network;
- you do not need a large network of intermediaries because technology is providing new ways of communicating with your customers and these will prove cheaper and more effective;
- these new methods of accessing customers (because they involve giving your customers more information) also provide a chance for you to establish a competitive edge – and if you do not exploit this opportunity, your rivals will.

Before we go on to look at each of these points in greater detail, it is important to stress that, when we think about new methods of communication, we should not confine ourselves to considering the Internet, however fashionable it may currently be. The working definition that we use throughout this book is that the information revolution is about all methods of communicating information, be they television, the telephone, the Internet or interactive TV. All these methods (and those which are yet to be developed) will play a part in revolutionising the way in which we sell goods or services to customers.

▒ QUESTIONS TO CONSIDER ▒

7. What methods of communication do you use in talking with your customers?

8. What other methods are you considering?

The end of geography?

For as long as people have traded, they have relied on networks of geographically dispersed agents. Visit the Anasazi sites in New Mexico and Arizona and you see the settlements built up at the crossroads of major trade routes, where the jewellery of one region was exchanged for the pottery of another. Agents perform two distinct functions: first, they collect information from customers and disseminate information about an organisation's products; second, they deliver the goods to the customer. A large geographic network of branches, shops or other outlets has traditionally been the only way in which information could be exchanged between a producer and consumer. Local bank managers were essential because they were the only people who had, or could obtain, the information about their local economic conditions to ensure that the correct decisions on lending and saving could be made. For a manufacturer, a large sales force was essential because this was the only means by which information could be given to and gathered from customers – and it was this information which ensured that the company's products sold successfully.

Since the late 1980s, however, this has no longer been the case. Simple credit scoring applications (filled in over the telephone and which can be matched against national, or even international, information) can provide better information about the likelihood of a particular loan failing than can most bank managers, even those with access to unlimited local information. It is acknowledged that linking a sales force to head office is at best a poor way to collect information about customers and provides no information in many organisations. What matters is not a local geographical presence but a reliable means by which a customer can connect to and interact with your organisation. What does not matter is where that interface is physically based, provided it is accessible to both existing and potential customers, so that you can understand their needs and desires and they can understand your product offering. The information revolution offers each and every organisation, big or small, the opportunity to create such interfaces at relatively little cost and at a considerably lower cost than those traditionally associated with setting up a geographically dispersed set of agents.

What has delayed the acknowledgement of this fact is the second activity performed by these agents – the distribution of goods. Most of these networks do not simply collect and disseminate information about goods and services. In many cases, such as retail outlets and bank branches, they have also traditionally acted as the location where customers and clients can collect goods and perform transactions.

Just because we have always combined information collection and distribution does not mean that we have to continue doing so. There is no reason why these two functions should not be separated: a ticket purchased through a travel agent can just as easily be sent through the post as collected from a travel agent's shop; larger items can simply be sent by one of the many carrier and distribution organisations that exist around the world. Indeed, the race is on to find an efficient means of transporting low-value goods directly to the consumer, thereby obviating the need for retail outlets at which customers can collect items that they have purchased.

■ QUESTIONS TO CONSIDER ■

9. What are the functions of your intermediaries?

10. Could the functions of your intermediaries be split off?

11. Could some of the functions be handled by the new technologies that are emerging?

The first organisations to acknowledge and accept that the information revolution had removed the need for a geographical presence were the financial services organisations such as banks and insurance companies. These organisations sell products that consist, almost entirely, of information. They supply their customers loan or savings accounts, abstract entities that consist largely of information about the customers' ability to draw money from an account. The physical elements of the transaction are minimal, consisting in most cases of a paying-in book, cheque book or plastic card, all of which can be transported through the postal service. Until the mid-1980s, however, these organisations still relied on a massive geographical network of branches to enable customers to perform the basic transactions with their accounts. Customers had to travel to a physical branch, fill in a form and then queue to hand the form to a cashier in order to perform each and every (however basic) transaction with their account. Even to organisations as conservative as banks, this was a rather inefficient and expensive way of doing business. As a result, banks have been at the forefront of using the information revolution to change their methods of sales and distribution. When automatic teller machines were introduced, they met with immediate success: customers no longer had to go to a remote branch to obtain money, but could now obtain it from a more convenient location with the use of a card. Even more importantly, they could obtain money at any time of day or night and on any day of the week. However, even with the introduction of automatic teller machines, banks still failed to appreciate the extent to which customers dislike using their precious spare time to queue for money. Customers also do not like being without money just because the bank at a particular location is closed, and they do not like having to travel somewhere just to order something. Customers much prefer a full range of services, provided 24 hours a day, located within their own sitting room – an ideal to which telephone banking is getting closer. The use of information technology (in this case telephones and sophisticated computers) not only means that geographical presence is unimportant, but also offers a way of enhancing the service offered by banks. It is not surprising that consumers are flocking to this type of banking wherever it is introduced.

Despite the widespread success of virtual services such as telephone banking in the financial services industry, the reaction we most often encounter when we discuss these issues with executives in other industries is that, while it is obvious in retrospect that such changes were bound to occur in the financial services sector, they could not possibly happen in other sectors because of the physical nature of most goods. Who, for example, would buy vegetables or meat that they could not see beforehand? We would want to know that they looked fresh, hygienically packed; we would want to be able to discard bruised fruit or limp vegetables. A decade ago, this attitude would have been completely understandable: we were all accustomed to living in the physical world; many of us did not quite trust computers. Today, the situation is very different: since the early 1990s people have been flocking to sign up for home shopping services in the USA, the UK and Europe. Home shopping services now range from specialist outlets – buying your chilli sauce from a company in California – to mainstream grocers, such as Shopco (see the case study below). What is important here is not the scale of the operation but the fact that each of the retailers concerned has been able to provide its customers with the information they require in order to make their purchases with confidence. This takes several forms. Many people now have access to local organic vegetable producers who deliver direct to their doors. They may not know exactly what vegetables will be delivered each week as this will be dependent on seasonal availability, but they do know that the goods will be fresh and organic. In this case, the information they have generated and communicated to their customers is strong enough for them to embrace the concept: customers do not need to see, touch or smell the goods to be satisfied that will be what they want. The co-operatives themselves do not need a massive geographical presence to be able to advertise the goods they have for sale. The exchange of information takes place in the virtual domain without the requirement of a physical presence – all the co-operatives have to do is find a cost-effective method of distribution. The point is not to emphasise the essentially niche aspects of the service that is being provided. Clearly, organic (and relatively expensive) goods are not going to be to everyone's taste. However, just as with financial services, it illustrates that it is possible to provide home deliveries of relatively low-cost but still bulky items. Larger retailers may use slightly different tactics – they may, for example, rely on their brand to be able to convince shoppers that they can be trusted to deliver high-quality goods.

And if the business model is successful for these goods, what is stopping this same business model from being applied to other goods and services?

Case Study

SHOPCO

Shopco was started in 1990 and provides a food shopping service over the Internet to local customers in Canada. The service does away with the shop as a physical place to view and collect food, and replaces it with the Internet site www.shopco.ca – as the place to view and purchase the food – and a warehouse and fleet of vehicles to manage the distribution. Shopco has recognised that you can separate the virtual aspects of the shopping experience from the physical and has divided its business along the same lines.

Many, many people have argued, and continue to argue, that shopping is a physical experience that consumers have to undertake in order to convince themselves of the quality of the goods before purchasing. Shopco, implicitly at least, acknowledges this but provides a virtual alternative. Rather than sell all food, Shopco sells only branded goods and top-quality meat, and it combines this with a no-questions-asked money-back guarantee. The company has identified the physical aspects of choosing and purchasing, and replaced them with a virtual equivalent – the customers' knowledge of what they will be buying, backed up with a guarantee (a virtual promise) that their purchases will be satisfactory.

It appears to work. Shopco claims an 85 per cent customer retention rate, far higher than most traditional grocers, and is one of the fastest growing companies in Canada.

Not only that, but once this division between the virtual and the physical has been made, and the processes by which goods are chosen and purchased are transferred into the virtual domain, these processes can themselves be improved. Customers receive e-mails of weekly Shopco specials, automatic reordering of their staple purchases and other added value services. The retailer has the opportunity to analyse shopping behaviour to ensure that it stocks the correct range, and increases its sales by bringing goods to the attention of the customers most likely to purchase them. Because the process has been transferred to the virtual, we can expect further improvements to the shopping process to be added, and, once the initial development costs have been amortised, the cost of providing these improvements will be negligible.

Home shopping is set to grow... the pioneers are demonstrating that, just as with electronic teller machines, many consumers neither need nor even particularly enjoy the physical aspects of the shopping experience. Economic logic then takes over: why have a large, geographically dispersed and expensive set of physical intermediaries (namely shops) when a better customer dialogue and a cheaper distribution service can be achieved without them?

Clearly, there are issues to be overcome, not least the fact that many existing outlets double up as distribution centres. However, by acknowledging that the function of marketing and selling your goods or services is different from that of distributing them, you open up the opportunities to revolutionise your business. Why have your own geographically distributed network when others (postal services or parcel carriers) might be able to distribute your products more cheaply and more effectively? Why invest enormous sums of money in distributing information to customers through your sales force or branches when you could provide it a single place in the virtual world of information?

Disintermediation, or the end of the middle man?

If the information revolution means the end of the need for your physical networks, then pity the poor middle man, for whatever applies to the end of geographically dispersed agents surely spells the beginning of his end.

The middle man or broker essentially developed to bring together customers and producers in order to effect a sale, and, in doing so, he took a commission. Such a commission inevitably either reduces the profits the producer makes, increases the price that the consumer pays or does both. However, the middle man's role was necessary for two reasons. First, it provided a solution to any physical or logistical problems with the desired transaction: the middle man could reach locations and customers that might not have been accessible to the original producer – he might, for example, have been an overseas agent giving the producer access to a new and unfamiliar market. Second, the middle man was an information broker: he decided what information to give customers and what information to relay back to the original producer. Much of this broking came in the guise of expertise. A middle man of this type might be a share broker who used his knowledge of the stock market to buy and sell shares on his customers' behalf. He might be a consultant, selecting those management techniques and methodologies most appropriate to his clients. Under almost any economic model, if there is a method for removing an intermediary function of this sort, it will in the end disappear. And the information revolution, because it provides new, interactive methods of communication whereby a customer can receive information from and send information back to the producer, is currently the primary means by which many of the traditional intermediary roles for business are being made redundant. Once again, financial services have led the way. We are already seeing the demise of professions such as insurance broking, as technology has meant that it is easier for consumers and insurance companies to exchange information about insurance products directly. Customers can telephone a company's call centre and, by answering a few brief questions, can obtain a quote and buy their insurance – all in a matter of minutes and with no middle man in sight.

Case Study

DIRECT LINE

One of the best known cases of this disintermediation is Direct Line in the UK. This direct insurance company was started in 1985, and by 1993 had become the largest private motor insurer in the UK.

The basic premise on which it was based was simple. People do not need or want to visit an insurance broker in order to purchase their motor insurance. This premise was confirmed: not only do people not need an insurance broker, but also many actually prefer to deal with an operator and their computer system via a telephone. The benefits to the customer are a simpler service. You telephone and obtain a quote, which you can accept or reject all from the comfort of your own home. Visiting a broker, in many people's eyes, involved an implicit obligation to purchase, in order to compensate for the time the broker had expended on their behalf as well as the considerable physical inconvenience that the visit created. No wonder people prefer to telephone. In the UK the traditional brokers are trying to fight back by setting themselves up in the same manner, so that they too can provide a virtual service.

By dealing virtually, with the absence of a large network of intermediaries, Direct Line also managed to reduce costs, and, because of the ability to handle information quickly, they were also able to pick and choose the risks that they wanted to cover. This, in turn, meant that they could offer a narrower product range (which also brought lower costs), but one which was much more precisely matched to the needs of its customers.

Again, we see the benefits of moving into the virtual domain. Consumers, or at least an extremely large proportion of them (in the UK over 30 per cent of motor insurance is now sold direct), prefer to choose and purchase in this way. Immediate cost benefits can be obtained because intermediaries and physical systems can be done away with. And finally, because the information is held virtually, it can be manipulated in new ways, in this case enabling the insurance company to pick and choose the risks it wanted to take on in a more sophisticated manner.

Bypassing the middle man like this is now spreading rapidly to other sectors: it is no longer necessary, for example, to go to a travel agent to buy a ticket to travel by aeroplane. Look at Sabre – the airline ticketing and reservation system on the Internet. Typing details of your dates, destination and ticket requirements into Sabre instantly finds you the cheapest seats on offer. The transaction is simple, can be done from your own home and takes no more than a couple of minutes. The travel agents would, and do, respond by saying that they provide added value that will ensure that they stay in business. They argue that they do not just act as a distribution agent (providing tickets to the customer), but also provide information: helping them to choose their destinations; explaining the options available; providing add-on services such as travel insurance; and reducing risk by being accredited with various travel bodies. This is undoubtedly true, but travel agents remain faced with two, almost irresistible, trends. First, the commission structure by which the travel agents get paid is under threat. This commission, which in the UK amounts to approximately 10 per cent of the ticket price, is the largest non-operational cost that an airline incurs. In February 1995 several US airlines joined together to take the bold step of capping commissions, and it has since been reported that the German airline, Lufthansa, intends to take this one step further by reducing the commission on tickets sold electronically.[1] If actions such as this mean that a significant differential emerges between the price of a ticket purchased electronically and that bought in a traditional outlet, the move away the high-street outlets towards electronic means of access will become inevitable. In fact, the real question facing the travel agents' industry is not whether such a move will take place but when. At the moment, most tickets are still sold through travel agents, and the latter therefore still wield considerable power with which to combat the airlines. However, the technology needed already exists and is being used, and the number of customers able to access the technology is rapidly increasing. It can only be a matter of time before the cost differentials appear that will erode the power and profitability of travel agencies.

■ QUESTIONS TO CONSIDER ■

12. Why would your customers prefer to use an intermediary rather than come to you directly?

13. If you are an intermediary, how can you add value to the transaction chain to ensure your survival?

14. What could you do to entice your customers away from their reliance on an intermediary and come to you direct? What additional information could you obtain, or disseminate, if they came to you direct?

Adding value in the information domain

So far, we have effectively focused on how information technology will supersede the communication of information through geographically dispersed agents or middle men. However, it is unlikely that simply by replacing your existing channel to market with a new virtual one will you achieve any real or sustainable competitive advantage.

In order to be able to acquire new customers and to access them on a long-term basis, organisations need to be able to exploit the information revolution to provide new, added value services rather than just provide a new way to access customers. As these added value services increase, and even if the price remains the same as other channels, customers will migrate away from the physical domain (retail outlets) and start to do business in the virtual domain. At its very simplest, the advertising campaigns for telephone banking emphasise the ability to access your accounts 24 hours a day, 365 days a year from the comfort of your own home. These added value components enabled telephone banking to increase rapidly its market share even though it did not offer any particular price advantage over the traditional bank account. Furthermore, such an advantage appealed particularly to a highly valuable market segment – those people who did not have time to go to a bank because they were too busy working hard and making money. Banking via your personal computer has further advantages in that it enables you to do more with your account – and it saves the bank money by getting you to perform tasks that it would otherwise pay a teller to do. It is this imaginative approach to changing a basic product or service – a massive revaluing of the traditional marketing propositions that are put to customers – which is threatening many existing organisations (among which may be your organisation).

Once again, we encounter a degree of cynicism when we discuss these ideas with executives. This is a trend that will be confined to predominantly information-based industries like financial services, we are told; it will never happen here. Not true! Many other organisations selling physical products are already adopting a similar approach to adding value.

Even when customers buy on the basis of cost, this does not mean that there are no ways of adding value in the information domain. Anderson Consulting have developed a new technology, for example, called Bargainfinder;[2] this enables the user to input details of a product, and the program will then search co-operating stores to find the cheapest price that is on offer. People may not be too concerned about finding the cheapest price for a CD, but the power of this software to transform the structure of sales dealerships that compete largely on price – car sales, for example – must be immense. Other organisations have reversed this approach. Rather than have individual consumers search out the cheapest product on offer, they search out the consumers willing to pay the highest price. Airline tickets can now be purchased by auction over the Internet. You type in the amount you are prepared to pay, and the top (say 100) bids win seats on the flight. Once again, it is important to stress that these organisations are not simply replicating the traditional methods of selling goods and services but are searching out and developing new methods that either add value to the organisation selling or to the consumer purchasing. Either way, they are adding value to their marketing proposition by getting rid of the middle men.

■ QUESTIONS TO CONSIDER ■

15. How is your organisation directly monitoring the development of technologies and methods for communicating directly with the consumer?

16. What alliances has your organisation formed, or is it considering relinquishing, in order that communication with the customer is performed as effectively as possible?

The final defence of the sceptical executive is that not many people have access to these methods of communication, or that the transfer of money is too insecure, or that the technology has not yet been sufficiently developed. Again, the answer has to be 'not true'. There is an irresistible trend towards the development of new methods of communicating with customers: banks and software houses are desperately working together to produce secure payment systems; multimedia companies are desperately working to deliver these services over new forms of communication such as interactive television, satellite television, telephone developments and a whole host of other technological combinations. Enlightened strategists are working within many producer organisations to work out new ways of adding value to the proposition.

We do not know exactly how this primeval soup of technology, ideas and approaches will evolve, but we do know that it will and that those organisations unprepared to take advantage of it will fail.

Summary

Most business have traditionally operated through intermediaries, but they no longer need to do so:

❑ Geographical coverage is being replaced by information networks that in many cases (for example, credit scoring) can be more effective than local knowledge. Furthermore, distribution – the other function of a geographical network – increasingly is direct from the manufacturer to the consumer.

❑ Technology provides a much more effective and cheaper means of communicating with your customers.

❑ Communicating with your customers in the virtual domain opens up new opportunities to add value to your products or services.

Notes

1. Jurgen Burchy, Lufthansa Senior Vice President, quoted in *TTG*, 1 November, 1995.
2. http://bf.cstar.ac.com/bf/.

10 Virtual Marketing: the Economics of Difference

The importance of being different...

Throughout the 1970s and 80s, companies were told to slim down the differences in their organisation: reduce the number of different products for sale, reduce the number of different customers, reduce the number of different markets in which the products were sold. Although this undoubtedly helped companies to increase their short-term profitability, this reduction in difference, and therefore reduction in customer choice, has turned out to be something of a blind alley.

In an ideal world – in our world, even – customers want more choice rather than less, and ultimately those companies that can provide the desired differences will be successful. In this context, difference is about branding (that is, selling *different* products), positioning (to *different* markets), style (in a *different* way) and micro-marketing (to *different* customers). It is about being *different* from other products or organisations. The ability even to contemplate such an approach is in stark contrast to the earlier part of the 20th century, when mass-production meant that making individual, hand-crafted goods was no longer commercially viable – and it remains the case in many industries and organisations in the late 1990s.

The change that makes this possible is the information revolution, and with it the ability to collect, analyse and act upon the vast quantities of information that are now available. No longer do organisations have to rely on selling mass-produced products to masses of consumers; they can instead collect information that enables them to target individually produced products to individual consumers. Those which are already embracing this change are already seeing sales increase at the expense of those organisations which are still trying to sell undifferentiated products to a mass of undifferentiated customers.

This chapter of the book examines one aspect of difference and looks at how some of the problems of supplying different products – mass-customisation – can be resolved by using information-based selling, in the form of micro-marketing.

Mass-customisation – what exactly is it?

The arrival of information technology on the factory floor has meant that, for the first time since the late 18th century, the basic economic model of manufacturing production has changed. Computers minimise the set-up time for machines; they can alter designs almost instantly and assemble products to order. Differentiation now costs little more than standardisation: we have entered the age of 'mass-customisation' in which it is possible to tailor products to the specification of individuals. At the same time, consumer taste has diversified – more people want more individual goods – so that FMCG (Fast Moving Consumer Goods) companies, for example, are having to design different products for smaller and smaller market segments. No longer, for example, is it sufficient simply to have one type of children's spaghetti: varieties now come in the shape of Barbie dolls, Thomas the Tank Engine and many other children's characters to suit each particular segment of the children's market.

This catering to ever-smaller market segments with different products specifically developed for the purpose was first called mass-customisation in the late 1980s. Since then, there has been a renaissance of interest in the subject, with the number of books and articles appearing on the subject proliferating. Between 1971 and 1980, approximately 20 articles a year were published on customisation; this rose to over 200 articles in the next decade, and since 1990, more than 2,000 articles have been published.

Current levels of mass-customisation

Some aspects of mass-customisation have already been implemented. We can order a new car in a particular colour and to a particular specification – a long way from Henry Ford's offer of 'any colour so long as it's black'. Going into a Levi's store, we can order a pair of jeans that exactly matches our measurements rather than having to select from a set of standard sizes. Mail-order computers are assembled and loaded with the specific software that we want installed.

However much the practice of mass-customisation is starting to impact on our everyday lives, it is important to recognise that it only goes so far. It is important to recognise that mass-customisation allows customers to choose, but only within certain parameters that the manufacturer prescribes: it does not free customers to make their own choice. For example, while we can tell Volvo that we want a certain model, size of engine, type of steering wheel and so on, we cannot get them to install the seats of a Saab. Mass-customisation is not necessarily about giving customers what they want, but is currently about giving them a limited choice within a set of rules that the manufacturer defines.

Standardisation ←——————————————————————————→ Customisation

Manufacturer	Product design Manufacture Distribution Sales	Product design Manufacture Distribution	Product design Manufacture	Product design	
Customers		Sales	Distribution Sales	Manufacture Distribution Sales	Product design Manufacture Distribution Sales
Typical products	Pharmaceuticals Soap powder	Cars	Financial services	Self-assembly furniture	Do-it-yourself business cards

Figure 10.1 Levels of mass-customisation

To this extent, the concept of mass-customisation does not represent any radically new or different approach to meeting customers' needs. It is simply a different point on a continuum from standardised to customised products where the level of difference is always defined by the manufacturer rather than by the customer.

The benefits of mass-customisation

But, if this is the case, why bother? The answer lies in the ways in which manufacturers can use mass-customisation concepts to increase their sales.

First, although mass-customisation does not offer consumers complete freedom to design their ideal product, it does give them a degree of choice in areas where they may have had none. This allows the manufacturer to come nearer to closing what has been called the 'full-potential gap' in their products – that is, the instances where a sale is lost because aspects of the product do not meet the needs or preferences of potential purchasers. A simple example would be where a jumper manufacturer allows customers to select their own colour for a particular style. This extra degree of choice means that customers are won who might otherwise have bought an alternative product. On this basis, we might say that any product has 'core customers' (those who would purchase it anyway) and 'peripheral customers' (those who are attracted to the product but not to the extent that these overwhelm other needs or preferences they may have). For any product, the ratio of core to peripheral customers varies. Giving consumers the opportunity to specify some aspects of their purchases themselves will not increase the sales from 'core customers': this group would buy the product irrespective of other preferences they might have. It will, however, increase the sales from 'peripheral customers' because it means that a product is more likely to meet their other, equally important, preferences.

▨ QUESTIONS TO CONSIDER ▨

Where do your products fit on the mass-customisation graph?

1. The first step to mass-customisation is to consider where it might possibly be applied. Compare your products with your competitors. Which contains the greater degree of difference? What additional degrees of difference could you incorporate with your product?

2. Even at this early stage, it is also worth considering what the customer might want. Which difference in your product do your customers most value? Which difference do they value the least? Can you order the differences in your current product range by their importance to the customer buying decision? What additional differences do customers ask for?

Second, mass-customisation is based on the premise that allowing customers greater freedom to choose (even within prescribed limits) is a key way of increasing their loyalty. Why should a Levi's customer buy their jeans from The Gap when the Levi's pair is guaranteed to fit their shape precisely? And, moreover, once you have entered your measurements on to Levi's system, what incentive is there for you to switch to an alternative manufacturer? The effort of re-entering all those details is likely to deter you from moving to another brand of jeans.

Third and finally, mass-customisation is a means by which companies can handle uncertainty in their trading environment, as Joseph Pine, Bart Victor and Andrew Boynton recently observed:

> The highly turbulent marketplace of the mass-customiser, with its ever-changing demand for innovation and tailored products and services doesn't result in a clear, shared vision of that market. A standard product or market vision isn't just insufficient; it simply doesn't make sense. In a true mass-customisation environment, no one knows exactly what the next customer will want, and therefore, no one knows exactly what product the company will be creating next.[1]

Mass-customisation institutionalises flexibility: it allows manufacturers to respond to market needs as they change rather than some time later. Its greatest use, therefore, is thought to be in unstable and unpredictable markets where traditional product development lifecycles and marketing plans are irrelevances. Conversely, it brings little advantage in markets where customers' needs remain the same year on year. Being better positioned to respond to customers' needs means that the company will make sales (of new rather than existing products) that it would not otherwise have made.

In summary, mass-customisation is about making difference work to a company's advantage. It is about taking the degree of difference that can be associated with a collective brand or an individual product and exploiting this to increase sales by:

- using it to gain a higher proportion of peripheral customers;
- exchanging it for customer loyalty;
- winning additional customers with new products.

▓ QUESTIONS TO CONSIDER ▓

Understanding your current processes for handling mass-customisation information

Virtually all companies customise their products to some extent; even Coca-Cola offers a diet version for those interested in slimming. Virtually all companies, therefore, have some processes for handling mass-customisation information.

3. Consider what systems your organisation has to handle mass-customisation information:

   ❑ How do you get information from the customer to customise your products?

   ❑ How do you convert it into a product description?

   ❑ How do you convert the information in the product description into a product?

4. What changes would be required to convert your current processes so that a greater level of mass-customisation could be incorporated within your product?

To make it happen requires that a company uses the opportunities opened up by the information revolution to redesign the processes that it uses to handle information. It needs to re-examine how to obtain the necessary information from a customer, convert that information into a product description and then pass that information to whatever unit of production is going to develop the product. The principles are the same for all industries, from consultancy, where a consultant is undertaking a particular study, to manufacturing, where a particular product is being developed. Without the appropriate flows of information, mass-customisation cannot and will not work.

Before everyone rushes out to incorporate a greater degree of customisation within their products, it is therefore also worth considering some of the drawbacks (see the case study below).

Case Study

TOYOTA

Toyota first began experimenting with mass-customisation in the early 1990s, but by 1992 the project had run into trouble: production costs had risen and product life-cycles had lengthened. Part of this deterioration in performance was blamed on external factors, such as the Japanese recession. However, equally at fault were internal process and management, which had failed to appreciate – and, there-fore, adapt to – what turned out to be 'a very unfamiliar way of doing business'. Unlike total quality management, which looks at the manufacturing process as a linear activity and focuses on discrete areas of improvement within this, mass-customisation depends on a dynamic network in which manufacturing compo-nents come together as and when required: the key to success is having flexible and interlinked teams. The project was also a failure in the eyes of Toyota's customers: 20 per cent of the varieties produced accounted for 80 per cent of sales. So much for giving the consumer more choice.[2]

What these experiences illustrate is that mass-customisation is often not implemented correctly. If the right processes are not put in place to ensure that the correct products get to the correct customers, experiments in mass-customisation will lead to significantly increased stock levels as the manufacturer or distributor will end up having to hold all the possible combinations of products that a customer may request. If the manufacturing process is not quite as 'just-in-time' as thought, or if customers' desires are actually much more restricted than anticipated, then, again, stock levels will increase. To succeed, mass-customisation needs to be timely. The links required between processes need to be flexible, low cost and seamless. Above all, people working in this environment need to work in small but inte-grated teams, linked by common databases and knowledge.

However, this is to see mass-customisation's drawbacks solely in terms of where and the way in which it is implemented. There is a more fundamental criticism of the concept: that it mass-customises the manufacturing process at the expense of consumer preferences. A common theme that emerges when one examines current attempts at mass-customisation is that the degree of choice introduced is always defined by the manufacturers, based on what they can accommodate within their physical processes. While this is the cheapest way of approaching mass-customisation (that is, you limit it to those aspects of products that you are most able to manage within your existing company systems and structure), it can (as we have seen with Toyota) be expensive because it is still the manufacturer's view of what customers want. If the customers do not want the same aspects of the product customised, manufacturers risk being left with stocks of unwanted goods. Furthermore, they are not only likely to be left with unwanted stock, but may also not be successful in attracting any more new customers. In many cases, all that the manufacturers are effectively doing is increasing the number of possible choices in a given area. Nissan, for example, offered customers a range of 87 different steering wheels, but in practice customers disliked having to choose from so many.

This type of approach to mass-customisation fails because it addresses only half of the equation: if you customise your production, you also have to customise your marketing. As well as introducing *difference* in your product offering, you must also offer *difference* in the way in which you market and *difference* in the customers to whom you sell. At the moment, many manufacturers have simply exchanged selling one model to everybody, to selling all possible models to everybody. This has a number of implications:

- In the first place, stock levels increase rapidly because you have increased the uncertainty of your production processes while failing to reduce the uncertainty through your marketing.
- Second, you confuse people by giving them too much to choose from (anyone can choose anything).

If we start to think about the mass-customisation of marketing rather than products, solutions to these two problems immediately present themselves:

- Stock levels can be contained and even reduced if we focus on selling a particular product to a particular customer (not all customers at once).
- A customer's perception of too much choice can be avoided if that customer only gets to hear about those product options which are of interest (rather than all the possible options).

The easiest way to consider this is by referring to Figure 10.2. This shows how different industries approach the marketing of their products. A newspaper, for example, sells a single product variant to many different customers. A bespoke tailor or portrait painter sells many variants to a few customers.

What organisations have been unable to do until the advent of the information revolution is to design a set of information management processes that enables them to sell differentiated products to their differentiated customer base, in other words to target a specific product at one specific individual consumer and another (different) specific product at another individual consumer. It is only by combining mass-customised marketing with mass-customised production techniques does this become possible.

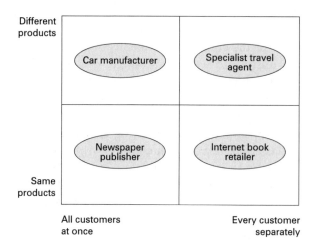

Figure 10.2   Different methods of marketing

■ **QUESTIONS TO CONSIDER** ■

What is the current attitude of your company to mass-customised marketing?

5. Refer to Figure 10.2 above. Where does your industry lie in this marketing segmentation? What is the smallest segment of the market that you can differentiate?

Mass-customised marketing

Our argument is that companies should not try to exploit the potential differences within their products without also exploring differences between their customers. Successful mass-customisation comes from marrying up these two aspects rather than from dealing with either of them in isolation.

Perhaps the most advanced sector is retailing. Predictability here is all important. Retailers have spent millions over the past few years in market research and in trying to segment their customer base so that they can target their advertising, ranging decisions and promotional discounts with ever greater precision. Despite this, they probably still feel that the old truism of marketing – half the budget is wasted, but nobody knows which half – still holds good. And it is here that the concepts of the mass-customisation of marketing and the economics of difference are most powerful.

Most sizeable retailers today operate a point-of-sale system that captures information about individual transactions (the products sold, the total basket value and so on). Since the mid-1990s, the number of retailers also offering some sort of loyalty or customer card scheme has soared, adding customer-specific information to that which is already being processed by the EPOS tills. Although capturing this information was, from the first, seen as one of the principal benefits of introducing such schemes, retailers' ability to use this information has, until recently, been limited. Even now, much of their analysis is confined to developing more sophisticated definitions of customer segments in order to target these on a more focused basis. Even here, it is, however, a rare retailer who has carried these more detailed segmentations through to implementation and increased profits. Leaving aside for the moment the technical and organisational issues posed by dealing with such large volumes of very detailed information, the problem seems to be three-fold. Retailers are finding it difficult to:

■ make sense of the data;
■ identify how they can be used to influence buying behaviour;
■ make customers behave differently.

Difference and the mass-customisation of marketing are the keys to resolving these issues.

Making sense of the data

As we noted earlier, one of the drawbacks of the mass-customisation of production is that the degree of freedom – difference – that consumers are allowed is determined by the producer. Similarly, when organisations start performing detailed market analysis, their first step is usually to try to fit all the available data into a predetermined pattern. In fact, what they should be doing at this stage is using the data themselves to establish what a sensible segmentation should be, based on the actual behaviour of the customers whom they are attempting to segment. In many instances, it will be case that the existing way of categorising customers is not applicable when selling differentiated products.

In fact, we would go considerably further in changing the method of analysis and ask whether traditional segmentation *per se* has any relevance. After all, segmentation is nothing other than an average, even though it is one that is calculated at a more detailed level; and every average necessarily contains summarised information. The details may have been incorrectly discarded. For example, a financial services company might carry out a segmentation of its customer base and identify that it was – for some reason – particularly well represented among young, single, professional men. In looking at the products sold to this segment, it might discover a high prevalence of a particular pension when compared with other segments.

There is, however, a problem with this type of analysis. Although it tells us the relative penetration of the product within each segment of the database, it does not tell us what to do. Should we be trying to sell more of this type of pension into the segment, or should we be trying to sell the same pension elsewhere? Traditional segmentation gives us no clues. Mass-customisation turns the traditional form of segmentation around. Rather than analysing customer groups and calculating penetrations, the approach of mass-customisation marketing is to divide customer segments into two categories: those who have bought and those who have not. Those who have are then analysed in considerable detail, sometimes down to the level of one, in order to understand exactly why they have bought. This analysis of their behaviour then dictates how the rest of the market should be approached and proceeds by analysing your market segments into groups that identify:

■ what relevant attributes differentiate purchasers from other groups of your customers;
■ the probability that marketing actions can change the behaviour of the other groups of customers;
■ the probable return if their behaviour changes;
■ the size of the group.

So, for example, we may have identified that the young men buying this particular pension product all work in similar professions. It may not be the fact that they are young but rather their job that is increasing their propensity to consume. By segmenting by behaviour and then examining individual circumstances in this way, it is possible to start to understand how to tailor your marketing to meet individual customer requirements.

Technology and much more detailed information are making this kind of individualised analysis feasible even for organisations with enormous numbers of customers. One technique used by retailers is market basket analysis, where the contents of a customer's shopping are analysed in order to identify 'affinity purchases', that is, those purchases which a customer makes because he or she connects the individual products (buying fresh orange juice with cold remedies being one of the most often-quoted examples). Using information on such purchases, it is possible to change the placement of products within a store to prompt people into making the connection (and thus purchasing an extra item) on a regular basis.

This approach has recently been extended. The Massachusetts Institute of Technology recently pioneered the development of collaborative filtering. This technique compares each individual's purchase behaviour with every other individual's purchase behaviour on a database to identify who is most similar. These groupings are then used to predict other purchases that each member of the group would be interested in. Note that there is no segmentation here, no potential throwing away of useful information. By performing comparisons at the lowest possible level, using purchase behaviour, much higher accuracy can be obtained. This approach is beginning to be included within commercially available software products such as Firefly, which is designed to track consumer preferences and make suggestions to customers based on their previous purchases and those of people with similar preferences.

■ QUESTIONS TO CONSIDER ■

How do you identify difference in different consumers' behaviour?

6. What information can you track at an individual consumer level? What changes could you make to your marketing mix as a result of individual consumer behaviour?

Both of these examples demonstrate how detailed individual buying patterns can influence the marketing of products. However, these approaches will only work if you can be sure that the changes that you make to your marketing mix will result in changes to your customers' behaviour.

Identifying how information can be used to influence buying behaviour

Understanding the likelihood of achieving change is central to mass-customised marketing. If you can predict behaviour, you are starting to reduce the uncertainty in your trading environment, and this will lead to a competitive advantage. If you can reduce uncertainty you reduce your costs by being able to concentrate on those aspects of the marketing mix which will lead to the greatest change in your customers' behaviour.

We have already discussed two ways in which the likelihood of change can be determined – identifying profiles of individual customers who are very similar and using these to highlight products that some but not others are buying, and identifying affinity purchases, in which it is probable that the customer will make the connection between two products placed together on the shelves.

Companies are beginning to realise the importance of this. Heinz, for example, ceased to mass-advertise in 1994. It is almost impossible to measure the effects of mass-advertising; what Heinz wanted, and what we applaud, was a more direct and measurable form of promotion. The same strategy has been adopted by Kraft General Foods:

> By applying [Kraft General Foods'] new model [of 30m households]… we plan to identify heavy using households and project their current value to the company… We want to go further. We think we can use modelling techniques to identify what KGF products these households should be buying and then we can customize marketing plans that will be significantly more impactful on their shopping.[3]

Another, potentially even more radical and powerful, approach is to identify a chain of events that indicate that a consumer already has or will soon have a need – as opposed to a desire – that will have to be filled. The aim here is to build up a profile of a customer over time rather than for a period as a whole. Using this information, we might start looking for the evidence that a customer is about to make a certain type of purchase. A do-it-yourself retailer, for example, might look for evidence that someone has just moved house (home improvement expenditure is closely correlated with home purchase). This might take the form of joining a loyalty scheme for the first time, starting to use an existing loyalty card in a different store or making purchases consistent with moving house (a sudden surge in decorating materials in an existing customer perhaps). This kind of activity could trigger direct mailing to the customer about the store's kitchen design service, for example. Once again, this kind of analysis can only be carried out on customer-level data. One can take this further by combining customer information from different sources. The home improvement chain's own evidence that someone has moved house may in practice be fairly weak – that sudden surge in decorating might just as well be connected with trying to sell an existing house as it is with buying a new one. A more certain way of obtaining the same predictive evidence would be by collaborating with local estate agents and sending out mail-shots to all newly arrived homeowners within a store's catchment area. However, in both cases, the aim is the same – to use individual customer data to identify where incremental sales are most probable.

▓ QUESTIONS TO CONSIDER ▓

How does your company identify need?

7. What does your company do to identify individual consumer preferences?

8. What does your company do to identify individual customer requirements?

9. How does your company exploit this information?

One of the most telling examples of the effectiveness of this approach has been the 1997 UK general election, won by the Labour Party in what was one of the most substantial election victories achieved by any political party in the UK since the Second World War. It is being seen as the first election to be won be 'telepolitics': the Labour Party gathered several hundred volunteers and installed them behind banks of telephones in its headquarters. Clearly, telephoning every eligible voter would have been logistically impossible, and the Labour Party therefore focused its attention on the much smaller number whose choice would be decisive under the UK's 'first past the post' political system. Every night in the 6-week campaign, 20,000 voters in key marginal constituencies were contacted. By the end, it was estimated that 25–30 per cent of voters in these areas (and a much higher proportion of floating voters) had been directly contacted. As a result, the swing towards the Labour Party was much higher in these marginal constituencies than it was in seats that were traditionally either strongly Conservative or strongly Labour. 'This is just-in-time politics', commented *The Financial Times*, 'delivering the right message to the right people at the right time'.[4]

Making customers behave differently

Understanding the likelihood that a specific customer segment may change its behaviour and identifying what factors may influence this (and therefore increase the probability that a desired event happens) are only two steps in the process of achieving the desired result. All the analysis in the work is irrelevant if you cannot get people to do what you want them to do.

Getting people to do something can take several forms. You can intervene directly – offering them money-off vouchers or a free holiday when they buy a car – or you can intervene indirectly, as when a law firm launches a newsletter for its clients in the hope of nurturing long-term loyalty. You can also use a variety of channels through which to make these interventions, from conventional mass-media to precision mail-shots. But, whatever the message you send out, whatever the medium you use to send it, the more you make use of the preferences and behaviours you have identified among *individual* people, the greater will be the return. This is not just because you have a more accurate view of people's needs and desires but because you can start to monitor the changes in an individual's behaviour that result. This is because the key aspect of getting people to do something comes from creating a 'virtual dialogue' with them.

What do we mean by a virtual dialogue? Imagine taking a single customer (for example, a customer of a bank). By monitoring his or her behaviour over a period of time (cash withdrawals and other transactions, reactions to prior promotions and so on), we may conclude that there is a high probability that this customer will be interested in a new type of flexible loan we are offering. Using other information that we have collected about how he reacts to different types of marketing approach, we may also be able to infer the most effective way of informing this customer about the new service. It may be, for example, that he responds particularly well to a direct approach by telephone, so, accordingly, we ask a personal account manager to ring the customer at home one evening to discuss the offer. Doing all this might allow an increase in our take-up rate from 1 per cent (for a conventional mail-shot) to, for example, 25 per cent – a very significant improvement.

Our argument is that you should not stop here: your objective should be a 100 per cent success rate. How can you do this? By continually adding the customer's responses to different marketing activities to the individual profile that you have already started to construct, and using all this information when you next come to promote a service. At the moment, most companies tend to stop once they have quantified the overall success rate for a given promotion (usually within a fairly short timescale). Some go further and carry out qualitative research on the reactions of a sample of the people approached. All companies should take this one step further. We believe that companies should be monitoring promotions across *all* the individuals involved, both those who have responded and those who have not. This would mean that, having telephoned the customer about your new flexibile loan, you would monitor the result (whether successful or otherwise) and feed it back into your customer information. This is where the detailed customer information comes in. Rather than using top-level analysis to give you an overall success rate, you can use customer-level information to build up an increasingly sophisticated – and differentiated – picture of the individual concerned over time. At each stage, you are taking the reaction of the customers into account in constructing your picture of their preferences, allowing you to target your promotions with increasing precision and effectiveness. However, you are also actively learning from the customers: you may not be talking to them in the conventional sense, but you are certainly making their behaviour speak to you – the 'virtual dialogue'. This is the key difference between this type of customer targeting and more conventional – although still detailed – methods such as micro-marketing, which tend to be a 'monologue' from the company to its customers.

Again, the information revolution has only recently enabled such complex interactions to be recorded and acted upon, and indeed the techniques required to make sense of the data are still in their infancy.

The information revolution has opened up new opportunities for the exploitation of any organisation's customer base. By collecting and analysing information at an individual customer level, it is possible to identify what products each customer would be most interested in purchasing, develop products to match their requirements and identify what would be the most effective way of marketing to each customer. This mass-customisation of a customer base enables the issues associated with simply increasing a product range (such as the necessity of holding high levels of stock) to be overcome and significantly higher returns to be achieved.

Summary

❑ Mass-customisation means the development of *different* products that are marketed to *different* consumers in *different* ways. Mass-customisation is about exploiting the *differences* in your marketplace.

❑ Some of the current attempts at mass-customisation have failed because they exploit only some of the differences that occur in the marketplace. Simply offering customers an increased range of products, for example, may not succeed because it requires significantly increased stocks.

❑ Mass-customisation must examine and understand the differences in consumers' purchase behaviour and use this as a basis for generating differences in their products, customer base and marketing approaches.

❑ To be truly successful, mass-customisation approaches must collect individual consumer's responses to each and every marketing approach that is made. Only by doing this can each element of the marketing mix be tailored to suit each individual consumer.

Notes

1. Joseph Pine II, Bart Victor and Andrew C Boynton, 'Making Mass-customisation Work', *Harvard Business Review*, September–October, 1993.
2. Full details of their case are given in the above article.
3. Lorraine C Scarpa, 'Fast, Flexible, Computerized, That's Today's Analytic World', *Brandweek*, 15 November, 1993.
4. *Financial Times,* 30 April, 1997.

Part III
Exploiting the Virtual Potential of Your Business

11 A New Way of Managing

While the number of companies experimenting with the kinds of idea we have discussed in the previous section is growing, there are many more companies who still think only about physical business. However, if we think the writing is on the wall, how is it that these organisations do not seem to be able to read it?

Our experience suggests that the problem is not so much that they do not see what is happening, although there is almost always a significant minority who think that their business will be exempt from these changes. The problem is more that, having read the writing, they simply do not know what to do next. The possibilities (and dangers) are numerous. How do you decide what to do? Things could go wrong; how do you assess the risks? Your organisation is not designed to work like this; how can you change it?

These are the questions we want to address in this section of the book. Much of what we have discussed will require a change in mindset. When FedEx enabled its customers to monitor parcel movements across the Internet, this was not just a question of setting up a website, but a change in the way in which the company positioned and marketed itself. When British Airways decided it wanted to have more direct dialogue with its customers, it was a question not just of setting up a customer relations department, but also of empowering the people who worked in it to enforce improvements across the organisation as a whole, and of initiating a company-wide training scheme for all staff.

Making such a change is not helped by the fact that many of our traditional tools of management are not suited to a virtual environment and do not encourage this new way of thinking.

Management is an activity that is focused on the physical – the visible, concrete aspects of our business, those which we can monitor and measure

We have centuries of experience in managing factories, machinery, buildings and so on, so much so that, as managers, we have been very suspicious of intangible areas. The reputation of many in-house IT departments, for example, is so poor that 'management' and 'information technology' seem mutually exclusive terms. In fact, many mainstream business people have long subscribed to the notion that IT is inherently unmanageable; these same people now suspect that knowledge will be equally so.

There are two reasons why this state of affairs cannot be allowed to continue. First, as businesses become more and more virtual, we cannot simply label them unmanageable, 'no-go' areas, where strategy is little more than a matter of blind faith. Second, if we continue to manage only our physical assets, we will be blinding ourselves to the opportunities of the virtual economy. Initiatives such as developing a company website will be no more than mass-marketing in a new media (and this is what most websites are in practice); exploiting the infosphere of a product will involve nothing more than sticking a bigger label on it. To exploit these opportunities for what they are worth, we need to be able to put the virtual part of our organisation at its heart rather than seeing it as some sort of fringe activity on the margin.

Management is a high-level activity – strategy is synonymous with importance; detail is what other, more junior, people deal with

Business cannot carry on thinking like this. As we noted much earlier in this book, the division between strategy and detail is based on a series of premises that are now mostly outdated. And out of touch. Understanding our customers as individuals means that we are all going to have to start rolling up our sleeves and plunging into detail. High-level market segmentations will not work in a world that can 'mass-customise' its products. Conventionally, we have aggregated detailed information so that we can make sense of it, but every time we do this – every time we look at an average customer, a benchmark lead time for delivery – we are missing opportunities to create new services or radically improve our performance. The market leaders of the future will be determined by the effectiveness with which they manage the *detail* of their operations, rather than being the ones with the better high-level strategy. In fact, we predict that the whole nature of strategy will have to change to accommodate this. In the 1980s a good strategy might have sounded something like 'Move into X or Y new market'. Today, something along the lines of 'Target young adults who are just about to have their first child, have just moved to a more upmarket neighbourhood, and who like the colour green' is more appropriate.

Our traditional distinction between strategy and detail is already starting to blur and will continue to do so.

Management is a means of breaking an organisation down into discrete units

Every manager has his or her span of control; he or she can only manage a finite number of projects, processes or people, so the larger organisation has necessarily to be broken up into – literally – manageable pieces. But does decomposing an organisation as complex as a business into parts really make sense? To understand the potential of a business, we need to see it as an integrated, interactive whole.

This is especially true when we start to think about the way in which a virtual business – because it is based on massive quantities of disparate information rather than a comparatively small number of people, processes or plants – is potentially a much more complex entity. In medieval Europe, a sheep farmer sold sheep; there was not much more to the process than that. Translate that same farmer into Europe in the 1990s, and the essential process of sheep farming – breeding, rearing, selling – will not have changed much. What has changed is all the information that now surrounds the process: the pedigree and health record of the animals, the administration of complex EU subsidies, rules and regulations about care and transportation. If we just tried to manage only the physical aspects of sheep farming today, we would be omitting the major part of the job; and, if we broke the process down into components, we would not be seeing the whole picture. Moreover, we can only really understand sheep farming today if we see it as a system that is interlinked with many other systems (neighbouring sheep farms, the retailing market, distribution channels, government policies, changing public tastes for lamb and so on).

Try an experiment. Find a pack of cards and build two houses with it. Now find some glue and stick together all the cards in one of the houses. If you now picked up the house you have stuck together, nothing changes – all the cards stay where you have stuck them. Now look at the other house. Even knocking it slightly will move some cards and may bring the entire house down. Traditionally, when we think about managing a business, we think we are dealing with a house of cards in which all the cards can be stuck down: moving into a new market is like sticking a new card on. In practice, however, your ability to put a new card on top of the house is determined by many factors, not all of which may be within your control – the surface of the desk, the flatness of the floor, whether a colleague inter-rupts. Our businesses, like a house of cards, are complex systems, but conventional management thinking tells us to keep things simple.

We manage people rather than intellectual capital

These days every company sees itself as a 'people-business'. What it means is that it invests time and money in staff recruitment, training and career development, so that it can attract and then retain the highest calibre employees. What this boils down to in practice is that we manage physical people – we send them on training courses, give them appraisals, promote them; what we are not managing is what is going on in their heads, which is ironic given that it is this intellectual capital that we are really after.

Nowhere is this distinction clearer than in professional service firms. It used to be the case that consultancies in particular recruited (or trained) specialists who would then sell their experience to clients. In other words, clients were paying for the individual concerned; it was all very personal. However, the 'people model' for doing this has some serious drawbacks. In the first place, you are very dependent on individuals; key staff leaving can destroy an entire business unit. Second, it becomes difficult, if not impossible, to achieve economies of scale: how can you improve leverage when the basic building block of the service you deliver is a person? Third, what do you do when you run out of people, when you cannot recruit enough people to fill your ambitious growth plans? How can you grow a business when its essential raw material is in such short supply? These problems have become increasingly apparent since the early 1990s, particularly since the consultancy market is currently enjoying a global boom.

The response of consultancies has been to develop knowledge networks, aimed at making the individual more productive and spreading information around the organisation so that no one person is the sole guardian of it. While many are making progress, it is probably fair to say that very few have done much more than begin to scratch the surface of the possibilities. One of the key obstacles they face is that it is difficult to manage something as ephemeral as knowledge using tools designed for the physical world. By default, therefore, we think about the technology, we become obsessed with databases, we worry about networks. However, these are all just the physical tips of what is in fact a very virtual iceberg. Unless we find new ways of managing that iceberg, its opportunities will always elude us, just as its threats will always surprise us.

We value physical goods rather than intangible assets

Most of us recognise the importance of performance measurements: if we want someone to sell, we give them a sales target, but giving them a sales target does not mean that they will do all the other things we want them to do – it will not make them a team player or a self-starting manager; it will make them a salesperson. One of the most common obstacles for companies that are in the process of changing is that their performance measurement system reflects the *ancien régime* even while the culture is changing. As long as the old performance measurements remain in place, the people working in an organisation will not believe that their employer has truly changed.

If this applies to organisations in general, it applies equally to the notion of the virtual business in particular. No matter how much we change our businesses to exploit the virtual opportunities that we perceive, few people either internally or externally are going to take our efforts seriously unless we can assign some value to our activities. However, our accounting standards are designed to count completed transactions or physical assets. Applying these standards to something as fluid as information or other forms of intellectual capital can only mean that we devalue it. It would be like trying to assess depth of colour using a black and white paint chart. If the virtual business requires new ways of managing, equally it needs a new method of valuation. The outlook, then, looks bleak for what Charles Handy has called 'the gods of management'.

In this, the final section of the book, we want to look at some alternative ways of managing a business. These are not so much tools as ways of thinking differently about the subject, ways to challenge your organisation to change. They are also designed to compensate for the weaknesses in conventional management approaches which we have noted above:

- *Zero-based physical budgeting* is a technique we have developed for helping companics to move away from managing only the physical parts of their business.
- *Electronic commerce* looks at how information – and the ability to exchange it across the Internet in particular – can radically transform how we sell and market.
- *Complexity and computer modelling* looks at how we can exploit the vast quantities of information we now have at our disposal without either being overwhelmed by it or over-simplifying it, and the role that computer modelling plays in this.
- *Work–Learn–Share* addresses the issue of how we can most effectively share knowledge within our organisation.
- *Getting the foundations right* deals with a different issue – how we can make best use of the technology now available, without allowing technical issues to set our corporate agendas.
- *Selling your virtual assets* is the logical conclusion of much of what we have covered and looks at the issues around converting the virtual aspects of your business into hard cash.

12 Zero-based Physical Budgeting

Throughout this book, we have given examples of organisations that have changed the rules of an industry by moving processes from the physical domain to the virtual domain, by converting a physical process into information. We believe that all industries (see below) will be subject to this type of revolutionary change, and that those organisations that embrace these changes will prosper and those that do not will fail. The subject of this chapter is how to identify when and where such changes might occur and how you can be first to exploit them.

Case Study

THE UK ELECTRICITY MARKET

When the UK electricity market was privatised in 1990, the old regional electricity boards, which had been established after the Second World War, were converted into separate companies with two distinct functions: supply of electricity over the physical network and distribution (service and pricing). Since they were privatised, these companies have been immensely profitable, and their shares have significantly out-performed market norms, so much so that, when constraints on merger and acquisition activity were lifted in 1995, the majority of companies were snapped up, either by their competitors or by overseas utility companies, all of whom were attracted by the super-profits being generated by these quasi-monopolies (competition for business users was still low, and for domestic consumers non-existent).

Despite sporadic concerns over price, service or the high salaries that the executives of these firms have chosen to pay themselves – despite even a windfall tax on the utilities being levied by the new Labour government – the share prices of these electricity companies have remained high. The domestic market might be being opened up to competition in 1998, but the companies have yet to see this as a major threat to their long-term profitability.

There is no reason – we might think – for these new owners to be worried, but we think they should be. Why? Because you can now buy a software package that allows you to sell gas to up to 100,000 customers, and it is only a matter of time before a similar package is developed for the electricity market. This means that one person, working out of her backroom, will be able to perform the same function as an electricity company with all its overheads of management, buildings and technology. Of course, the company will need to 'rent' space on the existing supply network, but its focus – on selling, billing and customer service – represents the most profitable functions of the established electricity companies. In fact, the new companies will not just be able to beat the incumbents on the basis of lower costs: because they will be almost completely virtual, they will also have greater flexibility to offer a service that is customised to suit the needs of individual consumers and preferential tariffs that reflect a customer's usage. In a classical application of the idea of increasing returns, they will be able to use this flexibility to reduce the incentive for any customer to shift to an alternate ('If this company is giving me exactly what I want, why look elsewhere?'): customers will effectively be locked in.

The situation is also an example of how a virtual business can quickly make inroads into even an apparently very physically based industry, thereby changing the fundamental rules of competition.

But with all this evidence, why aren't people responding more quickly? Why aren't the directors of these electricity companies quaking in their boots? Why aren't more people taking advantage of what we regard to be obvious opportunities? Part of the reason is what we could call the NIMBY (not in my back yard) syndrome – not believing that this problem could affect their industries, their 'back yards' (the UK electricity industry being a good illustration of this). Part of the problem is ignorance – many companies just do not appreciate the extent to which this is already happening around them. However, most of the problem is habit. People are used to thinking in terms of their physical environment; how else are most business processes organised and budgets decided? The physical world is the one to which we are accustomed, it is the one most of us have grown up managing and in which we have invested many years of our lives. It is the one that our systems and cultures are designed to manage. Our accounting systems, for example, have elaborate techniques for measuring the worth of physical assets, the way in which they depreciate over time and their contribution to profits. There are, however, few techniques, and certainly no generally accepted procedures, for measuring the worth of a virtual asset or for putting a value on the information in your business.

Even where people have taken on board the idea of the virtual value chain, and embraced the concept that they can use information to understand and then replace their physical processes, very few have looked beyond this horizon towards the true opportunities of the virtual business. Few have even started to consider what possibilities could be open to them if, rather than 'tweaking' their existing processes and systems, they reinvented their entire organisation as a virtual business, one founded on information rather than one that uses information as a substitute for physical reality.

To us, this kind of thinking is both the natural extension of automation and business process re-engineering (BPR) and a paradigm shift away from these approaches. When computerisation was introduced into business on a wide scale in the 1960s and 70s, much of the work involved automating existing manual processes. As Michael Hammer pointed out, in his seminal 1980 article in the *Harvard Business Review,* 'Re-engineering Work: Don't Automate, Obliterate', the aim should have been not to convert what was already being undertaken but to review the purpose of the physical process at the same time. Not doing this meant that major opportunities to improve efficiency were lost.[1] It is now almost 20 years since BPR arrived on the management scene, and, during that time, countless companies have used the technique to break down internal barriers, cut costs and improve customer service. The results have, it is now generally acknowledged, been variable: for every company that claims to have realised significant benefits, there is another that complains that the process has yielded little of value.

However, whether you believe the re-engineering approach has succeeded or failed, you will probably acknowledge that it is beginning to look a little old fashioned. There are several reasons for this beyond the negative publicity that the approach has recently attracted: its cost-cutting focus, for example, has little to contribute to a company that is launching a new product or exploring a new market. BPR was designed to help large, slow-moving companies become more agile, rather than changing the competitive rules. It was a focus that clearly appealed during the late 1980s and early 1990s when world recession meant that many companies needed to downsize in order to survive, but it is less useful to companies that are succeeding in the current, expansive economic environment. It is also much less interesting in a world where – as we have noted throughout this book – the essential rules of competition are changing. BPR gives you better goal-posts but it cannot move them.

Why? Because it has effectively fallen into the same trap its predecessor – computerisation – fell into 30 years ago. The weakness in conventional automation – as the re-engineering gurus pointed out – was that it took what was there and automated it; it did not first consider the efficiency of the process itself. We can see the same fault with BPR. It has been re-engineering the physical process; but it has not challenged the assumption that physical processes are necessary. In fact, it is our experience that you cannot make this challenge retrospectively. You cannot look at a process and decide whether you need it or not, because you have already started with a mental model saying that at least some physical processes are necessary. Tell that to the start-up electricity company, run by one person from a shed in a back garden. Tell that to the newest entrant in your industry. 'What good will it do to… follow the rules when some companies are re-writing them?' asks the US management guru, Gary Hamel:

> Never has the world been more hospitable to industry revolutionaries and more hostile to industry incumbents… What if your company is more ruling class than revolutionary? You can either surrender the future to revolutionary challengers or revolutionize the way your company creates strategy. What is required is not a little tweak to the traditional planning process but a new philosophical foundation: strategy *is* revolution; everything else is tactics.[2]

So how do you ensure that your organisation is the one that is leading the industry, the revolutionary rather than the ruling class? In getting companies to start thinking about the ways of rewriting the industry rules, we have found that the challenge is to make people ask, not 'How can we convert this physical process into information?' but 'What – if any – physical processes do we truly need?'

If you want to be truly revolutionary, you have to start with a blank piece of paper rather than with your existing physical processes. The technique that we use to help organisations is one that we call 'zero-based physical budgeting'. We start with the assumption that, in the increasingly virtual business world, *any* physical element has to be ruthlessly justified. After all, any physical process that we use will cost us money to maintain or produce and be difficult to change; every physical process in our business represents a constraint or limitation on our business and a hindrance to change.

Suppose, for the sake of illustration, that you decided to start a consulting company specialising in a small but hopefully highly profitable field. You should be asking yourself the question, 'What physical assets and resources do I really need?' You probably do need some office space in terms of meeting rooms and presentation suites for clients, but you do not need to house your staff, who (as many consultancies have already learnt) will often work more productively and comfortably from home. Do you need consultants or sales teams to go to clients' offices? In the short term, you undoubtedly do, but some smaller, newer consultancies are building their client relationship via e-mail, video-conferencing and the Internet, instead of having consultants physically based on the client site. Everyone wins: you do not take up valuable accommodation in your client's office and you waste much less time travelling. So far so good. But the question you should really be asking yourself is, 'How many people do I need?' 'None' clearly is not a viable proposition, but if you develop an efficient network for disseminating and 'productising' your particular skills and knowledge, fewer people should be required (or you will be able to do more work with the same number of consultants) because the chances of wasting time reinventing the wheel – an issue that continues to plague many consultancy firms – are significantly reduced.

The objective of the exercise in zero-based physical budgeting is to attempt to create a business in your industry that is entirely virtual. That business then becomes the blueprint against which to compare your organisation. Each physical process or asset within your business can then be challenged by asking what advantages are gained by maintaining that process or asset in a physical form. If no advantages can be discovered, apart from perhaps that it is the way things have always been performed around here, you have identified an opportunity to change the rules. Some generic examples are shown in Table 12.1.

These zero-based physical budgets are usually built up in considerable detail and help not only to highlight 'quick wins', in which an organisation can make a cheap but effective change, but also to identify the areas of an organisation where they might find themselves vulnerable because they are unable to change quickly.

Whether or not you end up with a completely virtually business, and few manage this on their first attempt, it is still a process that can be immensely valuable by challenging your preconceptions about both your industry and your own organisation. The benefits that we perceive are:

- First, it can help you to develop an overall strategy that does away with goal-posts altogether rather than simply moving them.
- Second, it gives you a much more radical model for restructuring your organisation than traditional BPR can.
- Third, it can help you to explore new strategic opportunities for your organisation.

Table12.1   Some examples of virtual approaches to traditionally physical processes

Processes	Possible virtual replacements
Marketing	
Distributing information	*Faxback* – A system where people telephone a number and receive information automatically back on a fax machine. *Internet* – Can be used to distribute large volumes of information
Sales	
Taking orders	*Automated order taking* – Many organisations now provide computer systems that enable customers to purchase their goods electronically
Billing	
Calculating charges	*Self-recording electronic metering* – Can be used so that meter readers are not required for services such as electricity and gas
Receiving payment	*Direct debit* – Enables money to be directly debited from an account, saving time and effort in checking cash and cheque receipts
Distribution	
Stockholding	*Just-in-time techniques* – Convert the requirement for holding stock into requiring information about sales patterns
Transfer of goods	*Electronic transfer of goods* – Many goods consist both of information and physical elements. Are the physical elements necessary? Perhaps the information elements could be transmitted in advance? *Does there have to be a physical delivery at all?* What benefits do your products confer? Do they have to be provided in a physical form at all? Is it possible to imagine an electronic alternative?

Doing away with your goal-posts

Let us take the first of those aspects. What is your company's ultimate aim? What does it really sell to its customers in order to survive and flourish? A few years ago, most people would have said things like 'better-quality, lower-price food', 'more reliable washing machines', 'clean windows' or 'enjoyable holidays'. Many organisations have since recognised that they are servicing a need rather than simply manufacturing a product. We want reliable washing machines because we want clean clothes; we want clean clothes because we want to look well dressed; we want to look well dressed because that's how we think we should look and because we want to move in well-dressed circles. And so on. In fact, when we start to consider it, very few of our final 'products' are physical: they are more likely to be aspirational and emotional, making us feel good, safe or happy. So why, if this is the case, do we always think about the physical side of our business when this is clearly a means to an end?

For example, ask an airline the question 'What physical aspects of your business could you really not do without?' and it will probably cite aeroplanes, airports, baggage handlers and so on. However, when you stop to think about it, airlines are essentially performing just two functions: they move people to where they want to be (holidays, family visits and so on) and they move people to where they have to be (business travellers, those with problems at home and so on). Does this really have to be done in physical terms? Anyone who has seen the film *Total Recall* will remember that the Schwarzenegger character takes a virtual reality vacation; he doesn't go anywhere near a plane. And surely, the biggest competitive threat to airlines' lucrative business travel market are things such as video-conferencing. Why spend time travelling when you can talk to global colleagues from your local office? Of course, video-conferencing has yet to take off in a substantial way, and we are clearly very far from being able to offer virtual reality holidays that are anything like as much fun as the real holidays. We are not suggesting that every airline should sell its fleet tomorrow. However, at the same time, it is important for them to recognise that, although tomorrow's competitors may not have aeroplanes or access to airports, but they may still be able to steal a sizeable amount of the existing air travel market. And we should always remember that these new entrants – precisely because they will not be encumbered with expensive and inflexible physical assets – will be much more adaptable to change and have much lower costs.

Nobody in their right mind would set up a postal service today: they would give their customers cheap and easy access to e-mail. Nobody would set up a bank with an extensive branch network: they would provide their customers with a telephone- or Internet-based service. Is there anyone seriously thinking about moving into grocery retailing just as home shopping and door-to-door delivery seem to be about to take off? We believe that the only way in which to consider the opportunities offered and the threats posed by the virtual economy is to go back to that proverbial blank sheet of paper and think what physical assets you are really going to need in the 21st century.

Radical restructuring

As well as making you challenge your preconceptions, the second aim of zero-based physical budgeting is to make you look – in the short term – at the balance between the physical and virtual in your organisation. Effectively, this is one step down from reinventing what your business will be 10 years from now. It focuses more on the present and on the immediate future. The question to be asked here is 'What physical processes do you really need to run your current business?' Most organisations would say that they needed most of them: they need factories in which to make products, trucks to distribute them and people to sell them. But is this really the case?

Let us look at an example, in this case a government department. In the UK, the Department of Social Security (DSS) pays out more than £90bn ($145bn) to over 20 million claimants per year. Each year 12 million benefit claims are handled and more than 1,000 million payments are made. In total, the DSS's expenditure accounts for more than a third of central government's expenditure, or 12% of GDP. Historically, this scale of operation has demanded a huge physical infrastructure: the department has 420 local offices and 64,000 full-time staff. Like other government departments – indeed more so, simply because of its massive budget – the DSS is under pressure to find operational efficiencies. Since the early 1980s, it has been involved in a massive computerisation and restructuring programme. Like other public and private sector organisations, the department has looked to automation to reduce existing processing costs and time.

Typically, it has taken existing processes, rationalised them and developed the software tools to support them.

An alternative way of looking at this issue, using our zero-based physical budgeting approach, would be to work from the basis that everything has to be information based and that the physical aspects of the organisation – people, buildings and so on – should be used only where absolutely necessary. Essentially, the DSS performs four main functions (Figure 12.1):

- It develops and implements the government's welfare policy, deciding, in negotiation with the Treasury, how much money the country can afford to spend and on whom that money should be targeted.
- It decides who is eligible to receive what in terms of benefits (testing them against income thresholds and so on).
- Once this is decided, it organises the payment of the benefit to the individual concerned.
- It (increasingly) monitors the overall system for abuse, removing benefits from those who are in fact ineligible, paying more or less as appropriate.

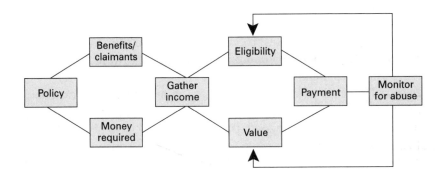

Figure 12.1   Re-engineering social security?

The only aspects of this system that are unavoidably physical are those which involve people, and people matter at two points: somebody has to decide the overall policy, and somebody, at the very end of the process, has to receive the benefit to which they are entitled. Everything else, we would argue, can happen in virtual terms.

For example, once an overall policy has been developed, deciding who is entitled to what (within the spending limit agreed) is better modelled by a computer than it is estimated by people. Such a model would hold details of everyone in the country, their current income, dependants and eligibility in relation to certain criteria, and would be capable of modelling different scenarios – changes to certain classes of benefit and so on. It would in effect be a top-down version of the current system of welfare expenditure. Rather than deciding who should be entitled to what and then adding up a total bill, payments would be calculated on the basis of how much money was available in total. Taking this a step further: rather than setting eligibility rules in advance, a computer model could work out what they should be, based on overall policy direction and available resources.

Offices where people go to make a claim could be replaced by telephone-based systems, common queries being answered automatically. Payment to claimants could be made through automatic bank transfers rather than over the counter as at present (the DSS, like many other social security departments worldwide, are experimenting with this and/or smart card systems in order to reduce their transaction processing costs). As we use electronic cash transactions more, and physical money less, it will even be possible in the future to monitor for abuse of the system using information rather than investigating officers. Although we may not relish the prospect for other reasons, we would be able to monitor claimants' expenditure to ensure that those who were claiming unemployment benefit were not earning income via other means.

A social security system of this nature would clearly be expensive to build, nor is it ever likely to involve no people or buildings. However, that having been said, this quasi-virtual system would, once implemented, be cheap to operate (as transferring information costs almost nothing) and easy to change, long-term advantages that will far outweigh the short-term costs. Equally clearly, it could not be built overnight – the transition from the present large and complex infrastructure would take time. That does not, however, invalidate the need to have thought through this type of overarching aim rather than trying to think through how each individual process can be best automated or re-engineered.

Identifying new opportunities

Whichever route you want to take – whether you want to rethink the future of your industry or simply exploit the opportunities to be virtual in the present – zero-based physical budgeting is also aimed at helping you identify what additional opportunities there could be for your organisation if it were virtual rather than physical. Returning to our air travel example, an airline that starts to provide video-conferencing services will learn new information about its customers, information, in fact, of a type to which it has never before had access. It will know which individuals and which organisations talk to each other; it will know how often they need to talk; it will know when they stop talking to each other and start talking to someone new. This information could have immense value. It could, for example, allow the airline to price its conferencing service more precisely, reflecting the needs of individual customers. It could be sold to other companies – to professional services firms, for example, which want to make sure that they are focusing on the individuals within an organisation who network most effectively with their international colleagues, so that ideas and proposals from the firms can be disseminated throughout their global clients.

Conclusion

The challenge when performing zero-based physical budgeting is to be imaginative. Everything should be questioned, every physical process, every physical asset should be thrown into the pot, stirred and then recreated as a virtual process or a virtual asset. There should not be, must not be, any hiding place, any *a priori* reason why something should be kept in the physical domain. Only by challenging the existing order will you and your organisation ensure that you are one of the revolutionaries, the survivors into the future.

Summary

- ❏ Organisations find it difficult to imagine how physical assets and processes can be replaced by virtual, information-based equivalents.

- ❏ Our entire culture, management and accounting tools, and techniques are based on a physical world; there are very few generally accepted tools or techniques that enable us to manage the virtual world of information.

❑ However, only those who perceive the opportunities will survive. Current management theorists predict ever more revolutionary changes to the accepted way of doing business.

❑ One approach is to start with a blank sheet of paper and develop a virtual organisation. This virtual organisation can then be compared with your existing organisation to challenge the necessity of keeping physical processes and assets. We call this approach zero-based physical budgeting.

❑ Such an approach provides three key benefits. It:

- Challenges your existing goals;
- Identifies ways of radically restructuring your business;
- Identifies new opportunities.each individual consumer.

Notes

1. Micheal Hammer, 'Re-engineering Work: Don't Automate, Obliterate', *Harvard Business Review*, July–August, 1980.
2. Gary Hamel, 'Strategy as Revolution', *Harvard Business Review*, July–August, 1996.

13 Electronic Commerce

Almost without a doubt, the most over-exposed new marketing concept of the 1990s will be the Internet and the promise of electronic commerce. We are bombarded almost daily with articles extolling the virtues of the Internet as a way of doing business – that 30–70 million on-line users are beginning to constitute a viable on-line market. You are encouraged to build your own on-line presence now, in order to be sure of addressing this market in the future. If you do not, the argument goes, you will miss the shift from the physical world of shopping in shops and shopping malls to shopping in cyberspace. The implication is unmistakable: miss this boat and your business will never recover.

As always, the truth of the matter is somewhat more prosaic. Some people are making money on the Internet, but at the moment they are not those who are particularly looking to do so. Just as in the great gold rush of the late 19th century, the people who are making money are not the prospectors themselves but the people who have dedicated their organisations to servicing the prospectors. In the 19th century, these types of organisation were providing prospectors with food, equipment and transportation; in the 1990s, they are providing the Internet prospectors with computer hardware, telecommunications connections and website designs. The service providers are thriving, while few, if any, of the prospectors have shown a return on their investment.

Take a typical example. Argos, the UK catalogue stores company, developed a web presence some years ago. In the past 2 years of operation they sold 10,000 items over the Internet. Recently, they opened a telephone call service. In the first two weeks, they took over 32,000 orders. The comparison and conclusions are inescapable. The

Internet is not currently a major new marketing channel for this particular line of business.

This experience is reflected in the estimates of total sales over the Internet. Although these figures are notoriously difficult to compile, they reinforce the conclusion that the Internet is not yet a major new marketing channel. One estimate, for example, suggested that the total sales over the Interent amounted to $436m in 1995. Compare this with the total USA retail sales of $1.5 trillion. The Internet clearly still sells only a minute portion of the total goods and services sold around the world.

So why bother? Because we believe that the advantage of the Internet will come not from trying to replace your existing sales channels (such as providing a website that looks like a virtual shop) but from exploiting the virtual possibilities that the Internet brings to add value to your customers. To return to the Argos example, at the moment it is telephone shopping that most easily adds that kind of value (not least because the number of consumers with telephones far out-number those with an Internet connection) because it enables customers to order what they want from the comfort of their own home. The challenge for Argos will be to find a way to exploit the Internet that goes beyond the added value of telephone shopping. Simply translating your physical marketing channels to the virtual, or translating your physical presence into a virtual presence on the Internet, is not going to generate additional sales.

What is needed is a new way of approaching customers that exploits the opportunities that virtual sales and marketing provide. The purpose of this chapter is to:

- identify the opportunities that marketing over the Internet provides;
- outline some of the perils and pitfalls of electronic commerce;
- help you outline a strategy so that you can be one of the prospectors who makes at least a modest return on your investment.

Why translate your current marketing strategy to cyberspace when this approach will not work? It has been instructive to watch the development of trade on the Internet. Initial attempts were all structured around conventional physical marketing models. Companies developed virtual shopping malls that linked together disparate retailers much as a physical shopping mall does and which, similarly, were aimed at assisting consumers to browse and shop. Almost without exception, these malls have been less successful than anticipated. Consumers neither have, nor particularly want, to go to a single location on the Internet to do their shopping. Nor is there any significant passing trade: linking different sites selling very different goods together does not provide any guarantee that people viewing one site will then go on to view the other.

The first and most important lesson that has to be learnt when considering trading on the Internet is that sales that depend on geography will no longer work. Supermarkets, for example, with their departments that examine in great detail the demographics of an area before a new store site is developed, have no advantage in cyberspace. Any site can be accessed from anywhere in the world. Equally – and perhaps to the chagrin of the early Internet prospectors – any site can also be ignored from anywhere in the world.

There is, however, an even bigger issue with marketing on the Internet. Not only is it difficult to select and purchase a prime site, in a good demographic area away from your competitors, that virtually guarantees you sales, but it is also increasingly difficult to differentiate your offering from the offerings of companies that are maybe a tenth, or even a hundredth, of your size.

The costs of maintaining a presence on the Internet is declining by the month. Even 2 years ago, it was estimated that the cost of establishing a serious Internet presence might be around $1m. Now, a respectable presence can be established for as little as $15,000. You can buy a complete banking system that enables you to set up as a bank on the Internet for less than $1m; you can buy the software that would enable you to set up as a gas trader with perhaps 200,000 customers for as little as $100,000. However, the fact that the price for an Internet site has fallen so markedly poses a problem for larger, more established companies that are accustomed to using their superior spending power to maintain their position in a given market. But how much money can you spend on a website, especially since extra cash will not necessarily result in much visible difference? Whatever the resources you may command, how are you going to differentiate yourself from your competitors and indeed from those companies that had no opportunity to compete with you when commerce took place exclusively in the physical domain?

Given that conventional approaches to marketing are not effective on the Internet, the answer has to lie in identifying a new approach.

Indeed, many of these existing approaches paradigms will be a handicap to organisations attempting to implement a virtual sales presence. But finding a new approach will clearly not be easy. You will only be able to do so by:

■ acquiring an in-depth understanding of the nature of the Internet;
■ identifying how the characteristics of your services and products can be adapted to achieve footfall in this new sales medium;
■ finally, converting the marketing theory into an actual sale.

We will now consider each of these points in turn.

■ QUESTIONS TO CONSIDER ■

1. Does your organisation have an Internet presence?

2. If it does, what marketing strategy has been developed to support sales over the medium?

3. How much of the strategy is a translation or reflection of the marketing strategy that you use to achieve sales in the physical domain?

The key characteristics of the Internet marketplace

What is it that is different about the Internet? What are the characteristics that can be exploited? What can – and, perhaps more importantly, cannot – be sold on the Internet? In our experience, there are four aspects that you need to consider as a matter of priority:

■ security;
■ intangibility;
■ Internet demographics;
■ fulfilment.

Fears about security

An obvious but fundamental point is that the Internet is new. Indeed, it is perhaps the first genuinely new marketing channel to have emerged in the past 40 years. Newness brings with it a set of characteristics. Consumers view the medium with a certain amount of suspicion: they will, in the main, be reticent about using it, and, as a result of this suspicion and fear, they will be concerned that they will not receive the goods or services that they have purchased.

This is true of any new product or service, but, so far as the Internet is concerned, such fears are compounded because consumers will be purchasing goods via a system that they do not fully understand. In fact, consumers are already worried about the security aspects of the Internet. There are scare stories of computer programs that watch for credit card-sized numbers being passed over the Internet and then capture these numbers so that they can be used illegally. While there is undoubtedly some truth in these stories, the majority are likely to be greatly exaggerated. Credit card numbers can just as easily be stolen every time you use them. A waiter in a restaurant who takes your card away, out of your sight, to prepare the credit card slip, has a much easier task of taking your number – and he can do it with no more powerful technology than a pencil and a piece of paper. However, we tend to be less worried about having our credit card number stolen in a restaurant because it is a familiar experience, both in the sense that we may know a particular restaurant on a personal basis, or because our previous experience in restaurants tells us that we do not need to be concerned. Neither of these types of familiarity exists for would-be purchasers on the Internet.

Payment security is an issue, but it is one which can be resolved: in the short term, pre-paid accounts can be set up, credit card details can be given over the telephone, customers can be invoiced. Even the security aspects of the payment system can be fixed. Indeed, many of the major banking organisations are frantically working to get their payment system accepted as the norm. Methods exist to solve the problem, although they are, as yet, not being widely or consistently applied. Fears about the security of payments are, therefore, something which, in our view, can be resolved and dealt with.

A more genuine fear arises from the very nature of the Internet. Because of its virtual nature, it is not possible to touch the goods that you are purchasing physically, and you might – quite reasonably – be concerned that the goods you are buying either are not as good as they look on screen or even do not exist at all. How can a consumer buy a product that they cannot touch, or trust an organisation that may have no physical head office? There have already been scams in which an organisation sets up with an address that is very similar to a *bona fide* organisation and then seeks payments for goods that it has no intention of supplying. A typical trick is to use a genuine address but add the suffix .co.uk (representing a company based in the UK), rather than .com (representing a commercial company) or vice versa. These companies may not last long, but of course they do not have to. They can be disbanded and reformed without the perpetrators having to leave their desks.

Describing the goods

As we have already stated, the Internet is a virtual medium: it has no physical manifestation. Like every opportunity, this brings with it corresponding problems. How do you convince people to purchase goods that you cannot show them physically? One answer is that you only try to sell the kind of goods that people do not need to try out physically before purchasing (music, software and so on). There is already a lively debate about which goods can be successfully sold over the Internet. One argument is that goods such as clothes cannot be successfully sold in this way because people will want to try them on before buying. However, this is clearly a fallacious argument: there are many thriving mail-order clothes businesses, all of which are succeeding on the basis that customers are, in fact, prepared to buy before they try. So why shouldn't clothes be sold successfully on the Internet?

We believe that what customers are seeking is some confidence in the goods that they will receive. Thus, a reputable clothes manufacturer – preferably one with a strong brand – will attract customers and achieve sales. Levi's, for example, maintain a highly regarded site that promotes sales of their jeans. What will be much more difficult will be for a new clothes retailer to establish a presence on the Internet. Simply putting a site on the Internet, however powerful the graphics used to describe the goods, is unlikely to generate very many sales.

There are, of course, some goods that do not need a powerful brand in order to achieve sales. The sales of books, videos and CDs, for example, depend much more on the artist who produced them than the brand qualities of the retailer who is trying to sell them. Anyone can set up – and indeed many already have – websites that sell such goods.

One of the key characteristics of the goods and services that are capable of being traded successfully on the Internet, therefore, is that they are recognised and understood by the consumer. This means either that they must have a strong brand (so that the consumer knows what to expect) or that the goods must be of such a nature that the consumer knows what they will receive.

The demographics of the Internet

While the population that can be addressed by conventional physical sales and marketing is constrained by geography, that of the Internet is constrained by the number of people who both have access to it and make active use of it (these not necessarily being the same thing).

Estimates of the number of people who use the Internet vary widely, although a consensus seems to be emerging that currently (1998) tens of millions of people do indeed use the Internet. What there is no disagreement about is the type of people who use the Internet. At the moment (and this will change as the user-base of the Internet expands), they are predominantly young, under the age of about 40, male and relatively wealthy. It should come as no surprise, therefore, that the pornography industry is one of the few industries that appears to have developed a successful business model for selling on the Internet. Another key aspect of the demographics of the Internet is that every one single person using it owns, or has access to a computer. Users are likely, therefore, to have an above average interest in technology. Computer companies, both hardware and software, are, therefore, also extremely well represented on the Internet.

It is thus important that particular attention is paid to the appeal of products that are sold over the Internet. Retirement homes for the elderly are unlikely to be a bestseller; conversely, sales of gadgets for young men are likely to do well.

The fulfilment of the purchase

We said earlier that the Internet was a virtual medium without a physical manifestation, and that this means that the constraints imposed by geography can be broken. Of course, at the end of the sales process, the consumer has to receive his goods. Goods that are large relative to their price, furniture for example, are unlikely to sell well, simply because the shipping charges constrain the population to which they can be offered. Goods and services that have no physical manifestation, for example dealing in stocks and bonds, are ideally suited. The fulfilment of the purchase of a stock or bond requires simply a certificate to be sent in the post or, at best, no physical manifestation whatsoever.

Achieving footfall

There are many thousands of sites on the Internet, which makes it considerably more competitive than your local shopping mall or high street. Getting people to enter your site is as difficult as, if not more difficult than, getting people to purchase your goods from a retailer. While one of the major advantages offered by the Internet is that – as a manufacturer, for example – you no longer have to do battle with retailers and competitors to obtain the best shelf space in a physical outlet, the down-side is that many of your traditional tactics for being noticed have disappeared. You may have complete control of the sales process, but you also have a much more difficult task of persuading people to enter your site when there are thousands of other sites on the Internet. Consider the following equation:

Probability of a random visit to your site = Number of people on the Internet × Number of sites they visit randomly/ Number of sites

When the number of sites is growing faster than the number of people on the Internet, the probability of a random visit declines. When the number of people is growing faster than the number of sites, the probability of a random visit to your site increases. At the moment, the rate of increase in new sites is higher than the rate of increase in the number of people joining the Internet, which means that the probability of someone making a random visit to your website is falling – and that number was probably already so small as to be close to negligible.

ESTIMATING THE SIZE OF THE MARKET

Using the above factors, it is possible to start to get an idea of the size of the possible population to which you might be able to sell your goods or services.

Let us imagine, for example, that we are trading fine wines from a famous château in France. An example of the numbers that might be filled in are shown below.

Estimate	Example	Your figure
1. Enter your estimate of the total number of people on the Internet. (Use a value of 30 million if you don't have a more up-to-date estimate)	30,000,000	
2. Enter the percentage of your sales that you expect to make to men under the age of 40	20%	
3. Enter the percentage of the Internet population that you can reach without excessive shipping charges (this might be very small for large objects. It might be 100% if you are distributing software over the Internet). Assume that half the Internet population is in the USA if you don't have a better estimate	10%	
4. Enter the percentage who will not be scared off because they don't trust the Internet. (This number will be close to 100% if you are a reputable company with a good brand name. It will be smaller if you are trying to sell to people who do not know you)	90%	
5. Enter the percentage who don't have to feel and touch the object before they buy it	100%	
6. Multiply these numbers together and you have an approximate size of the total market on the Internet for your product or products	540,000	

For our château selling fine wines, these figures suggest that approximately 2 per cent of the total Internet population might be interested in purchasing fine wines over the Internet. The figures would, of course, be considerably higher if you were selling computer hardware or software, and considerably lower if you were selling large hand-crafted goods from your own, unknown retail outlet.

Figure 13.1 Estimating the size of the market for your product on the Internet

The issue facing all traders on the Internet is that passing trade is close to zero. There are not thousands or millions of people out there who will simply come across your site, take a look inside and buy something. Anyone placing a site on the Internet with this delusion will almost certainly fail.

▥ QUESTIONS TO CONSIDER ▥

Your firm's strategy for achieving footfall on the Internet

4. Most companies do not have a coherent strategy for the achievement of footfall on the Internet. Does yours?

5. What is your firm's strategy for getting people to visit your site?

6. How does it differ from your traditional marketing strategy?

7. How have you estimated the potential increase in visits from your strategy?

There are, essentially, two different methods for achieving footfall at your site. The first is to use the traditional media for advertising to make people aware of your site and the benefits that it brings. The second is to use the Internet itself to increase footfall. We will not dwell on the traditional approaches that people are using to advertise their websites, except to say that the approach most organisations are currently taking is simply to include their website address on their traditional advertising and promotional literature. Whether this is enough is open to question. We suspect that, although this is probably sufficient to persuade your loyal customers who already have access to the Internet to have a look, this will be insufficient to persuade people who are not interested in your product to notice your name. It is, however, clearly better than nothing.

Many organisations – especially the small ones hoping to compete in this new channel – do not have the luxury of this method of achieving recognition. They have to rely on the Internet itself to generate trade, something that is forcing them to find increasingly inventive ways to achieve footfall. Three such methods currently predominate:

■ registering with a search engine;
■ advertising on other sites;
■ persuading other sites to carry links to your site.

The first and most pervasive method of using the Internet itself to increase footfall is to register with one (or preferably more than one) of the Internet's search engines. By doing this, your site will appear on a list of possible sites to visit when a user of the Internet types in a key word. So, for example, to go back to our example of a château, when a user types in the word 'wine', the site is likely to be registered (along with thousands of others) as being of potential interest. The problem with this method is that there are likely to be literally thousands of other sites listed. In this instance, for example, we counted almost 200,000 sites. Analysis of which sites people choose shows that they tend to select sites from the first hundred or less. If your site is listed after this, it is much less likely to be picked.

The trick is to ensure that the right keywords are included and that the number of times that they are included is maximised (it tends to be the case that the more times the keyword is included, the more relevant the site will be deemed by the search engine, so the higher up the list it will appear). Marketeers will often include a section on their site with a blue background on which they have written (in blue) the keywords that they hope people use. These words are invisible (being blue on blue) to people visiting the site, but are not invisible to the search engines, so increase the chances that the site will appear high up on the list. Not unnaturally, the providers of the search engines frown on this practice and have threatened to take action against anyone found to have done this.

An even more effective trick, however, is to include the names of your key competitors somewhere within your site. When a competitor's name is typed in, your site will be listed, again increasing the chances that your site will be visited. This is especially effective for a small start-up company that is trying to break into a market. An established competitor may have spent millions of dollars trying to get their site established; by incorporating their name within your site, you can, to some extent, piggyback on their efforts.

The major benefit of registering with the search sites is that it is – at least at the moment – free. The disadvantage, of course, is that your name will only appear to those people who are actively searching for your product, and even then the likelihood of someone actually visiting your site, especially if your site appears low on the list of hits registered, is small.

A second, much more powerful method of making your site visible is to advertise on one of the search engines or other frequently visited sites. At the top (and in some cases in the middle and at the bottom as well) of each page of these search engines, there is an advertisement. If the user clicks on that advertisement, they are then linked to your site. There are essentially two methods by which these advertisements can be displayed. They can be displayed all the time whatever a user types in as his keywords on which to search, or they can be displayed only when a certain key word is entered. For example, when we typed in 'Pangkor Laut' (the name of a holiday resort in Malaysia) we were rewarded with not only a list of people offering trips to this resort, but also an advertisement for cheap flights.

Advertising in this way will undoubtedly increase the number of visits that your site achieves. Instead of being buried in a list, your site will be displayed prominently at the top with whatever words or graphics you choose to show. However, there are three disadvantages to this. In the first place, it costs, probably on the basis of a mix of fixed fee and 'click-thrus' (that is the number of people who click on the advertisement to visit your site). Second, people may use a different search engine, or even a 'meta-search' engine, which is capable of exploring more than one search engine at a time. These will strip out your advertisement and show their own instead, thereby reducing your advertisement's effectiveness. Third, some users deliberately ignore these advertisements, preferring to rely on the content of the sites they visit to dictate what links they follow.

The third major way to developing footfall to your site is to persuade other sites to carry links to your site. For example, our château making fine wines would clearly benefit from having a link from a site promoting books on wine and vice versa. There are many, many cases of reciprocal linking on the Internet, and this is clearly an effective way of passing on information about the availability of complementary sites. However, once you have agreed links with the half dozen sites that are obviously complementary and non-competing, what do you do next? The answer – and this practice is growing rapidly – is to incentivise other sites to carry links. Thus, for example, Amazon books will pay other sites a proportion of the profit on a book that is sold through a link to the other site. If, for example, you have a site offering book reviews, and at the bottom of each review you include a button that says 'To purchase this book press here', which takes the customer through to Amazon books, your book reviewing site, Amazon and the customer all benefit. It is estimated that Amazon have around 2,000 sites that link in this way.

ESTIMATING FOOTFALL

It is possible to estimate the approximate footfall that your site might receive from each of the methods described above, and therefore get an estimate of the total traffic that your site might receive. The example figures are based on our fictitious château selling fine wines.

Factor	Example	Your estimate
1. Enter the size of the total target market that has Internet access	540,000	
2. What percentage do you expect to capture using traditional advertising and communications? *The château does not traditionally advertise except at trade fairs and local celebrations*	0%	
3. What percentage do you expect to come via people searching using search engines? (Use 5% of those making a search if you think your site will feature in the top 100 sites shown in a search, 0.5% if you think it will appear lower down the order) *The château does not know enough about the Internet to be able to ensure that its name will appear high on the Internet searches. It expects that 10% of its target market might make a search about wine, and that half of one per cent of those will then click on its site*	0.5%	
4. What percentage will come from advertising on the Internet? (Use 10% of those making a relevant search) *The château is not prepared to make such an investment at this time*	0%	
5. What percentage (or number) will come from having sites with similar links? *The château was introduced to this concept by a leading French wine publication, which has offered complementary links. This site receives approximately 30,000 visits a year. The château has assumed that 10% of those visits might also visit the château's site*	10%	
6. Multiply the target market by the total of the percentages and/or add together the number of visits that you have calculated	2,700	

Based on these calculations, the château can expect approximately 2,700 visits in a year. An examination of the visitor counters shown on many sites suggests that this figure is slightly above average for a poorly promoted site.

Figure 13.2   Estimating footfall

To achieve footfall successfully requires that you adopt a comprehensive strategy for the Internet. Simply creating a website, however much or little money you spend on it, does not mean that people will visit it. Without an approach that exploits the singular opportunities of the Internet to increase footfall, creating a website aimed at increasing your sales is a strategy that is doomed to failure.

Making the sale

Once you have succeeded in getting customers to visit your website, you still have to get them to buy something. This is the area in which the Internet, with its interactivity and versatility, starts to win over traditional sales methods. The virtual nature of the Internet means that you can use different methods for achieving sales – methods that cannot be applied effectively in a physical environment. Ironically, however, most websites fail to take advantage of these methods. The Internet has been constructed by computer experts, not by marketeers, but its future, whether the computer geeks like it or not, is going to depend on the speed with which an effective model emerges that allows commercial organisations to sell their goods and services. There is no such thing as a free lunch, and unless the marketeers can find a way of making it pay, then the Internet is doomed to grind to a halt.

There are four areas which, we believe, you particularly need to consider:

- price;
- interactivity;
- volume of information;
- new methods of selling and buying.

Price

One issue that we have touched on throughout this book is price. Although not necessarily playing to the Internet's strengths, price nevertheless remains an extremely powerful method of encouraging (or discouraging) consumers to buy. If the prices on the Internet are lower than in the physical market, this advantage will go a long way towards increasing sales. But, to be sustainable, lower prices clearly need to be matched by lower costs if the profitability of a business is to be maintained.

It is one of the key – but comparatively under-exploited – aspects of the Internet that it provides you with an opportunity to lower your costs as a precursor to reducing prices. As such, the Internet enables you to pursue a low-price strategy while maintaining your profitability. There are industries in which this is already proving possible: indeed, in some sectors we are starting to see wholesale migration from physically based methods of doing business to virtual methods. One of the best examples is the brokerage industry for stocks and shares. The *Wall Street Journal* recently reported that there are now some three million on-line accounts at brokerage firms and mutual fund companies – almost double the number in the previous year.[1] The reasons for such a rapid increase are obvious: the target market of the affluent young (often men) fits well with the demographics of the Internet; regular surfers on the Internet are highly likely also to hold stocks and shares. Once a trade is initiated on the Internet, the remaining physical costs of the business are extremely small and the potential to reduce costs is accordingly very high. Finally, the speed with which the transaction can be completed is far quicker than that using the traditional methods of telephone or letter. It is, therefore, not surprising that analysts predict that the percentage of broking business that is conducted over the Internet will continue to grow rapidly.

However, not all business falls into this category and, for that reason, price should not be the only weapon that you wield on the Internet. There are many more, much better weapons.

Interactivity

The key factor that differentiates the Internet from other forms of marketing is its interactivity: consumers are not passive recipients of a broadcast marketing message – they can interact with it. At its simplest, consumers can choose which areas of the message to explore. Sites can be laid out so that consumers can be led down a particular set of pathways depending on their particular interests.

Sites can, however, also be developed to provide different information to different consumers. 'Cookies' – small pieces of information that are placed on your computer giving details of the parts of the

Internet that you have explored – can be picked up and used to generate the site content that is displayed. Imagine a music retailer who provides free samples of different bands. By analysing and recording which bands you have listened to, the company can display advertisements that reflect your areas of interest the next time you visit its site.

Used in this way, the Internet can begin to resemble the marketeer's dream of one-to-one relationship marketing, where individual content is generated for individual customers depending on the information that is carried about each person's individual preferences.

Volume of information

One of the other major advantages of the Internet is the volume of information that can be stored and the ease with which it can be updated. This enables new services to be provided in a way that was not economically feasible before.

A good example of the use of the Internet in this way is to keep rapidly changing catalogues on-line. This enables, for the first time, the opportunity to bring grocery shopping out of the grocery store, supermarket and superstore. By uploading the daily catalogue of goods and prices that are available, stores can now enable consumers to buy their goods without having to go round the store to collect them. In an environment in which time is precious (the young affulents who use the Internet also tend to work extremely long hours), the advantage to the consumer is undeniable.

Not only that, but the concept can reduce costs too. The warehouse that stores the goods which a customer wants can sort and pack these goods considerably more efficiently than the store and can be located out of town in an industrial park or other area where cheap rents are available. Moreover, staffing requirements are lower, the incidence of in-store theft is reduced, and the hours of operation can be extended.

It is no wonder, therefore, that organisations, such as Groceries to Go in the US, are being set up to exploit this opportunity, while, in the UK, retailing giants such as Tesco's and Sainsbury's are all running trials which – the signs suggest – will soon be extended to a much wider base of customers.

New methods of selling (and buying)

This interactivity also gives rise to new methods of selling and purchasing, primarily by giving purchasers and sellers new ways in which they can interact. One of the best examples of this is General Electric, which is rapidly moving all its different business units to purchasing via the Internet.

Case Study

GENERAL ELECTRIC

Perhaps one of the most successful ventures on to the Internet has not been a retail venture at all. General Electric, the USA's and the world's largest diversified manufacturer, decided (in the interests of efficiency) to start purchasing via the Internet. Until that time, suppliers had to submit tenders via paper or via the firm's proprietary EDI electronic links. The problem with this was that it meant that the supplier had to have the same proprietary EDI link. By launching GE Trading Process Network, which links a secure website direct to their resource planning software, the time taken to purchase goods can be drastically reduced. Not only that, but because of the openness and ease of access, supplier prices have been reduced by up to 10–15 per cent. As Orville Bailey, the global director of purchasing and supplier productivity at GE Information Services, comments:

> Suppliers aren't sure who else is out there bidding... . The immediacy is causing more competitive pricing earlier in the process.[2]

Essentially, the change in the method of purchasing has, because of the openness of the Internet, led to an increase in competition and therefore a reduction in prices.

This approach can also be used by organisations that want to sell as well as buy. The use of auctioning, for example, is becoming more common on the Internet. These auctions started with the sales of surplus computer equipment. Purchasers were invited to submit their bids for each item, and these bids were then displayed for all to see. When the auction closed, the purchasers with the highest bid were offered the goods. This method of selling is now being investigated by other industries as well. A number of airlines have held auctions of surplus seats on the Internet. Again, the method has proved to be successful, drawing numerous bidders interested by this new approach, as well as maximising the price that could be obtained for the seats.

The Internet is extremely seductive to marketeers. It promises a large customer base, a cheap method of communication and all the advantages that a truly interactive medium can bring. It is no wonder that barely a day goes past without some new hype that is making organisations jump on to this particular bandwagon at the rate of literally hundreds a day. Yet few of these organisations have given any thought to the peculiar nature of the Internet and how they can maximise the return they achieve from it.

If you do not have a marketing strategy for the Internet, your efforts, however impressive your website might look and however much you might have invested in its development, will be disappointing. Take a look at the way in which the four key 'P's of the marketing professional relate to your physical business. Success on the Internet is not about reapplying your existing thinking but about formulating a new approach to these core issues:

- **Price:** Does selling your product over the Internet confer a price advantage over selling via other channels? If not, what are you going to offer to persuade customers to move to this new marketing channel?

- **Product:** Is your product enhanced or diminished when you sell it over the Internet? Can the speed of the Internet and its interactivity add value to the product? Does the lack of the ability to touch and directly examine the product diminish its value?

- **Place:** How are you going to ensure that you get enough visits to your website to create the requisite amount of sales needed to produce a reasonable return?

- **Promotion:** How is your product going to be promoted and differentiated from the other products that are for sale on the Web? How will you differentiate your products both from those of your existing competitors, and from those of new competitors who may be exploiting the Internet?

It is the interactivity – the ability to communicate with the customer – that is drawing marketeers to the Internet. You do not need to forget the basic rules of marketing – you just need to reinvent the way in which they are applied to this new, and genuinely different, medium.

Summary

❑ The opportunities of Internet-based commerce seem considerable, but few companies have yet succeeded in exploiting them profitably.

❑ Such success is dependent on acquiring an in-depth understanding of the characteristics of the Internet and matching these with the characteristics of your existing products or services.

❑ In considering the nature of the Internet itself, there are four key aspects that need to be considered:

- managing consumers' fears – reasonable and unreasonable – about the security of Internet-based transactions;
- overcoming issues surrounding the intangibility of Internet-based shopping either by using your established brand to give consumers confidence or by trading in the kind of goods that people feel comfortable buying remotely;
- playing to the demographics of the Internet, which are skewed towards young, male and well-off individuals;
- ensuring that, at the end of the day, your physical goods can be delivered successfully to your remote customer.

❑ To exploit the opportunities of the Internet, you need – like any retail outlet – to maximise footfall. However, this is much more difficult on the Internet (where there is negligible passing trade) than in a shopping mall. Most companies are attempting to overcome this issue by mass-marketing, but smaller companies are finding more inventive ways of using the nature of the Internet itself to help promote their services.

❑ Any strategy you adopt – however clever – will be worthless if you do not convert visits to your website into actual sales. To do this, you will need to think about how you can exploit the Internet to:

- reduce costs and ultimately prices;
- improve the information you have about customers;
- provide much more up-to-date information on your products and services;
- find new methods to buy and sell (such as on-line auctioning).

Notes

1. *Wall Street Journal,* 5 September, 1994
2. Clinton Wilder and Marianne Kolbasuk McGee, 'The Net Pays Off', *TechWire,* 28 January, 1997.

14

Computer Modelling and Complexity

Survival through simplification

'Chaos' and 'complexity theory' are some of the key business buzz-words of the 1990s, reflecting not just the emergence of a 'new' science but also a more general shift in our culture away from simple certainties. However, it is a change to which business has come comparatively late. Much of what we do is still based on comparatively simple assumptions, some of which we have already discussed in this book, such as the dichotomies between strategy and detail, and between information and knowledge. We keep things simple because this is how we get things done. Tell someone to do one or two tasks and there's no problem; tell them to do 20 and, all too often, nothing ends up being completed. Like economists, we all know that the real worlds of our businesses are rarely as clear and logical as our planning models; we all know that things do not always turn out as we expected. We simplify to survive: it is a necessary part of management.

The question that concerns us here is what this process of simplification involves. On what basis do we decide what constitutes the most important parts of our work, which we therefore retain in our simple management model? Do we exclude what appear to be less important elements because they do not appear to have any visible impact? How reliable are our perceptions?

There are three key ways in which we simplify what we manage:

- *We minimise the number of things with which we have to deal*: We are all guilty of this. A company whose customer base is growing rapidly will usually start to group customers together so that the numbers of submarkets to which it is selling remains 'manageable'. As a result, it gradually ceases to treat customers as individuals. A music company launching a new pop video may think hard about the launch date, about how many copies to ship to which stores, about the advertising directed at its prime target audience, but it probably pays little attention to the impact that word-of-mouth recommendation has on potential purchasers.

■ *We tend to see the things that we manage in isolation*:   A popular computer game of the early 1990s was called 'Railroad Tycoon'. Players became the owners of small railways, transporting a variety of goods and passengers and competing with rival companies. Their objective was to build the most successful network by exploiting differences in the profitability of alternative payloads, using rolling-stock efficiently and minimising risks. What started off comparatively simply – you might have just a couple of engines and lines – soon become very complex to manage: every few seconds a train might be taking on a new load or changing route for reasons beyond your control. Gradually, as your ability to keep track of things declined, the network would become over-loaded, some orders would go unfulfilled while stock-piles of other goods would grow. It was a lesson in just how difficult it is to manage multiple variables (in this case, trains) in a system in which the success of the whole was dependent on the effective integration of all the component parts. In our working lives, most of us do manage groups of interrelated variables (what else, after all, is a team of people or the launch of a new product?), but we only manage them by limiting the number of interrelationships between variables. We may make our department the most productive in the organisation, but we will not necessarily think how what that department does impacts on anyone else. We may run an immensely successful business, but that does not mean that we stop to think about that business's effect on the environment or the local economy.

■ *We assume that things are predictable*:   Finally, even where we do recognise that the things for which we are responsible are made up of a host of variables, many of which are interrelated, we usually assume that we can predict the end result.

These are hugely important issues because they touch on fundamental assumptions about how we, as individuals, work and manage, and how the organisations in which we work function. Clearly, the way in which such assumptions influence us vary from activity to activity, and from organisation to organisation. The assumptions of a shopfloor worker about, for example, the composition of metals in the bolt that he or she is manufacturing have very little direct impact on either the process of making the bolt or the completed bolt, because the process in which they are engaged is primarily a physical one. However, the assumptions of the bolt designer or of the person who laid out the production line potentially have a much greater impact – assumptions about what a bolt looks like, what it is supposed to do, the acceptable rate of error and so on. This is because the design process, even in heavy manufacturing, is primarily an information-based process that happens on paper, in computer-generated proto-types, in people's heads. The more virtual the process, the greater the impact of assumptions.

Perhaps the most virtual process in any organisation is strategic planning, and this is where our mental models have the greatest influ-ence. Strategy development is a virtual process in the sense that the future does not exist in physical terms: the scenarios we create are based on extrapolating the information we have on past and present trends. For example, the chances are that you are planning on a linear basis ('If we do A and the competition does B, then C will happen'); the assumption you have made – whether it is how much food to buy from your supermarket this weekend or which market your company should move into next – is that events are consistent over time and are therefore predictable ('If D happened last time we did E, it will happen again the next time we do E'). However, as we all know from planning, things do not always turn out as we anticipated. Thus while we simplify to survive, it is often at the cost of having an inaccurate picture of even the most immediate future. But if we had this picture, we probably could not function effectively because everything we looked at would be too complicated for us to be able to make a deci-sion. As children, we learn to discard detail and develop high-level concepts: we can talk about a bird without worrying whether it is a sparrow or starling. An autistic child never learns to develop such concepts: she may be brilliant at mental arithmetic but she cannot make the leap from the detail to its practical application. Having too much information on the present or future has always been seen as the management equivalent of autism. Successful executives rise above the detail.

Information and information technology are making redundant these three ways in which we simplify our environment in order to manage it. Just because we can be overwhelmed by detail does not mean that computers are. Where we simplify, they can make complex, and this – we believe – constitutes a major business opportunity. To exploit it, we need to reverse the three ways of thinking we described above. We need to:

■ increase – rather than decrease – the number of variables we control;
■ see these variables as interrelated rather than as isolated entities;
■ recognise and exploit the fact that their behaviour can be unpredictable.

Tools for looking at each of these aspects are discussed below.

Using micro-management to increase the number of variables under our control

In this book, we have inevitably talked a lot about information: how you can exploit it, who you could sell it to, the kind you need. However, none of the information-related opportunities we have highlighted can be realised if you do not *manage* information.

This may sound like a self-evident truth, but business has in fact generally shown a marked reluctance to do anything of the kind. Information management – insofar as it has existed at all – has been the responsibility of IT specialists (who have approached the subject from a purely technical perspective) or accountants (who have focused only on financial data). Neither of these attitudes will get you very far in the virtual economy: business now needs to manage information from a much more strategic perspective. Business needs to start to match its strategic vision and sense of direction (built around the business as a whole) with precise analysis – at a detailed level – of the information from which it is composed, whether this information concerns customers, employees, products or processes.

We have traditionally managed business from a strategic perspective: the chief executive looks after strategy, and, as a result, 'strategy' becomes the aspiration of all the talented and ambitious people who work within the organisation. How often have we all said, 'Don't bother me with the detail'? Promotion and career development are about moving away from detail and into strategy; strategy is a status symbol. It is only failures – the bean-counters – who get left behind in this particular evolutionary ladder.

It is worth pausing for a moment to consider why we think like this. Why do we see strategy and detail as opposites? Why is this distinction so important to us? The person running a corner-shop does not distinguish between strategy and detail because such a distinction is irrelevant. The 'strategic' decisions that he or she takes are also necessarily detailed ones: 'Which shelf should I put the soap powder on?', 'Should I buy a new cold storage unit?' The strategy/detail dichotomy comes into play only as an organisation gets bigger. In fact, we could probably say that the larger the company, the greater will be the perceived gap between detail (the responsibility of the people at the bottom of the hierarchy) and strategy (the preserve of those at the top).

However, the strategy/detail split is not so much a function of size but of what size entails. When large companies first appeared on a common basis, during the Industrial Revolution, they did so in an environment where the principle of the division of labour was gaining widespread acceptability. Greater size meant that activities had to be divided and managed, something which in turn gave rise to formalised organisational hierarchies. Given the increasing size and complexity of business, it followed that their owners could not know everything about them. To a lesser or greater extent, the information that they had to run the business had to have been filtered: they could not be expected to know everything about everything. This meant that they had to have either fewer bits of detailed information or all information but in a summarised format. In practice, there was no real choice: to be able to run a business on a few, very aggregated performance measurements, you need to know which measurements – which bits of information – will be important; you have to be able to prioritise. It was therefore easier and safer for the factory owners to adopt the second approach: because they could not be sure what information was important and what was not, they had to know a bit of everything.

Two factors, then, drove this division between strategy and detail. In the first place, growing increasingly complex businesses meant that the information required to run them had to be summarised – the detail had to be converted into the strategic. Second, the people who managed these businesses had no framework by which they could work out what was important; they had no means of identifying the important 'detail'. To these two entirely understandable, perhaps inevitable, factors we need to add a third – status. The strategy/detail division legitimised management – it was a visible sign that what a manager did was different from what his staff did.

Of the three factors, the first two are pretty much redundant today. As we have already noted, increasingly cheap and powerful computer technology means that we can handle large volumes of information comparatively easily. Furthermore, because we can handle all this information, it is less imperative to decide from the outset what is important and what is not – computer systems can warn us when a factory's output has fallen under a particular threshold or tell us when an individual consultant's utilisation has been unusually good.

What remains is status. Thus, when we assume that strategy is the most important activity of a business – the one to which we all aspire – our attitude is a product of historical accident rather than any reflection of genuine merit. Moreover, it is an attitude that is quite simply out of date.

Micro-management is an approach that turns this on its head: it can perhaps best be defined as the strategic management of detail. The next time you install a new management accounts or financial reporting system, you should invest time in identifying how you might make use of your most detailed data before you decide what consolidated information you need. Suppose you are responsible for managing the surgery of a group of doctors. Conventional management thinking would tell you that you should decide what your key – usually high-level – performance measurements should be: number of patients, average length of appointment, average length of wait for patients, cost per patient and so on. While these are valuable figures in their own right, they do not constitute much more than a thumbnail sketch of the practice and they could mislead you if you tried to make changes. You might, for example, decide that the surgery hours should be more efficient and that you want to bring down the average length of an appointment to 2 minutes. You talk to the doctors and support staff, you install a better computer-based system for taking notes during an appointment, calling up repeat prescriptions and so on, but nothing happens. The length of appointment remains – in your view – obstinately high. The micro-management approach would be to look at all the individual appointment lengths and see whether you could spot a pattern in the data that the overall average might conceal. In this example, it might show up that it is a very small minority of patients who have very special needs who are keeping up the average.

The doctors and the support staff are concentrating on reducing the time each appointment lasts when they should be focusing on this small subset and understanding why these patients take up such a disproportionate amount of time.

Patterns, like this, at a very detailed level tell you things that an average never could. The purpose of micro-management is to replace this aggregated analysis with more detailed analysis that provides additional insights and benefits to an organisation.

Some of the best examples of micro-management come from the retail industry, where a combination of factors (planning restrictions on new stores, intense competition, the introduction of 'category killers') have combined to make increasing revenues from existing stores, as opposed to adding new stores, very difficult. In the USA, the average 'register' (that is, trolley of purchases) has been falling for the last few years, partly because higher-value items are being increasingly purchased in warehouse clubs and the growth of managed health care schemes has meant that the purchase of expensive, over-the-counter medicines is also declining. Retailers are now focusing on how to increase that average register again, as small percentage point increases here have a significant impact on a chain's overall turnover. This means micro-managing activities such as category development and pricing.

Micro-management takes many forms, but, in every case, it uses detail to generate a strategic advantage; the conventional division between the two does not apply. Although we would not necessarily think about it in such terms, dealing in the financial markets is another form of micro-management. The whole concept of arbitrage – the exploitation of small differences for financial gain – is a good example of micro-management in action. It is not surprising that the first exponents of micro-management were the financial services companies. They deal in products that consist almost solely of information. Their information-handling infrastructure is the most advanced of any industry. There are, however, also plenty of sectors where the opportunities of micro-management have been largely ignored. Many of the major consultancy companies tend to put up prices across the board, leaving individual partners to negotiate the actual fees for assignments in practice. More effectively, they might try to understand the extent to which price elasticity varies by service and sector, and adjust prices on this basis. Even in those companies which do use some aspects of micro-management, there are plenty of under-exploited opportunities. This is because people assume that what applies at a strategic level also applies at detailed level. They believe, in other words, that the detail is just a smaller version of the strategic (this being an assumption that underpins much of our thinking about management, organisational design, delegation and so on). In fact, we would argue that, as you delve more and more into the detail, the more the rules of the game start to change.

Exploiting the potential complexity of your business does not, therefore, have to stop with micro-management. Two things happen when you start to use information at more detailed levels. In the first place, you will find that many of the aspects of your business that you thought you could look at in isolation are in fact interrelated. Second, some of the results you observe will be unexpected – the world of detail turns out to be a lot less predictable than the world of strategy.

Systems thinking and information

Systems thinking is an approach that has been pioneered by the Massachusetts Institute of Technology and which was summarised by Peter Senge in his book, *The Fifth Discipline*:

> Business and other human endeavours are... systems. They... are bound by invisible fabrics of interrelated actions, which often take years to fully play out their effects on each other. Since we are part of that lacework ourselves, it's doubly hard to see the whole pattern of change. Instead, we tend to focus on snapshots of isolated parts of the system, and wonder why our deepest problems never get solved. Systems thinking is a conceptual framework, a body of knowledge and tools that have been developed over the past fifty years, to make the full patterns clearer, and to help us see how to change them effectively.[1]

This book is not the place to give an extensive or in-depth analysis of systems thinking; there is a growing body of material on this subject. Our purpose here is to look at the way in which the theory can be applied to the way in which we exploit information.

Systems thinking sprang, in part, out of a reaction against the linear assumptions that have been made by much of science since Newton. The 17th-century philosopher, René Descartes, for example, argued that we live in a mechanical, 'clockwork' universe. When our analysis of this universe produced unexpected results, scientists have tended to put this down to 'noise on the line' – an impurity in a chemical experiment, for example. Science, like management, has effectively evolved on the basis of simplification. Systems thinking starts from a different assumption – that our world is fundamentally non-linear; things do not happen as planned because the number of variables involved is high and the interaction between them both complex and fluid. It looks at the world very differently from conventional science.

Take two scientists, one a conventional chemist and the other interested in systems thinking, looking at a bowl of fruit. Each one would see it differently. The chemist would see individual pieces of fruit, he could measure and analyse the composition of each. The complexity theorist would see the fruit and the bowl as a single system, each piece of fruit dynamically supporting the others in a unique way – take one away and you would have, not one less piece of fruit, but a different system. Systems thinking, therefore, sees the world in terms of interactive systems rather than isolated atoms. It is the interaction of parts of the system (the pieces of fruit), rather than the parts themselves, that are important. These interconnecting parts act together as a whole, so that the overall system changes if you take pieces away: cutting a piece of fruit in half does not mean that you end up with two smaller pieces of fruit. Equally, doubling a system does not mean that you get a system that is simply twice as big, because the behaviour of the system depends on the structure as a whole rather than on its individual components. This means that, to change a system successfully, you may have to change its structure, as changing the parts in isolation will not always produce the desired outcome. It also means that you cannot predict the properties of a complete system by taking it to pieces. Conventional analysis (where we pull things apart) needs to be replaced by synthesis (where we put them together).

An organisation is a good example of this. If you cut your company in half, you would get two new and different organisations rather than two smaller versions of your existing company. When we merge companies or departments, we habitually talk of economies of scale and synergy. We believe that the whole will be greater than the sum of the parts, in other words that, when we add the two 'systems' together, we get a third, new 'system'. We should not be surprised, therefore, that it is in the field of organisational design and culture that systems theory has found the most practical business applications. Organisations are complex systems. Why else is it that a particular CEO can turn one failing company around, but not another? Why does a process that worked well in one department fail dismally in the next? 'The simple truth,' two business writers, John Sofinis and Beverly Goldberg, recently concluded 'is that there is no single, best "solution"':

> the inescapable truth is that the changes necessary to become so fluid that you can survive requires a new understanding of what constitutes an organisation and an understanding of the organisation as a complex and adaptive system.[2]

Rather than treating organisations as simple, linear systems ('If we run an internal PR campaign, we'll be able to get the staff behind us'), we should be thinking of them more as organisms, single entities in which all the parts are interrelated and which change and adapt over time. Organisations evolve only very slowly (they have their genetic blueprint as much as we do). Their complex structure makes them difficult to change. How many times have we seen new recruits sucked into the dominant culture of a company? Like cells, an organisation replicates itself and organises itself – informal communication channels are often much more influential than formal ones. In fact, one of the interesting, although apparently perverse, conclusions you reach in thinking about organisations as systems is that every organisation is perfectly designed. Even that restaurant you visited last week (where the service was atrocious and the food even worse) was perfectly designed to produce those outputs (poor service and bad food). The problem was that these were not the outputs you wanted.

From our perspective of exploiting information and the virtual business, systems thinking is important in three ways:

■ Our habitual process of simplification matters most where we are relying on information rather than physical entities. The process of producing a bolt may, in fact, be just as complex as designing one, but the impact of that complexity is more marginal. We may not understand why a particular bolt is imperfect, but the rate at which these imperfections occur is within a tolerable level and does not, therefore, hold up the assembly line as a whole. In contrast, any decision about the design of the bolt – if it turns out to be wrong – can cost millions. An information-based process, such as strategic planning, is heavily influenced by our assumptions, our mental model of the organisation in which we work and the market in which it operates.

- Simplification has a more significant impact on virtual companies and processes. The more information we have, the more options we have and the more complex our world is. If our mental models cannot keep pace with this new level of complexity, a potentially serious problem arises: how can we grow new markets, launch new products and acquire new customers if we are approaching a 21st-century world with 19th-century attitudes about how those markets, products and customers interreact?

- If information is part of the problem, it is also, however, part of the solution. What systems thinking enables you to do is examine the information to establish and then exploit the links between each part. We believe that the massive quantities of information that we are generating and storing today will only become truly useful if they can be linked together, if connections can be identified between previously segmented departments, products or customers. Taken in isolation, each 'unit' of information gives us only current physical properties. If we analyse information on our customers, we will learn who they are, where they live, the demographic categories they fall into and so on, but we will not learn anything about what they will buy next. This is the crucial difference between isolated and linked information: isolated information can only tell us what is, but linked information can tell us what *may be*. Moreover, it is important to recognise that the links between units of information are dynamic and interactive: it may be that positive changes in some areas of the business can have negative impact elsewhere.

Developing an in-depth understanding of the levers in a business is crucial. Everyone is used to looking at sales figures, but these are purely output measures. If there is a problem with them, it has already happened and we cannot affect it; we might be able to affect next month's figures, but we cannot change those already past. Using the concept of micro-management, business information would be used, first, to identify all the factors that influence the outputs (such as sales), and second, then to understand the potential influence of each of these factors. The key difference between this process and other forms of analysis is that it has to be carried out at a detailed – possibly the most detailed – level.

To continue our example. The sales figures will almost always be driven by the number of items sold multiplied by their price, and these factors are, in turn, driven by others – the number of customers, competition and so on. The further back in this chain we can go, the earlier we will be able to have an impact on sales. Thus we may identify that if one of our competitors reduces the price of a product, our volume of sales will go down; if we reduce our price at the same time, our volume of sales will remain static (assuming that we also match our competitor's price promotion or other marketing tactics). However, the more 'micro' we can go, the greater the impact we can have. Looking at a yet more detailed level, we may see that our competitor's price reduction appeals only to a certain type of customer (those, for example, who have easy access to the competitor's products; in other words, the discount is not sufficient to attract customers who do not have this access). In this case, our proposal would be to restrict our own price reduction so that it applies only to those customers who have easy access to the competitor products. By doing this, we can minimise the impact of our competitor's actions on our overall margins. By using historical information to produce forecast trends in behaviour, we can also act as such a price reduction occurs, rather than waiting for it to come through in terms of lower sales figures.

▓ QUESTIONS TO CONSIDER ▓

---

1. What is it that your company is optimally designed to output? (You can be reasonably confident that it will not be conventional products or services.)

2. How do you make decisions?

3. How often have things turned out differently from the way you expect?

4. How far into the future can you really see? Next year? Next month? Tomorrow?

A second important aspect of systems thinking is that we can identify the relative importance of factors such as price, competition and ease of access, again at a detailed level. The concept of price elasticity is familiar: its basic premise is that raising or reducing the price of a product will have an impact on its sales – where the price is inelastic, small increases will be followed by a small fall-off in sales; where it is elastic, sales are affected even by small price increases. In practice, the relationship between price and sales volume is likely to be a complex one and will vary according to a host of additional factors such as type of customer and time of year. Understanding the relative importance of this factors means that you will know what to change when in order to achieve the maximum impact; it means that you will be able to identify the minute changes that will have a significant impact on your business. Systems thinking, by identifying such factors, enables us to have a disproportionate impact on our businesses.

Exploiting the dynamic behaviour of your business

Look around your business. You will see many areas in which its dynamics are being ignored. This can take many forms:

- the way in which marketing budgets are allocated to different media, based on gut-feel rather than a comprehensive understanding of why some channels succeed when others do not;
- the decision to launch a new product on a specific date or in a specific place, which is based on the past experience of other products;
- attaching a single price to a single product.

Whatever the precise form, they are all likely to be instances of when a potentially complex situation has been simplified in order to allow the human brain to encompass it. But every time we do this represents a lost opportunity. If the dynamics are understood, much less money would be wasted in the marketing budget; products would be targeted more precisely and launched more effectively; profits would be higher. We have already noted how this is the case when you deal with detailed customer information, where the aggregation of the data into 'averages' conceals individual differences in behaviour that, once recognised, can be exploited in other marketing terms. This same approach, however, can be applied to other areas of a business.

Consider the way in which Hollywood blockbusters are released. The overall number of films released is rising rapidly, even in traditional off-peak seasons. However, studios' profits are becoming increasingly dependent on the summer blockbuster season: a successful film or two here can be the difference between surviving and going under. Moreover, the number of people who see a film in its first few days is playing an ever-increasing role in determining the ultimate success of a film: in 1996, *Independence Day* was shown at all-night screenings in order to have maximum impact. With so much going on and so much attention focused on a relatively small number of weeks, knowing exactly when to release a film is becoming like a game of multidimensional chess. Among the pieces on the board are: how many cinemas should you open at (too few and you lose impact; too many and the half-empty stalls will create a bad impression); which cinemas; the audience at which your film is aimed; which competiting films are being released at the same time; what the weather is likely to be; and who is starring in it, plus who is starring in the competition. You cannot intuit the best result. Too many of these factors are interrelated, and, in any case, the situation is clearly complicated by the fact that all your competitors will be trying to take this kind of decision as well. What is needed is a computer model that can take all these variables, combine them with the 'rules' that constitute gut-feel and experience in the industry, and then use advanced modelling techniques such as genetic algorithms to explore the millions of possible options. Modelling the interaction between the different variables – the number of cinemas in which to open, the target audience, competitors' films and the number of weeks they will have been in cinemas, for example – provides a much deeper insight into the impact of small changes on the 'system' as a whole, which substantially increases the likelihood of a studio launching its film at the optimum – most profitable – moment.

The process is no different from building the arbitrage model in the financial services sector, to which we referred earlier. The only reason that things like this have not been done with this degree of sophistication is that we continue to assume that processes such as deciding which advertising slot to put where, or which film to launch when, are too subjective – that is, too complex – to be captured effectively by something as dumb as a computer model. Clearly, computers cannot as yet replace human judgement, but much of what we perceive to be judgement – and television advertising, film launches and bond-dealing all fall into this category – are in fact rule-based 'games'. Judgement may still play a role, but many of the rules (once we see them as such) can be carried out much more effectively by a model.

■ **QUESTIONS TO CONSIDER** ■

One of the areas in which the interrelated dynamics of a business are most commonly ignored is pricing. We described earlier the example of airlines using yield-management systems to change seat prices depending on the popularity of a particular flight, but this kind of thinking is used only to a limited extent in other sectors.

5. How complex is your pricing structure?

6. How often do you vary prices, and on what basis do you vary them?

7. Do you look at the prices of groups of products across your customer base as a whole? Or do you price individual products for individual customers?

8. How much more money would you make if you used differential pricing?

In fact, we would take this argument a stage further. Computer modelling does not just help a business to exploit its inherent dynamics – dynamics that have hidden opportunities to increase profits or cut costs. It also provides a tool that helps you to understand, even gauge, the ways in which this dynamics may have a pronounced and unexpected impact on your business or the external environment in which it operates. Such techniques are not the stuff of fantasy. Systems thinking is a discipline that enables organisations to use computer models to predict the behaviour of their own complex organisations, and, as such, it is starting to gain widespread acceptance in mainstream business. The proof of a pudding, though, inevitably comes from eating it; similarly, the test for systems thinking lies in being able to exploit it for commercial advantage.

Exploiting the non-linearities of your business

One of the most valuable results of using systems thinking is that it allows you to identify the points of greatest leverage within any organisation, the points at which you can have the most impact. Most of what we do when we develop a strategy for a business, or even just try to change things that are going on inside one, is effectively to assume that when we push Button A, Effect B happens, and that if we push Button A five times, we get five times as much of Effect B. As we have already discussed, this assumption is predicated on the basis that we are dealing with a comparatively simple and static system, which is rarely the case in practice, but what this attitude also misses is that Button A, if it only ever has Effect B, may not be the right button to press in the first place. In other words, unpredictable events may be important not just because they need to be understood, but also because they offer the potential for much greater improvements in performance than the more predictable areas of a business. If a part of your business is predictable, this implies that the 'system' that constitutes that area is an established one with many checks and balances. Such a system is inherently hard to change. However, if the performance of another varies wildly, this suggests that the 'system' in this context has not yet settled down. There are fewer checks and balances, which means that changes may be easier to effect. Thus a hospital that has performed consistently poorly for 20 years will be harder to improve than one whose performance has varied markedly even though it has performed, on average, worse than the first, more consistent hospital. Unpredictable behaviour implies that the under-lying system is non-linear – if we push Button A, Effect B may happen on some occasions, but on others it will be Effect C or D.

■ QUESTIONS TO CONSIDER ■

9. How non-linear is your organisation? Where do these non-linearities reside?

10. Does it take a lot to make your organisational systems change the perfor-mance of your business? Can your particular camel's back be broken by just a small straw?

11. Can you predict the impact of even the smallest changes? How much time did you give over in your last planning cycle to following through the complex implications of your actions?

Busy roads are another example. We have all driven along roads where the sheer volume of traffic and the variability of the rate at which cars travel mean that the traffic comes to an abrupt halt every now and then for no discernible reason. The principle is the same: it takes only a small number of additional cars over a tolerance level to bring a busy road to a complete standstill. It takes only a small change in the input (the number of cars) to a non-linear system (the road) to make a large change to the output (a traffic jam). Similarly, it does not take much to make a complex system chaotic. If we can use systems thinking techniques to identify the non-linear aspects of a business, we can use these as levers with which to change the business. Also, precisely because small changes will have a disproportionate impact on the business around them, we will be able to make bigger changes – realise more radical strategies – than if we focused on simpler, more predictable areas.

But can you convert this type of behaviour into an opportunity? As with exploiting the dynamics of a business, it is information which makes this possible. Just as – we have argued – the number of inter-relations in an organisation increases as it or its component parts become more virtual, so does its potential for non-linearity. You only need to look at the results of Internet-based companies over the past couple of years to see this. The performance of an information-based business is more volatile than that of a business that is still primarily physical. This is because you can change more of the variables more quickly, more easily and more extensively. Even now, it still takes time to retool an assembly line; an insurance company could in theory change its entire investment portfolio, running into billions of dollars, in seconds (and the increasing volatility of the international stock markets is testimony to the scale of the impact that this can have).

Most organisations habitually see such volatility as a threat, and not unreasonably so. The value of stocks and shares is still heavily depen-dent on not just the absolute performance of a company, but also the reliability with which that performance can be predicted. However, volatility in some areas has its uses, especially if you can identify and to some extent ring-fence it, using information to exploit the opportu-nities and side-step the pitfalls.

One of the key areas in which we seen an approach like this working is corporate taxation. This may seem surprising; after all, those of us who do not spend our entire lives looking at tax issues often assume that calculating tax is a fairly predictable activity – how else could your advisors come up with tax-saving plans if they could not predict the results? When you stop to think about it, however, tax is – certainly for an information-based company – not so very different from film scheduling. There are areas in which we make choices (perhaps to adopt a particular taxation method), which sit above the complex system of inputs and outputs that constitutes our organisa-tion's tax position. It is the combination of these two factors (the number and interrelationship of the variables, and the extent of our discretion) that can turn a complex system into opportunities for profit.

Taxing a life assurance business is a good example. Under the UK tax regime, corporation tax for insurance companies is based on an extended calculation that takes into account (among other things) the kind of business the company is writing, its investment strategy, the way it prices its products and its forecast of future profits. A life insurance company is, however, an almost completely virtual business, in the sense that almost everything it does (invest, develop new products and so on) is information based and only touches physical reality at the point at which it sells a policy or pays out on one. This means that almost all the input variables to its tax calculation can be varied; in theory, everything in the business is a tax planning opportunity.

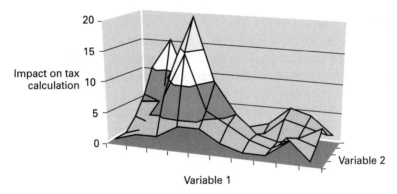

Figure 14.1   Looking for areas of leverage in tax calculations

Where the idea of volatility comes in useful is that, when modelled by a computer, it can help a company's tax manager to identify the best opportunities for tax planning. Think of a company as a landscape in which the contour lines of hills are based on the extent to which a particular area has an impact on the company's final tax position: the greater the impact, the higher the hill (Figure 14.1). Looking across the business as a whole, there will be flat areas where the activities have little impact on the amount of tax paid, but it is also likely that there are hills – even mountains – where the impact of even tiny changes can have a disproportionately significant impact on the tax owing. Being able to distinguish between the mountain ranges and the flat plains helps the tax department to identify areas of the business where small changes can have a hugely favourable impact. In a virtual business, where more areas of 'land' can be changed more quickly, you would expect the proportion of mountainous ground to be greater than that of flat ground, but even the relative height of the hills can help to focus on the areas of greatest yield. As befits a complex, even chaotic, system, it is our experience that it is hard to predict which issues come to light in this way, but, once identified, they are an example of how 'keeping it complex' can actually help rather than hinder your business.

Applying this kind of thinking to tax is, to an extent, comparatively easy. After all, tax is a quintessentially virtual activity – it is all about applying rules to different pieces of information; physical reality (or indeed the 'truth') does not feature greatly. We can, however, equally well apply this approach to any areas of a business, providing of course that we can represent it in information terms (train scheduling, error rates on an assembly line, passenger flow at an airport) and then explore it using sophisticated computer models in order to understand the impact of small change to the input variables. If we can identify the aspects of a business where performance is highly volatile, these are the areas on which we should be focusing management attention. Why spend millions re-engineering a process that does not have the capacity for significant improvement? All processes are equal, but some are more equal than others.

Applying these approaches in practice

Each of these approaches requires that a model is built of the business and that the model is then used to explore and understand the relationships between the different variables that underpin the business. The techniques used by the different schools of modellers vary, but underlying each approach there are a number of common tasks. Any good modelling approach will:

- develop a conceptual model of the business based on the understanding of those involved within it;
- develop a computer representation of the conceptual model and calibrate it with historical data;
- accept inputs of information about the future to run the model and derive conclusions about how the future will develop;
- provide a method of interpreting these results.

Again, as we have stressed throughout this book, the key benefit that such approaches provide is the ability to manipulate the future in many different ways. Because the representation is contained within the virtual world, it can be quickly and easily altered. Different management structures can be developed and examined, different assumptions can be quickly input into the model, and the results, and more importantly the differences in the results, can be explored and understood. You no longer have to make changes to your physical structures of supply chains and channels to market to understand what to do in the future. Rather than performing costly and time-consuming experiments, different approaches can be tried on the computer and the results instantly assessed.

Just as with all information, the accuracy of the results in foretelling what will actually occur will depend on the accuracy with which the information represents the physical reality. We are nowhere near the stage at which we can predict the future with 100 per cent accuracy, but we are at the stage where such models are close enough to reality to provide some real insights into the future and, more importantly, to identify what to do about them.

Tools such as systems thinking and non-linear mathematics enable us to model the world in a much more accurate fashion than has previously been possible. The interactions between different parts of the system can now be taken into account, and the impact of non-linear relationships between different parts of the business can be accurately modelled and understood.

Managing the virtual business in the future will require computers and computer models to exploit the wealth of opportunities that arise from managing in detail and understanding the interactions between different parts of the system. The emerging discipline of business modelling will be an essential part of the armoury of any business that wants to take full advantage of the opportunities offered.

Micro-management, systems thinking and non-linearity – the wealth of detailed information we now collect about all aspects of our organisations makes tools such as these not just useful, but also essential if we are to compete effectively. Our old model of doing business – in which we simplified our environment in order to understand and manage it – has little relevance in a virtual world that the wealth of information available has made more complex and difficult to grasp.

Summary

❑ Traditional management techniques rely on three types of simplification:

  ■ minimising the number of variables with which we have to deal;
  ■ treating each variable as independent so that we do not become overwhelmed with the complexity of even our most immediate environment;
  ■ assuming that the links between variables – where they are recognised – are staightforward.

❑ Information and the virtual business that is built from it cannot, however, be managed effectively in this fashion. Information means that we have many more variables to manage, all of which are linked together either directly or indirectly and often in complex, unpredictable patterns.

❑ A virtual business, because information is inherently both detailed and flexible, is more complex than a physical business.

❑ There are three techniques that business should start using in order to respond to this kind of environment:

  ■ Micro-management involves looking at the detailed information a company has, rather than aggregating in order to manage from a strategic standpoint.
  ■ Systems thinking provides a means of understanding how this growing plethora of variables link together.
  ■ Assessing the non-linearity of a business identifies the areas in which comparatively small changes will potentially have the greatest impact on performance.

❑ Computer modelling tools provide a method of understanding, making sense of and exploiting this information and its interrelationships.

Notes

1. Peter Senge, *The Fifth Discipline: The Art and Practice of the Learning Organisation*, London: Century Business, 1992.
2. John G Sifonis and Beverley Goldberg, *Corporation on a Tightrope: Balancing Leadership, Governance and Technology in an Age of Complexity*, Oxford: Oxford University Press, 1996.

Work–Learn–Share: a Method for Increasing Knowledge

Why is knowledge important?

How much is the knowledge in your organisation worth? Is it worth as much as your physical assets? Is it worth more? Could your organisation survive without the knowledge that has been collected? How is that knowledge represented in your accounts? What steps are you taking to safeguard or augment your knowledge? Why is this such a fashionable topic as we approach the millennium?

The answer to the last question probably lies in the realisation that current methods of accounting fail completely to account for the key assets of an organisation. For example, at the end of 1996 Microsoft had a market value of approximately $85bn, but fixed assets of less than $1bn. How can we account for the remaining $84bn? From the viewpoint of the market, this represents the ability of Microsoft to leverage its physical assets to produce a return to its shareholders. Delving a little further, the question then becomes 'What gives Microsoft the ability to leverage its physical assets so successfully?' In the short term, this might represent the knowledge about its brand that Microsoft has managed to instil in its customers. However, in the longer term, the vast majority of that $84bn represents the knowledge that Microsoft either already has or is capable of generating in the future, which enables the company to exploit its chosen markets.

Take another example. When IBM purchased Lotus it paid $3.5bn for a company with a book value of $500m, and its share price went up. Why did the market react in this way to the apparent folly of spending $3bn dollars too much for a company? Precisely because it recognised that the combination of Lotus's knowledge of software products (in particular its knowledge of communications technologies such as Lotus e-mail and Notes), coupled with IBM's knowledge of computer hardware, could together realise far greater returns than could either company's knowledge in isolation. Why did the value of Saatchi and Saatchi decline when the Saatchi brothers left the organisation? Not because of their worth on the balance sheet but because of the loss of their knowledge of and ability to exploit the advertising market.

None of the above examples represents anything that is measured on the balance sheet, yet each had a far more profound effect on the market price of the company than any mere change to the physical asset base. For some industrial sectors – such as pharmaceuticals – various approaches for measuring knowledge are in the process of being developed. Analysts have started to try to measure the worth of patents and other intellectual property rights. However, for the vast majority of sectors and for the vast majority of different types of knowledge, such measurement techniques are still in their infancy.

▓ QUESTIONS TO CONSIDER ▓

---

1. What is the ratio of your company's market value to its physical assets?

2. How does this compare with that of your competitors in the same industry?

3. Can you explain the differences?

It is not surprising that, given the vast disparities that are beginning to emerge between the accounting and market valuations of companies, the concepts of knowledge and knowledge management are becoming fashionable. Barely a day goes by without some guru proclaiming that knowledge management is the key to success that will transform your organisation.

The truth, of course, is somewhat more prosaic. Knowledge management has been around for years. The largest and most successful companies have always practised it, and, in a large part, it accounts for why they have remained successful. What is true, however, is that the information revolution opens up new means by which knowledge can be acquired, shared and acted upon. It is these new opportunities that we want to discuss in this chapter.

■ **QUESTIONS TO CONSIDER** ■

4. Before going on to explore what we mean by knowledge and knowledge management, can you specify what techniques your organisation uses to acquire, share and act upon knowledge?

What is knowledge?

There are probably as many definitions of knowledge as there are knowledge management gurus. Our preferred model is the data–information–knowledge model. This model has the virtue of being straightforward, practical and useful; it is also the one which seems to be emerging as the standard definition. To this basic model, we would add one extra tier – insight – an addition that is best explained by way of an example. Consider a retailer's loyalty card scheme where information is collected from customers about their purchases in return for some form of loyalty card reward. In this type of scheme:

■ **Data** represent the base transactions, in this case that customer number 7859233 purchased goods to the value of $56 on Thursday 23 January 1998.

■ **Information** represents patterns in the data, perhaps that customers similar in demographic profile to customer 7859233 prefer to shop on Thursdays, or that they tend to purchase more than $50 worth of goods per shopping visit.

■ **Knowledge** represents the practical ability to exploit information – to take action as a result of the understanding gained. In this case, management might have realised that late-night shopping occurs on Thursdays and that customers such as 7859233 tend to be single people in full-time employment. The knowledge here is that by targeting single, full-time employed people with advertisements about late-night shopping, more will visit on a Thursday evening.

■ **Insight** is the ability to derive knowledge from similar types of information, that is, the ability to identify how to create knowledge from information.

Surprisingly, perhaps, most people find it extremely difficult to answer basic questions – like those posed below – on where their knowledge comes from. Yet for most organisations, the market views the knowledge held within an organisation as one of its most valuable assets.

---

5. What data are collected by your organisation?

6. How are those data converted into information?

7. How is knowledge extracted from that information?

8. Who is the most insightful in your organisation?

The basic model for creating knowledge

We believe that there is a simple model that underlies all knowledge management techniques. We call this model the Work–Learn–Share model.

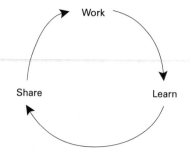

Figure 15.1   The Work–Learn–Share model

The basis for the Work–Learn–Share model is extremely simple. Everyone, during their time at work, is performing a series of tasks. From those tasks, learning can occur that will create knowledge – in other words, acquiring and interpreting information that can change the way in which the individual and the organisation act. An organisation that manages its knowledge effectively will ensure that knowledge is shared around the organisation, so that the next time someone performs a similar task, he or she can perform it more effectively.

Case Study

THE MICROSOFT SUPPORT FUNCTION

The purest embodiment of these principles that we have discovered is the Microsoft support function. Microsoft has to field many thousands of support calls each day. The way in which it handles such calls is as follows:

1. The support engineers ascertain from the customer the nature of the problem.

2. Using their own knowledge, the support personnel identify whether they can resolve the problem.

3. If this fails, they examine the knowledge base of all known user problems.

4. If the problem is contained there, they inform the customer.

5. If the problem is not contained within the knowledge base, they research and resolve the problem and (critically) write up the results of the research and resolution of the problem, placing it on the knowledge base.

In terms of the model that we are proposing, the support engineer works at the task of resolving customer problems, learns through examining the knowledge base or researching and resolving a particular customer problem and then shares the solution with the rest of the Microsoft team by putting the results of the research into a particular problem on to the knowledge base.

It is not difficult to imagine how quickly the number of customer problems that have not been previously resolved will tail off using this sort of model, thereby markedly increasing customer satisfaction by speeding the resolution of the problem and decreasing the costs of the support function by reducing the time required to resolve each inquiry.

There is no reason, of course, why this approach cannot be extended to many other functions within an organisation. It is not confined solely to sorting out customer problems. Indeed, the secret of good knowledge management is to understand how best such techniques can be incorporated throughout an organisation.

■ QUESTIONS TO CONSIDER ■

9. Most organisations have some form of customer support function. How does yours work? Does it implement any form of knowledge management?

10. What other functions within your organisation would benefit from implementing this sort of model?

11. Do they implement this model of knowledge management or some similar model?

The Work–Learn–Share model contains two key concepts, which we will examine in turn:

- the ability of an organisation to *learn* from the tasks that it performs;
- the ability of an organisation to *share* that learning.

How do you make learning happen?

We have argued, so far, that a considerable portion of many companies' value is tied up in the knowledge within the organisation. One of the key questions that every executive should be asking is, therefore, how do I create that knowledge?

Case Study

SHELL INTERNATIONAL PETROLEUM COMPANY

The principles enshrined in knowledge management and the creation of knowledge within organisations have been around for a long time.

Shell, arguably one of the world's most successful companies over a sustained period, has long incorporated leading edge principles both for the learning of knowledge and for its dissemination.

Take, for example, the career track of its more senior executives. Almost from the day on which these executives join the organisation, they embark on a career track that is designed to maximise their opportunities for learning. The average time in a job is between 2 and 3 years, just long enough to extract the knowledge required to perform the job effectively. The average stay in one country is probably only a little longer. The career path of Shell's senior executives is carefully defined to maximise the opportunities for their learning in a wide variety of different settings and hence give them enough knowledge to manage effectively one of the world's largest organisations.

Such opportunities, however, cannot be given to everyone. It is extremely expensive to move executives rapidly round the world. The costs of remuneration and benefits to compensate for the life-style can run into tens of thousands of pounds each year. Clearly, not everyone can be afforded this treatment.

Shell has not, however, forgotten the remainder of its management. Scenario planning, or planning as learning, was developed by Shell's group planning department during the 1970s and 80s as a way of educating Shell's management about the possible futures that they faced and how they might be addressed.

In this process, Shell's central planning function develops a series of coherent, plausible futures for the world and then disseminates them around the organisation. Managers are expected to read about these futures and then plan how their particular part of the business will react if these futures occur. This has become a mainstay in Shell's planning process. For example, all the more significant investment proposals are assessed in the light of the current planning scenarios. To be accepted, each investment proposal has to indicate how it would perform under each of the current planning scenarios and what steps would be taken to mitigate any adverse effects that might occur under each scenario.

The benefit of this approach is that much of the work is performed by only a small number of people in the central offices. It is, however, then shared widely across the organisation and used as a stimulus to promote further learning.

Shell is, of course, just one of the many companies that are attempting to embed learning (or knowledge-creating) principles throughout their organisation. Perhaps those which are trying the hardest are the companies that rely most on knowledge for the success of their business, obvious examples being software houses and management consultancies. This comment from Charles Paulk, the Chief Information Officer of Andersen Consulting, is typical of many:

> When one of our consultants shows up, the client should get the best of the firm and not just the best of the consultant.[1]

However, what is good for the knowledge industries will also undoubtedly be good for yours. When one of your staff performs a task, it would surely be better to incorporate all the learning of the organisation into performing that task more effectively rather than relying on the abilities of that individual.

Virtually every organisation contains some form of learning mechanisms. Many organisations have developed training courses to deal with specific tasks, or have embodied the knowledge of the organisation into manuals or procedures that have to be followed when a certain task has to be performed. The issue with these approaches is the static nature of the knowledge. It costs considerable time and effort to update a training course or to change a procedures manual, which means that such tasks are rarely performed. This in turn means that the currency – and therefore value – of that knowledge quickly degrades.

The priority must be to develop systems that encapsulate knowledge in a way that is more flexible and cheaper to maintain, as this is the only way of ensuring that learning can occur without a considerable amount of 'off-task' effort. One of the keys to this is to ensure that learning can take place in the virtual domain. Coopers & Lybrand, for example, have developed a product called TeleSim, which enables telephone companies to play out different scenarios within a computerised virtual world and see what the outcome of their actions would be. By playing in the virtual world, the action can be speeded up many times and the managers of these companies can rapidly increase their learning by trying out a number of different strategies.

Such virtual worlds can be taken a stage further. By incorporating the mental models that senior managers carry around with them about the economic and competitive environment in which they find themselves, these virtual simulators can be used to explore a wide range of different courses of action, thereby enabling learning on what would happen if different approaches were taken.

■ QUESTIONS TO CONSIDER ■

Methods of learning in your organisation

12. What are the main methods of learning that are employed in your organisation?

13. How have these been changed by the information revolution?

14. What steps is your organisation taking to incorporate new methods of learning within the organisation?

Sharing knowledge

Using tools like Coopers & Lybrand's TeleSim and other virtual tools, organisations have become increasingly good at capturing knowledge, although everyone would acknowledge that there is still a long way to go before we get anywhere near capturing all the useful knowledge that our organisations generate. However, even where we gather knowledge, almost all organisations are still chronically weak at sharing it. What use is it to gather knowledge and then do nothing with it? This lack of sharing probably represents the biggest waste of resources that takes place within the organisation, far outstripping any wasted monetary capital (which will ironically have been analysed to death within some form of capital approval committee).

■ QUESTIONS TO CONSIDER ■

Harnessing the learning within your organisation

Despite the fact that the virtual assets of many organisations far outstrip the physical, little attention is paid by many organisations to their management.

15. Who is responsible for managing the learning within your organisation?

16. What access do you have to learning within your organisation?

17. How do you contribute your learning to your organisation? Could it be improved?

One of the fundamental changes that the information revolution has brought about is a step-change in our ability to share our data, information and knowledge – via the virtual domain. We have already argued that those organisations which are the quickest to capture and capitalise their virtual assets are likely to far outstrip rivals who are unable to harness this asset. The same lesson applies to sharing knowledge. To make best use of their intellectual assets, organisations need to ensure that data, information and knowledge are taken out of the physical domain and moved into the virtual domain. While in the virtual domain, these assets can be divided, added together, viewed and manipulated, distributed and shared, all at little cost. As soon as these assets are translated into the physical domain, be this paper, microfilm or tape, they become hard to manage, hard to analyse and – most importantly – hard to share.

Keeping intellectual assets in the virtual domain is not a difficult idea to put into practice; indeed, many organisations are already moving their data, information and knowledge into the virtual domain. Retailers, for example, have embraced the use of EPOS systems. By collecting individual customer transactions in the virtual domain, as well as recording them on physical till rolls, they are able to compute stock levels and eliminate the need for regular stock counts. By providing electronic means of access, many organisations have eliminated the need to collect information in the physical domain at all, thereby reducing the costs of collection and the costs of making the information available for analysis and dissemination. Some companies have gone even further. Insurance companies, for example, are embracing the concept of scanning all physical communications such as letters as soon as they arrive and then moving them round the organisation using electronic workflow systems.

However, ensuring that intellectual assets are either kept or moved into the virtual domain is an important, but essentially preliminary, step to sharing them. Moreover, completing this stage does not mean that you have solved the problem. Simply converting data, information and knowledge into the virtual domain does not enable managers immediately to use it and thereby improve the organisation's performance. Indeed, many managers are already complaining of information overload – that they receive far more information than they can possibly react to, that using all this information is far too difficult. Instead of helping, making all this information available may be paralysing our decision-making processes.

So what can be done about it? There are essentially three strategies, being adopted by organisations today, for sharing knowledge, each of which is discussed below:

- the 'ownership' strategy;
- the 'push' strategy;
- the 'pull' strategy.

Each has their advantages and disadvantages. Indeed, most organisations are finding that some form of combination of these strategies is the best way to manage their knowledge assets.

The ownership strategy

This is the traditional method of sharing knowledge. In fact, it was the only method that organisations could adopt when their knowledge assets were retained in the physical domain. The strategy is very simple. Someone, normally an 'owner' of the information, decides what is important and makes it available, either at a central place such as a library or an accounts department, or duplicates it and sends it to those people whom they believe will benefit from its receipt. Middle management structures in the 1970s and 80s were created to perform this task, various departments jealously guarding the information in the belief that knowledge equalled power. Although such an approach is beginning to seem positively antedeluvian in this day of e-mail and electronic communication, many organisations have taken the same principles and applied them to electronic and other communications in the virtual domain. If you wish to adopt such a strategy, the principles underlying it are simple:

■ Identify what knowledge is important within your organisation.
■ Identify who will benefit from having that information.
■ Disseminate the knowledge to each person who will benefit.

The difficulty with this approach is that you will not necessarily know what information will be of value to which individuals. Why should an owner of information about an organisation's customers know what information to pass to other members of the organisation? Manufacturing directors may well be interested in what customers want them to manufacture, marketing directors in what image will cause customers to purchase, finance directors in what customers will be prepared to pay. Each director might benefit from information about a customer, but, at the same time, it is not easy for any one of them to understand all the others' requirements. Even more fundamentally, how can any individual know how the value of a piece of information can increase markedly when it is combined with information from elsewhere in the business, of which that individual was not even aware? When most information was collected and kept in a physical form (usually paper), this lack of awareness about information in other parts of the business was not a significant handicap as there was very little that could be done with that information anyway. However, now that such information is available electronically, and can be sent at virtually no cost to anyone in the organisation and then combined with other pieces of information to give insights into managerial decisions, this strategy of the 'owner' of the information deciding who will receive it becomes positively harmful.

■ QUESTIONS TO CONSIDER ■

The ownership strategy of information management

To illustrate the difficulty of implementing the 'ownership' strategy of information management consider, together with a colleague, the following questions:

18. What are the top five pieces of information or knowledge that your organisation possesses? Where are they kept? How are they disseminated?

19. What are the top five pieces of information or knowledge that your organisation should acquire? Who should be given them?

We have yet to come across any different groups within an organisation who have given remotely similar answers.

The problem with this approach is that the value of a piece of data, information or knowledge is not intrinsic: it depends on the use to which it is put and the ability of individuals to identify how it can be used. The only person who can really decide on that value is the person who is going to be using it, not the person who has collected it or made it available.

The 'pull' strategy

For this reason, many organisations are now looking to 'pull' strategies to share knowledge, which work in the opposite way to the traditional 'ownership' strategy. Those individuals in an organisation who want access to a piece of information 'pull' it to themselves. In the days of the physical storage of information, the only way in which this could be performed was for individuals to go to a repository of physical information – usually a library of some sort – and search through it until they found what they were looking for. Such a process used to take an enormous amount of time, however well organised the library might be and however good the skill of the librarians who administered it.

The introduction of information technology is rapidly changing the ways in which people can access such information. Five years ago, technology became widely available to enable people to search using keywords. True, the information still had to be indexed, but the searching of the indexes could be performed very quickly. It is still true today that one of the first applications that is usually converted to an electronic format is the company telephone directory. Why? The explanation is simple. In the first place, it is clear that everyone within an organisation requires it. Second, the cost of updating it – because of the frequent number of changes – is high. Third, and perhaps most importantly, the directory comes ready indexed, the keywords in this case being each person's name.

The telephone directory, and similar, ready-indexed information resources, had relatively crude search facilities (you looked up names in alphabetical order), but over the past 5 years and partly due to the vastly increased use of the Internet, many different tools have been developed that will help the people in your organisation to 'pull' information to them rather than waiting for it to be 'pushed' at them. One of the more exciting tools is the ability of packages to search through whole documents looking for the word or words that you type in. Developed primarily as a method of extracting information from the Internet, search engines are now available that will enable you to store all information on a single or multiple machines in one format, or in several, and then enable you to type in a keyword or multiple keywords and extract and view all the documents that contain such words.

The power of this technology is hard to comprehend. For the first time, machines are available that enable you to ensure that you have shared all the information available within an organisation on a particular topic, whether that topic is a customer, a particular issue or even a general view about the state of the world. For the first time, individuals are able to build upon what has gone before rather than having to reinvent, sometimes from the very beginning, the response to a particular issue.

Case Study

THE USE OF EXCALIBUR IN THE 1997 UK GENERAL ELECTION

One of the most impressive demonstrations of such technology was the use of Excalibur in the 1997 UK General Election by the Labour Party. Arguably, the weapon of 'rapid response', the technique of very fast, highly factual rebuttals of comments made by the opposing party had won Bill Clinton the US presidential election in 1992.

The Labour Party decided to develop such a weapon for use in the UK 1997 General Election. To do this, they selected a computer system called Excalibur that could store all references made by a Conservative politician (or indeed politician of any persuasion) about a particular topic. When the topic was being argued over during the election, the Labour spin doctors could simply type in a few keywords and all the comments that had ever been made on the subject could be pulled out and a suitable rebuttal developed.

The use of such a weapon gave the Labour Party an enormous advantage. Topics raised at the morning press conference by the Conservatives could be instantly analysed and inconsistencies exposed before the conference ended. On one memorable occasion, until the use of mobile telephones in the chamber of the House of Commons was banned, the Labour spin doctors were even able to supply a devastating question to a backbencher before a minister had even finished making his speech.

The power of such tools is clearly awesome. Imagine being questioned on a topic by someone who had instant access to all the other pronouncements that you had made on the subject. The combination of using computers for what they do best, searching through enormous volumes of data, and humans for what they do best, spotting the patterns and making the connections in the results, gives the questioner an almost overwhelming advantage. The use of such a tool was undoubtedly a significant contributor to Labour's success in the 1997 election and is set to become a standard tool in subsequent elections.

Organisations that want to capitalise on their information assets must start developing their own databases of information and indexing them. Storage space is cheap: disks containing gigabytes of information can be obtained for a few hundred dollars apiece. The computing technology is cheap: suitable hardware on which to run such a system can be obtained for a few thousand dollars. The only significant cost is feeding the system with information. We recommend that any organisation should:

- identify the most common formats for the information you want to index and select a software tool that can index them (if, for example, the company has a standard of using Microsoft Word for all written documents, ensure that a tool is selected that can index Word documents);
- select the hardware on which the system will run;

- design procedures to ensure that the information is captured and updated regularly (there is nothing worse than a system that does not contain the latest information); this is undoubtedly the hardest part of the process – failsafe methods must be devised to ensure that all the relevant information (which could also include external information) is captured, preferably automatically;
- implement the system and make it available to users within the organisation;
- monitor its use to ensure that the right people are getting access and that all the pertinent information is being collected.

The 'push' strategy

It is probably apparent that we have a strong preference for the adoption of a 'pull' strategy of information management, but we also recognise that the weakness of such an approach is that it relies on active information management. Information has to be managed; users have actively to seek out the information. However, some organisations are taking the view that this is too onerous a change to make to the way in which they share knowledge, and that a less active approach would be more appropriate. They appreciate that they still need to collect information and make it available in the virtual domain and that there is still a need for users to select what information they wish to access. However, they also believe that the organisation has to take a role in ensuring that knowledge is shared effectively so that managers do not suffer from information overload.

Perhaps the simplest approach is to arrange information around 'communities of common interest'. Users select where they wish to place information and which 'communities' they wish to access. This is the model that was adopted by the early Internet users who banded into different 'communities of interest' on the Usenet. People wishing to find out about a topic could scan the list of available groups and select those that they wished to subscribe to. Any postings to that particular group were then sent to all those who had a subscription to the group. Much the same approach can be taken within an organisation. Groups can be set up that cover a multitude of different subjects that are of interest to different groups within the organisation. The difficulty inevitably lies in identifying which groups should be set up. If they are set up along functional lines, there is a risk that cross-functional opportunities will be lost: if they are set up around topics, there is a risk that they will become too diffuse and individuals will have to scan too many groups to find out all the information about the subjects that interest them.

Newer technologies are being developed that may help to overcome some of these problems. The latest 'push' technology, for example, will enable you to specify a number of keywords. When a document is added that contains such a keyword, for example the name of a competitor, it is automatically sent to you by e-mail. Such technology can even be included with a screensaver, so that when you are not using your personal computer, the headlines of the relevant documents can be scrolled on your computer screen.

Such technologies remove the need for the user actively to search for particular items. They do, however, still require active management of the source documents. The implementation of such a system is similar to the implementation of a 'pull' technology:

- Identify the most common formats for the information you want to analyse and select a software tool that can analyse them.
- Select the hardware on which the system will run.
- Design procedures to ensure that the information is captured and updated regularly and preferably automatically.
- Implement the system and make it available to users within the organisation.
- Regularly review the system to ensure that it is getting used in the most effective way.

Summary

❑ The knowledge contained within organisations is worth a substantial amount of money. The value is not captured by traditional accounting techniques, but it is real and is recognised by the stock market.

❑ Knowledge is defined as the ability to act on information and data.

❑ Most knowledge management techniques are underpinned by a variant of the 'Work–Learn–Share' model. As individuals perform their tasks, they learn how to perform more effectively. This knowledge becomes truly useful when it is shared across the organisation.

❑ When such information is contained within the physical domain, it is hard to access and manipulate, and this acts as a major barrier to its use. If the information is transferred to the virtual domain, it can be shared quickly, cheaply and effectively.

❏ To prevent information overload, it is necessary to introduce an information management strategy. The traditional information management strategy in which the 'owner' of the information decided who should obtain access to it is ill suited to the virtual management of information. Two alternative strategies – the 'pull' and 'push' information management strategies – were described. Both have a part to play in the management of data, information, knowledge and insight within an organisation.

Notes

1. Charles Paulk, 'Mapping Corporate Brain Power', *Fortune Magazine*, 30 October, 1995.

16 Getting the Foundations Right

The information technology revolution is, literally, revolutionising the way in which we do business. Hardware costs continue to halve every 18 months; software applications are continuing to make our existing hardware obsolete (as we write this book, continuous speech recognition is rapidly appearing as the next hardware-killing application); accommodating new users and responding to new competitors demand new technological changes; new methods of collecting information continue to generate vast quantities of data that can be ignored only at your peril.

How, you may ask yourself, are we supposed to organise our technology? Indeed, what do we mean by 'technology' in this kind of environment? How, in a state of constant flux, can we possibly produce anything stable enough to enable us to continue – let alone flourish – in our chosen business?

What is needed – indeed, what the less technically literate users within all organisations are demanding – is the ultimately flexible system that enables anyone to do anything once they have had an idea. But, clearly, even the ultimately flexible system is going to have some characteristics that have to be chosen in advance. Critical to each organisation – critical even to its survival – will be the ability to make the right choices where choices are unavoidable.

This chapter describes what we believe to be the best way of developing a strategy within this environment of rapid technological change. It distinguishes the decisions that have to be made and those which can be ignored, and it lays down some common groundrules to be followed if your company is to embrace the virtual age successfully.

---

1. What are the major difficulties that you face in your organisation when developing a strategy for the introduction, organisation and exploitation of your information?

Developing the strategy

Most organisations' processes for the development of their information strategies approach the issue from the wrong end. Enormous effort is spent on deciding and then procuring the hardware that an organisation requires; some effort is spent on deciding what applications should be run on this hardware; almost no effort is spent on deciding what information will be held. If your organisation has an information strategy, and a surprising number do not, take a look at it. How many pages are devoted to the hardware, how many pages to the software and the applications, and how many pages to the sources of information that your organisation might use? We have yet to come across a strategy that devotes more than a tiny fraction of its total length to a serious consideration of the latter, even though the survival of all organisations – not just virtual ones – depends on it. It should be unnecessary, but sadly it is not, to have to remind organisations that the most important item in an information strategy is the information, and that the most important aspect of an information technology department is its ability to deliver the information rather than the technology.

As a final test, ask yourselves what your information policies are. Members of most organisations will happily say 'We only buy IBM (hardware)' or 'We're a Microsoft (software) organisation'. When you ask individuals what policies the organisation implements concerning the collection and dissemination of information, we confidently predict that the response will be a series of blank and uncomprehending looks.

---

2. Does your organisation have an information strategy? If yes, what proportion of the strategy is about information? What proportion should be about information?

3. Does your organisation have information policies? Should it?

The lifeblood of any organisation is the information that it uses. The development of an information strategy must, therefore, start with the information. Other issues – the software you need to process this information, the hardware you need to handle it and the organisation you need to support all of this – should all flow from your understanding of the information that you want to capture and exploit.

We will look below at each of these aspects in turn, starting with the information itself.

Information

The lifeblood of any organisation, especially the virtual organisation, its most valuable asset, is the information it collects and uses. Its unique competitive advantage arises from the use of information, especially private information (that is, information which is not available elsewhere) and its exploitation in the market. This might be information about customers, it might be information about chemical molecules, it might be information about pricing. This information may have no physical value. It can be stored on a floppy disk worth no more than a few cents. However, it is vital for an organisation to survive. It is what gives organisations their competitive advantage – something that will sustain them and cannot be easily replicated. Organisations that start to think about information in this way will soon recognise the mantra:

- What information have we got?
- How do we gain competitive advantage from it?
- How can we protect and augment it?

If information is so valuable, what do you currently do about it? The first task in an information strategy is to understand your current position by conducting an information audit. What information does your organisation possess, and how much does it waste each day? Pieces of information tend to be like grains of sand that pass through the organisation's hands each day: vast handfuls are picked up, but, at the end of the day, only a few grains remain to be collected.

Try this simple survey. Take one aspect of your organisation – its customers, for example – and ask all your departments to record the information they receive on a daily basis about their customers.

Certainly, the sales and marketing departments should have records of your customer transactions, responsiveness to promotional offers and so on, but so too should the finance department, and even the maintenance department. Take a note, too, of the extent to which the information recorded has been consolidated. Does the department have the information by individual customer? Does it know every individual purchase that has been made? Does it know the individual time each repair was made? Finally, ask each department how much of that information is formally recorded on a computer rather than just held in someone's head or scribbled down on bits of paper.

No one can tell you exactly what information your organisation needs to survive. What we can be sure of is that the more information you collect, the more likely you are to survive. Every organisation collects vast quantities of information every day, and every day it destroys these same vast quantities of information, either because the information is not recorded in a form that can be manipulated, or because the data are aggregated so that the fine detail is lost. Your information audit should record such losses and the means by which they occur.

Why do we recommend starting this way? Surely, you will be saying, I develop a strategy by deciding where I want to be and then investigate where I am. We have, however, found that organisations are still blinkered to the possibilities of the virtual world and that, by asking these questions, we can start to open management's eyes to the possibilities of working a new way.

Using this survey as background information, then – and only then – should you begin to ask what you should do with it. Again, you need to stretch the mind of your organisation to think in new ways. We are not simply trying to make the old ways more efficient: what we are looking for are new *virtual* ways of performing tasks. The question that we like to ask at this stage is 'What pieces of information do you require to make your job easier?' A salesperson might reply 'To know which customers are going to buy our products so that I can concentrate on our most likely prospects'; a maintenance engineer might reply 'To know when our products are going to go wrong, so that I can fix them before the customer complains'; a marketing person might reply 'To know the maximum price I can charge our goods at, in order to maximise profits'. To a traditional organisation, requests like these will seem impossible; in a virtual organisation, they will be commonplace and manageable. Take the first example –

how can you identify which customers are most likely to buy? One place to look at is which customers bought from you in the past, what products they purchased and the factors that might have influenced them? Have they been asked why they bought? Do you have any information on their defining characteristics? Can you link these characteristics to other potential customers? Can you provide this information back to the salesperson? Do you already have the information within the organisation? How up to date is the information? These questions underpin the development of an information strategy. More formally, they can be expressed as:

- What information do you require?
- What process will be used to collect the information?
- What process will be used to maintain the information?
- What links need to be provided to other information?
- Where (to whom) must the information be supplied?

It is important to stress that these are all questions about information. We have not talked about software, or hardware or the organisation required to support the information technology. Until you have a clear idea of the information you possess – or potentially possess – and the information that you desire, questions about hardware and software are more or less irrelevant.

■ QUESTIONS TO CONSIDER ■

---

4. How much information is used by your organisation each day? How much is lost and wasted?

5. What are the key items of information that your organisation requires? Why?

6. How many of your key information requirements could be met if you better used the information already within your organisation?

Applications

Starting in this way reveals an interesting fact. Most of the software applications used by an organisation consist of simply taking information in one form, performing some very simple transformations to that information (rarely more than aggregation and the usual arithmetical operations of addition, subtraction, multiplication and division) and then presenting the processed information in another form. Thus, at the highest level of abstraction at least, all applications are the same. What varies between applications is that different information is processed each time and that the information is processed in different ways. The underlying architecture of software applications that an organisation needs to best perform these tasks is obvious. There must be some form of flexible, central 'data store' containing all the information and data that are going to be manipulated, fed by a variety of information-gathering processes. Attached to this data store needs to be a series of manipulating engines that process and present information in different ways.

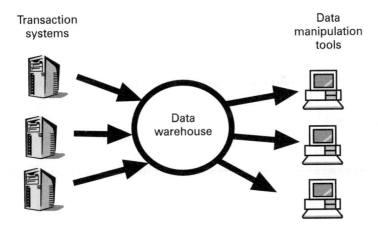

Figure 16.1   A typical data warehouse structure

   The information technology industry is currently promoting such a model in the form of data warehousing. Data warehousing applications essentially take information from transaction-processing systems (that is, the systems used to collect the information) and hold it in a data store, together with a description of what it is (called meta-data). Other applications are then hung on the back of the data warehouse to enable the manipulation of the data to take place.

Some refinements may be necessary to this basic model. There may be some types of information that will never need to be manipulated together (we might assume, for example, that details of where a particular doctor did his or her medical training will never need to be combined with the pharmaceutical properties of a particular mole-cule). In these cases, it may be more appropriate for separate data warehouses to be developed. There may also be issues about the size of the data warehouse and the speed with which analysis will need to be performed. This may mean that specific application architectures have to be developed. However, in all the cases that we have come across, the basic principles remain the same: the most appropriate architecture is a flexible data store (or data stores) together with an application toolset that enables users to access, manipulate and present the data quickly and easily.

Having agreed and developed a structure for the data store, the next question is to agree precisely which applications will be needed. Depending on the exact nature of the tasks that your organisation performs, these could be anything. It is not possible to give specific advice, but there are four general principles that generally apply:

- Every application must deliver benefits to the users.
- Users must feel comfortable with the way in which the system manipulates and presents information.
- You need to plan for the support of a system before purchasing or developing it.
- You need to be able to develop and implement any system quickly.

First and foremost, the applications that are developed and acquired must deliver benefits to the user. This is easier said than done. Information technologists still speak a different language from the rest of the organisation, and this lack of a common language prevents organisations from explaining what they want to the information technologist, just as it prevents the information technologist from explaining what it is that the organisation will receive. This misunderstanding is probably the most common cause of failure in IT projects.

But it doesn't have to be like this. Methods are now – painfully – beginning to emerge that provide a common language for both those who will use the technology and those who are charged with implementing and supporting it (see one example, the 'ability to' language, which is described in the box below).

THE 'ABILITY TO' LANGUAGE FOR
COMMUNICATING WITH YOUR IT DEPARTMENT

Current IT development methodologies usually consist of asking what the users want in immense detail and then translating those requests into large documents with titles such as 'Business Requirements Documents', 'Functional Requirements Documents' and 'Technical Design Documents'. These documents are then given to the future users of a system, who are asked to agree that they reflect their requirements.

This is plainly a nonsense. No user can realistically be expected to specify exactly what he or she wants or to understand, or even have time to read, the technical translation of those requests within large and impenetrable documents. Similarly, no IT department can realistically be expected to deliver everything a user wants in exactly the way in which a user wants it, given the technical constraints imposed by the hardware, software and conventions used within the organisation.

What is needed is a language that divides responsibilities more appropriately. The users of the system must take full responsibility for the functionality of the system that they require. The IT department must take full responsibility for the way in which it is delivered. This is where the 'ability to' language comes in. Rather than asking users to specify every function within a system, the users specify what they want to do with the system, that is, that they must have the ability to... Some examples of 'ability to's are shown below.

A user might specify that he or she must have the ability to:

- identify his or her top 100 customers by value;
- identify any customer whose spending exceeds a preset limit;
- identify any customers who have not paid their debts;

as well as the 'ability to':

- have guaranteed access to the system between 8.00 am and 8.00 pm;
- print out any report that is shown on the screen;
- download any report into Excel or other spreadsheet package.

Many of the 'ability to's' will be common across applications. By creating a library of these 'ability to's', templates can be created that can rapidly speed up the process of identifying what is required from the system.

The IT department then responds with their 'This feature will enable you to...'. Thus, following on from the 'ability to's shown above, the IT department might respond with:

- a report showing customers listed by value in descending order, which *will enable you to* identify your top 100 customers by value;
- a report showing every customer with their current expenditure and their preset spending limit, any customers who exceed their limit being highlighted in red, which *will enable you to* identify any customers who exceed their preset spending limit;
- a report showing the debts of every customer divided into 30, 60, 90 and greater than 90 days, which *will enable you to* identify any customers who have not paid their debts;
- a system that is maintained on two machines with automatic mirroring, which will ensure that there will never be more than 30 seconds during the day when you cannot have access to the system; this *will enable you to* have guaranteed access to the system between 8.00 am and 8.00 pm and so on.

The language might not be very elegant, but it does ensure that the right people perform the right tasks. Users concentrate on specifying what they want to do with the system, something they undoubtedly know best, and information technologists concentrate on what they know best – how best to use technology to deliver different functionality. Furthermore, a tight link is maintained between the user requests and the functions that are delivered.

If your information technologists are very able, they will provide not only a written description illustrating how they will meet each request, but also a prototype, showing what the end system will look like and thereby further reducing any potential confusion.

Perhaps this all seems very obvious, but we have seen many situations in which not only were the technical documents describing the system impenetrable, but also, in some cases, users were not even consulted about the design of the system.

▨ QUESTIONS TO CONSIDER ▨

7. What method do you use for specifying the requirements for your applications?

8. Does it divide the tasks appropriately between the various skill groups within your organisation?

9. Would the use of the 'ability to' language help to clarify requirements and how they were delivered?

The second principle worth stressing is that those using the applications must be comfortable with the way in which those applications manipulate and present information. Ease of use is probably the single most important factor that determines the effective use – and thus the success or failure – of a piece of software. If an application is easy to use, it will promote experimentation; users will develop new ways of manipulating the information in the virtual world and productivity will increase. Conversely, where users have problems performing even relatively simple tasks in an particular application, the incentive to experiment is slight and users will avoid using the software wherever possible.

The debate here – and it is one that is currently unresolved – is about how you should select applications that are easy to use. One method that goes part way to addressing the issue is ensuring that all your applications have a common front end, in other words that they present the same set of commands in the same way in every application. The most common standard for end-user applications is currently Microsoft's Windows. Every application that follows the conventions has a menu-bar at the top of the screen that starts with a 'File' menu; within that menu, options are found for saving and loading data, and for how to print information. Simply having those commands which are common between applications in the same place each time has radically reduced the time its takes users to learn a new application.

However, there is a new standard in the process of emerging, based around the Internet and the World Wide Web. This standard adopts a new and different command structure based on the conventions used within the Internet for access to commands and the display of information. Which convention, Microsoft Windows or the Internet-related equivalent, will emerge as the winner? We do not know. If the Internet increases in popularity so that every household uses it not only from their computer, but also from their TV, perhaps the Internet standard will then emerge as the most common. If the already installed base of applications remains dominant, people will perhaps prefer to remain with the current standards.

At the end of the day, it probably does not matter which of these two standards wins. Provided that your applications have a common front end, together with a common way of presenting information to the user, those working in your organisation will not find it difficult to adapt to whichever of these standard emerges as victorious. Going to the opposite extreme, there can be no doubt that having different methods for accessing the different applications is a sure way of delaying the introduction of new methods of working into an organisation. There is no excuse for presenting different interfaces to the user, especially given the proliferation of programming tools designed to enable standards such as Windows to be adopted, for bespoke or packaged applications, developed either in-house or by a third party.

The third principle of technology management is that you must ensure that any systems which are developed can be maintained. By this we do not just mean that they can be repaired when they go wrong, but that they can be altered as and when circumstances change. Circumstances will inevitably change in the future: users will require new features to be developed; new sources of data will become available. The systems that you develop must be able to adapt to meet these changes in requirement. In the past, this meant that you hired enough IT people with the right skills to make changes. Today, it is more likely that you will be relying on the suppliers of packaged software to maintain the products. Judging which the most successful suppliers will be is not easy, but whenever packages are selected, especially those that are mission-critical, attention must be given to ensure that enough support is provided.

Fourth, we think it is essential that applications do not take too long to develop. Gone are the days when one had the luxury of years to develop applications. If we wait for mammoth applications to be developed and implemented in today's business environment, we will find that the world has moved on, that the business model on which the application was predicated has changed, and that different applications will be needed. As a rule of thumb, if an application takes more than 6 months to develop and deploy, it will probably not succeed. Of course, you will always be able to find exceptions to this rule, but they will probably be fewer than you imagine.

▓ QUESTIONS TO CONSIDER ▓

---

10. What principles do you use for application selection? Do they meet the criteria that are described above?

Hardware

Many new applications are driven by the remorseless increase in computer power (something we discussed in the first section of this book). The choice of hardware required to support these applications is not crucial because its cost is small compared to the total lifetime costs of a particular application.

This is nowhere better illustrated than in the debates that are currently raging about the relative merits of personal computers and the new (lower-powered) network computers that will work by downloading applications from a network where they are stored. This might ostensibly appear to be a debate about the hardware that people will use to run applications, but this is not the case. The difference in hardware costs will be no more than a few hundred dollars at most. This is a debate about the lifetime costs of applications. The hardware of the PC is not the question; what is important is the ease with which applications can be changed and those changes communicated to a large community of users. The argument runs that if the applications are maintained in a single place and the users download them on to network computers each time they want to use them, it will be much easier and cheaper to upgrade them (because only a single copy will need to be changed). The real question here is about how the IT department plans to control applications, and the relative costs and merits of the different options.

This does not mean that there are no decisions to be made about hardware. For a start, the costs and the power of the hardware should be calculated from when they will be deployed rather than when the development of the IT strategy takes place. It is possible, and indeed it should be assumed as a base case, that the power/cost ratio of hardware will continue to improve. What may not be possible today may well be possible tomorrow. If you do not take account of this, it is almost certain that one of your competitors will.

It also means that your user community will almost certainly campaign for upgrades to their hardware to ensure that they can run the latest applications, and the costs of this must be built into the budget of any system. Our experience suggests that few users will tolerate having a machine that is less than four times as powerful as the newest machine, and therefore, based on the rate of increase in performance, machines will require changing every 3 years or so.

There is also a debate about whether all machines within an organisation should be changed at once or whether they should be changed on a rolling basis. The advantage of changing them all at once is that you can guarantee that all applications will be able to run on all machines without modification. The advantage of a rolling programme of replacement, for example one-third each year, is that your organisation will always have some of the latest machines, which will be required for running some of the newest and most powerful applications. We come down firmly on the side of rolling replacement policies. The truth of the matter is that many users will do little more than use their machines for word processing, for which a powerful machine is not required, and a rolling replacement scheme will give you some flexibility to distribute computing power to where it is most needed.

■ QUESTIONS TO CONSIDER ■

11. What hardware strategy does your organisation have?

Organisation

An area that must not be ignored within your technology strategy is how you will organise yourselves and your IT department (or its equivalent) to meet the demands of the virtual world.

There are two basic models to choose from: you can either outsource your IT department to a third-party supplier or you can carry out its functions in-house. Since the late 1980s, the pendulum has been swinging towards outsourcing, as companies have seized the opportunity to rid themselves of a part of their business that they regarded as non-core and inevitably troublesome. However, it seems possible that this pendulum will before long start to swing back again: indeed, many companies have already started to appreciate that the gains they foresaw (lower costs, better service) are not so easy to realise in practice. For this reason, it is worth examining each option in turn.

There is no doubt that the provision of the nuts and bolts of the hardware, the cleaning and maintenance of data and quality information, and the design and development of applications are all complex tasks that require specialist input. The case for the outsourcing of these tasks is, therefore, on the face of it obvious. Why go to the expense of maintaining expertise in these tasks when we can outsource them to a third party who has more specialist skills in these areas and who will therefore be able to improve the level of service we receive but deliver it at a lower cost? But – and it is a big 'but' – does this mean that you will be throwing the baby out with the bath water? Is it really true to say, in today's world and especially within the virtual organisation, that the ability to handle information in the virtual domain is not a core competence that must be maintained by the organisation. All processes run with the aid of information, and therefore the ability to handle information must surely be of critical importance to the organisation.

It is difficult to understand how, when these responsibilities are passed to a third party, you can maintain a long-term competitive edge. How will you build into your organisation the ability to spot new opportunities, the ability to move processes from the physical to the virtual world, if this capability is being maintained by a third-party supplier? The reality, however, is even worse. Many organisations do not even maintain an 'intelligent customer' capability, that is, the ability to challenge the supplier of the outsourced services about the present, let alone the future.

Of course, maintaining an in-house capability does not guarantee success. How do you organise your IT function so that it best serves the needs of your organisation? We have seen all sorts of model being tried, from the centralised controlling IT function to the small units devolved directly in line with the business functions. None of these seems to have been particularly successful. Times are, however, changing. There has been a growth in the number of intelligent users, those knowledgeable about both their business function and the technology needed to support it. These people must clearly be supported by the organisation. On the other hand, there has also been a recognition that there are some things that a centralised information department does best. Some standards are required, especially about the data which are acquired, created and used around the organisation. There is no doubt that a centralised information department is required to introduce and monitor such standards.

The division of labour that is emerging is that the information department deals with those aspects which cross departmental boundaries, ensuring that people have hardware and applications that can talk with each other, whereas applications within departments should be left, wherever possible, to the members of that department (which may or may not include specific information resources). The model is still not perfect, but the basic principles of dividing up responsibilities are sound. Give the information professionals responsibility for what they do best, and devolve as much responsibility to the users as they can handle. This way, new ideas can emerge and be incorporated within an overall organisational framework.

▓ QUESTIONS TO CONSIDER ▓

---

12. What organisational policies does your organisation adopt for information-related matters? On what principles are they based?

13. If your information technology functions are outsourced, how are your competencies in this area being maintained?

Organisations are becoming more and more reliant on the information that they collect and manage. The increase in power of computing technology means that this information is increasingly being maintained in a virtual form within networks of computers. Developing a strategy for your organisation to adapt to this method for the storage and retrieval of information is vital. The single most important point to remember when designing such a strategy is that it should be driven from the information requirements of the organisation rather than by the technological constraints of the hardware and software that you already possess or are considering purchasing in the future.

Summary

❏ Despite its critical importance, most organisations spend insufficient time and effort in considering the information aspects of an information strategy.

❏ When developing an information strategy, you must first identify the information that you wish to hold and manipulate. Only then should you consider the hardware and software required.

❏ Most organisations require a technological architecture to support their information handling that is based around an information store (or stores), together with a series of manipulation tools.

❑ The most important issue to consider when choosing or developing applications and tools to manipulate the information is to ensure that the user's requirements are accurately translated into a technological solution.

❑ This translation will only happen if your technical staff and users can share a common language for the description of applications. The 'ability to' language is one such language.

❑ When selecting hardware, you should consider a process of rolling replacement to ensure that your organisation has the flexibility required to meet the demands of its users.

❑ Although outsourcing your IT organisation has a number of benefits, organisations must ensure that they maintain a sufficient in-house capability in such a key competence.

17 Selling Your Virtual Assets

Valuing the virtual

None of the ideas or tools discussed in this book makes sense if we cannot convert them into profits: the virtual only becomes valuable in practice – rather than in theory – when we can translate its potential into hard cash. It therefore seems appropriate, in this last chapter on the toolkit for the virtual business manager, to address this issue explicitly.

In 1996 a survey by The Technology Broker, a UK company based in Cambridge, reported that only 24 per cent of the country's leading companies had assigned any value in their annual reports to their intangible assets; where intangible assets were included, they mostly took the form of goodwill.[1] However, in the same year, an OECD report, *Measuring What People Know*, argued that the long-term prosperity of many countries may depend on innovations in the way in which knowledge is measured. If most of a company's wealth lies in its intellectual rather than its physical assets, and if these assets continue to be ignored from a financial perspective, how will this company be able to raise capital? Why should anyone invest in it? What is needed, according to the OECD, are new accounting systems that recognise the importance of this type of asset.

It is, however, not just the means of valuing intellectual assets that are the concern here. Any valuation is meaningless – indeed, any intellectual asset is worthless – if the value is unsustainable. We may develop leading edge software that appeals to a mass-market, but if it can be quickly replicated and sold by others, its value to us is limited, as a recent article by John Perry Barlow in *Wired* concluded:

If our property can be infinitely reproduced and instantaneously distributed over the planet without cost, without our knowledge, without its even leaving our possession, how can we protect it? How are we going to get paid for the work we do with our minds? And, if we can't get paid, what will assure the continued creation and distribution of such work? Since we don't have a solution to what is a profoundly new kind of challenge, and are apparently unable to delay the galloping digitization of every thing not obstinately physical, we are sailing into the future on a sinking ship.[2]

In fact, all the qualities that we value in the virtual business – its flexibility, for example – make intangible assets especially difficult to value. Barlow cites three particular issues: information is an activity – we experience it rather than possess it; it is like a life-form in that it adapts to different circumstances; and, finally, it is a 'relationship' – information does not exist in isolation but is linked to meaning (the price/earnings ratio of a company tells us nothing unless we know what it means). What all of these points add up to is that information is an inherently unstable matter (certainly compared with tangible assets). It changes as its environment changes; its relevance to us is dependent on a host of interrelated variables. Information on a holding company that is planning to dispose of a subsidiary may be almost priceless to a company planning to acquire a foothold in that market but is worthless to another which has no such ambitions. The value of information is, like beauty, very much in the eye of the beholder.

In attempting to value information, we are faced with a conflict. On the one hand, the whole notion of valuation is based on the assumption that the value ascribed to any asset will be common to the parties involved and that it will remain static for at least a period of time. Thus, if we sell our house, both we and the purchasers have a reasonably common view of the value of the house. That price may be the result of negotiation, but it still represents a compromise that we both (perhaps for different reasons) find acceptable. In other words, the common value allows us to trade a commodity, in this example a house; if we did not have that common value, we could not engage in trade.

On the other hand, however, we have the nature of information itself, indeed the nature of all the intangible assets of the virtual company. These are flexible, variable and not necessarily sustainable: how can we expect to trade intellectual capital (and this is, ultimately, what is at stake here) if it is in what is effectively a continual state of flux? It is the equivalent of trying to sell a three-bedroom house for an agreed price only to discover that the house has suddenly acquired or lost a bedroom.

And let us throw into this already murky equation a third factor – the future. Much of what we think of as intellectual capital reflects an organisation's current products, markets and processes. As such, this is entirely in line with standard accounting practices that look at present, rather than past or future, value (such, for example, is the basis of depreciation and amortisation). This way of thinking is, however, more appropriate to the diminishing returns environment of the physical world than to the increasing returns of the virtual. We expect physical assets to decline in value (hence the need to write them down over a period of years), whereas information may become much more valuable, either because we have spent years investing in our customer database or because – quite suddenly – we hold a missing link in a particular chain of information (a maternity hospital that suddenly realises that the names of new parents are of value to the manufacturers of baby products).

In *Intellectual Capital: The New Wealth of Organizations*, US business writer Thomas Stewart identified two priorities if we are to come up with meaningful and acceptable ways of valuing intellectual assets. First, we need to find rigorous ways to track this kind of capital, which means that measurements of its worth can be comparable to conventional financial statistics. Second, these measurements also have to be useable outside an organisation in order to facilitate inter-company comparisons. The problem is a complicated one. A project to develop accounting standards for intangible assets has been the International Accounting Standards Committee's longest-running initiative (it took more than 10 years to produce the draft standards issued in November 1997). The pressure for the IASC to resolve the issue is mounting daily as, in many of the mega-mergers currently taking place, the principal assets involved are intangible. Yet, at the same time, intangible assets pose a challenge to our basic accounting model: what use, for example, are historical costs in an environment when the link between costs and value is much less certain?

So far, the IASC's proposals are hardly radical. They suggest that intangible assets should be included on a balance sheet only when they can be measured reliably. This may work for such assets that are purchased (typically goodwill), but would potentially leave, for example, software manufactures unable to include a captive market base, or drinks-makers unable to include the value of their brands. Possible means of measuring intellectual capital are numerous, the most commonly accepted perhaps being a company's market to book ratio:

Price per share × total number of shares / Equity portion of a company's balance sheet

Where the market value of a company is higher than its book value, the argument goes, the difference lies in the company's (unmeasured) intellectual assets. Precisely the key flaw in this and other methods is that they focus on this gap between expected and actual performance, and attribute this to intellectual capital; in other words, they have made the intangible the invisible. Intellectual capital is, therefore, all those parts of a business which we cannot see, touch or, by extension, measure directly. The only way to measure them is to quantify their impact on the tangible world, in the much the same way that we were taught at school to measure the mass of irregular objects by seeing how much water they displaced in a tank. Once again, this approach works well if all we want to do is to understand the here and now, but it will not answer any of our questions about future worth. What people do not seem to have fully appreciated is that they are not trying to measure the mass of an irregular object so much as that of a living organism that may grow or decay over time. And future worth is especially problematic when we think about intellectual capital because it is difficult to predict and is dependent on a whole host of known and unknown variables.

It all makes, you would think, for an insoluble problem, a problem we should continue to leave well alone – pretty much as we have for the last decade. But the cost (in terms of lost opportunities) of not finding a resolution is already high and is rapidly increasing. We looked, in the first part of this book, at how the rules of the business game are being changed by the information and the emergence of the virtual company. We looked, for example, at how the convergence between different industries means that information on customers will become one of, if not the, most important assets of the future. If you cannot rely on your products or market positioning being unique, you can have a unique relationship with your customers. But if this is the case, if customer information proves to be more valuable than buildings, patents or inventory, if it proves – as we think it will – to be even more valuable than brands, how are any of us (individual investors as well as corporations) going to make any money in the future? If a company cannot utilise an intangible asset such as this in order to raise capital for further investment (probably in that same intangible asset), how is any company going to evolve and grow? If we continue to account only for the physical world, this will be the only world in which we can expand. If we can find a means of valuing the virtual world, and then – crucially – making commercial use of that value, we can use the intellectual capital: we have to generate yet more intellectual capital. We can join the virtuous circle of – as we termed it – the them-that-have-gets. In other words, we can build not just the virtual business but the virtual economy.

We need to do this, however, by taking the unique qualities of the virtual world into account. Rather than looking at the past value of physical goods, we need to look at the future value of virtual goods, a process that involves looking externally (rather than internally) to estimate how much someone would pay for certain information or knowledge. If the accounting world cannot help us, we need to look elsewhere. Rather than attempting to value the asset using conventional means, we need to test that asset – or the individual parts that make it up – in a commercial market. If the market is prepared to pay, we have a basis for valuing the virtual.

Exploiting the market for the information

In our experience, there are three fundamental factors that you need to take into account in exploiting the virtual market. These are knowing:

- what you are selling;
- who will be interested in buying it;
- how much they will be prepared to pay.

What are you selling?

This sounds a simple question, but it can often be difficult to answer in practice. In a previous chapter, we noted how the manufacturers have realised that their physical products represent only a part of the 'package' that they are selling: camera-makers are selling memories, car manufacturers status and security, beauticians confidence. This way of thinking applies equally – if not more so – to virtual products. Suppose you decide to set up a company selling information about yourself and your immediate family and friends (it may sound bizarre, but the day this happens cannot be far away). What you would be selling is not information about you and your relations *per se* but, for example, information about how your attitudes, habits and behaviour are influenced when you go shopping, or information about who you tell when you have bought something you like. The customers of your company will (sadly) be interested not in you as an individual but in learning about the ways in which they can influence you. You are therefore selling not yourself so much as a methodology for increasing sales.

Various writers and organisations have tried to codify intellectual capital into different 'taxonomies'. In *Intellectual Capital*, for example, Thomas Stewart divides it into human (the skills needed by employees in order to meet customer needs), structural (market-related information) and customer capital, a model also used by institutions such as the Canadian Imperial Bank of Commerce. In our experience, these taxonomies – or at least the information that creates them – also fall into three categories:

■ *Information relating to internal processes.* This information can be used by the company that develops it to increase efficiency and to identify those physical processes which can be shifted into the virtual world. An example would be an optimised scheduling system. However, the problem with this kind of information is that the people who would be most interested in purchasing it are also the people you would least like to give it to – your competitors. This is because your process-related information would help them to improve the efficiency of their processes, wiping out any competitive advantage that you may have gained. At the same time, however, this information is of much less interest to the kind of organisation to which you would probably be prepared to sell it – companies in other sectors that could gain from your knowledge but not use this gain to compete with you. Process-related information is also rarely transferable between industries and, for this reason, is perhaps the least tradeable of the three categories of information.

■ *Information relating to products.* In contrast, product-related information has a much broader potential and is of interest to competitors and non-competitors alike. It could, for example, be used to add information to other people's products. An example would be a water company that has amassed huge quantities of information on the freshness and purity of its water supply; this information could be used by a manufacturer to design a gadget that people could attach to their domestic water supply and which would warn them if the water became contaminated for any reason. However, the practical difficulty with buying and selling this type of information is that companies are comparatively inexperienced in joint product development and may therefore find it difficult to exploit the more complex (although also more profitable) opportunities that will come from combining one person's physical product with another person's intellectual capital. We believe that this will happen, but we also think that it will take time for a market in this kind of information to develop.

■ *Customer information.* By far the most lucrative market in the short term will come from buying and selling information on customers. The goal of almost all companies at the moment is to 'get closer to their customers', but how can they do this if they lack even the most basic information on who their customers are and how they behave. A holiday company can find out from a utility's customer database who regularly goes on holiday when (they use less gas and electricity); a utility company can find out which people have just had children from a nappy manufacturer and use this information to offer discounts for high-volume usage to attract these customers.

Who is the final consumer for what product?

Closely connected to the question of what your virtual product is, or what it does, is the issue of who will ultimately be buying it.

In the physical world of business, the process by which a manufacturer purchases raw materials, converts them into a product and sells them to an intermediary who sells and distributes them to consumers is a very familiar one. Using assumptions we have built up from decades of operating in this mode, we find it comparatively easy to identify the nature and size of our final market. This is essentially because comparatively little is added to most products post-production: a book, once printed and bound by the publisher, will not be changed by the book store. The sheer flexibility and adaptability of virtual goods such as information means that it is almost inevitable that your customers will change what you sell to them before they then sell it to their customers. In the virtual business world, these changes add value (for example, two companies combining their information on a single set of customers). In the physical world, they only add cost, which is why such changes are likely to proliferate among virtual businesses. All this means that it is difficult to know not only what you are selling, but also who your market is.

How much is your virtual business worth?

As we discussed earlier, attaching a value to your virtual products is complicated by the fact that the concept of 'value' implies something that is comparatively static (or at least static enough for people to exchange good or services on this basis) and sustainable, whereas it is the very nature of virtual assets that they are flexible and renewable. Furthermore, virtual assets, unlike their physical counterparts, cannot be valued by reference to the past. Fundamental to resolving the dilemma that this poses is seeing a virtual asset as something that somebody else – not necessarily you – values. Information, for example, is often most valuable to the people who do not have it, especially since, while it is cheap to distribute, it can be expensive to collect. Organisations that own and exploit information resources are, therefore, more likely to enjoy increasing returns; those that do not, need to acquire similar assets to stay competitive. For the companies without information resources, there are, in theory, two options: they can either develop them internally or buy them from someone else. In practice, however, few companies have the luxury to develop such resources internally. Not only does this process often take time (how long will it take you to build up a picture of how a customer's shopping profile will change over the course of their lives?), but, if the resource you need has already been built up by someone else, you can be confident that your competitors will be trying to buy it, even if you are not. Selling information also makes sense to the company that owns it: having invested to develop the asset in the first place, selling it to a third party enables you to recoup some of your initial outlay. It may also provide the opportunity to explore joint initiatives with the purchasing company, initiatives that would not have been possible to either company independently. The economic pressure, therefore, is mounting from both the supply and demand side of the market to not so much share information but start selling it.

We see embryonic evidence for this already. The Air Miles consortium in the UK brings together a range of companies (banks, retailers, petrol stations and so on) and clearly has the potential to start exploiting the knowledge built up about customer behaviour across all these sectors. Similarly, we see retailers and utility companies combining to launch co-branded cards. Market research companies are launching databases of people's life-style that companies without their own databases can purchase.

Clearly, for these examples – loyalty card consortia and market research companies – exchanging/selling information is their *raison d'être*, but there is no reason why any information-owning company could not be selling its information externally. In our experience, there are still only two factors that you need to take into account in negotiating a price for your virtual assets:

- the investment required by the potential purchaser if they had to recreate for themselves the asset that you are offering to sell to them;
- the opportunity costs (sales and profits) of not having access to your asset.

To that extent, we fall back on the rather unsatisfactory 'let the market decide' approach.

Why bother valuing your virtual assets?

That agreeing a price is still a matter of negotiation is a reflection of the immaturity of this market. The price for goods – physical or virtual – is likely to vary more in an environment when the value of that good is still uncertain; the greater the uncertainty, the greater the volatility in price (Figure 17.1). Thus the price of bread or soap powder does not change much from year to year because its value is well understood. If we were suddenly to discover that a particular brand of soap powder also had a miraculous ability to prevent tooth decay, we would expect the share price of the soap powder to soar (and then perhaps plummet as counterclaims were made by rival manufacturers).

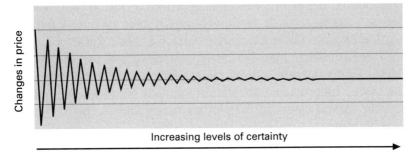

Figure 17.1   Uncertainty causes an increase in price volatility

We should not therefore be surprised that the value of a piece of information is so difficult to gauge. It may be worth a lot one moment and nothing the next; it may be valuable to one company and almost worthless to another. New information is always likely to have a rarity value, but other information will become more of a commodity. If you are an investor specialising in the electronics industry and you hear about a new entrant who has a patent on a machine that will make colour photocopying as cheap and accessible as black and white copying, you may think you should be investing in the company. The level of uncertainty may still be high (can the company convert its design into a workable piece of equipment?), but you may think even the promise of this opportunity is worth some investment. For the first few years, you can expect to see the value of the patent rise and fall, but, as time moves on and the product is launched and then emulated by competitors, the value of your patent settles down.

In an earlier chapter, we discussed an approach called zero-based physical budgeting. Its aim is to make companies think about the virtual side of their business rather than the physical side, not because the latter is not still important but because it blinds people to the potential of the former. Organisations could usefully adopt the same approach to understanding the value of their intellectual capital. Pretend for a moment that you could not sell any of your existing products or services – what information assets could you sell? How long would it take you to do it? How much would it cost? Who would be prepared to buy them, and how much would they be prepared to pay? How much profit would you make?

There are other benefits from this approach. Consider, for example, a clothes manufacturer. It is conventionally able to raise capital for expansion because the stock markets attach a value to the company's overall performance that can then be exchanged for the funding required. That valuation reflects many factors – the company's return on its assets, its projected profitability and so on. If we were able to add to the virtual assets of the clothes manufacturer, there would be three advantages:

- First and most obviously, doing so will add to the value of the company concerned (although, conversely, it could also reveal the extent to which a company is not exploiting its intellectual assets as productively as its competitors).
- Second, by adding to the sum of information that is known about the company, it reduces uncertainty and thus facilitates trade.
- Third, and we think most importantly, it raises intellectual capital to the status of tangible assets, which effectively means that it can (like tangible assets) be sold, mortgaged – and potentially arbitraged.

How would this work in practice for our clothing manufacturer? Let us suppose that the company has been targeting families with young children, offering them a quarterly magazine that – as the company's marketing becomes more sophisticated – is tailored with increasing precision to their individual needs and interests. All told, the magazine (and, through it, the company's products) have built up a loyal following, to the extent that the manufacturer can be confident of a certain level of take-up if it launches new lines (its own or those of other companies) via its magazine. At the moment, this exceptional degree of customer loyalty will not be reflected in the company's balance statement, even though it is more of a guarantee of long-term profitability than are the company's physical assets. Putting a value on the relationships it has built up with its individual customers would allow the company to borrow against the future profit stream that this relationship will help to secure. Equally, it will provide external analysts with more information about the company (and, in this case, perhaps the competitive edge it has over its competitors), which will further facilitate investment (by the company in others, or by others in the company itself).

So far, the fact that the manufacturer has an exceptionally loyal customer base will simply be another factor in helping analysts or investors to estimate the probable return on a particular initiative. The company may, for example, want to raise capital to build a new factory that will produce accessories matching its core clothing range. Accessories may be a completely new area for the company to move into (and as such is a comparatively high-risk market), but the directors are confident that, given its loyal following in the market, the take-up for this new line will be good. In effect, the information the company has on its customers (because it reduces the uncertainty of the new venture and makes success more likely) is translated into funding.

To some extent, this kind of transaction already occurs, although we do not necessarily recognise it as such. Companies use information to hedge bets; they use commercially available credit scoring facilities to ensure that, when they lend money to an individual or organisation, the chances that they will be repaid are good. They use company accounts to find out the prospects of a particular company. However, this approach is mainly confined to those areas in which intellectual capital has been – to a lesser or greater extent – standardised. As *The Financial Times* recently put it:

> The mass production of intellectual property retains strong elements of the craft era. But it is possible to identify... the outline of a new production paradigm... The system [of credit rating] is more important than the work of any individual analyst... the judgement itself is identical and interchangeable.[3]

However, we believe that this process can be taken further. Suppose that our clothes manufacturer wants to do more with its loyal customer base than simply give a few investors and analysts a warm feeling. If the company is effectively using the information it has on its customers (which helps it to maintain and increase loyalty) as some sort of collateral for its own projects, why could it not sell it to other companies as collateral for theirs? If a multinational buys and sells foreign currency in order to hedge the risk on its exposure to fluctuations in the exchange rate, what is to stop a company that is, for example, launching a new product hedging the risk that the product will fail by buying additional information on its customers that will help to make sure that its launch is a success?

In fact, if we look back at the history of business, arbitrage has always tended to become increasingly virtual – it is not just a recent phenomenon. Our early ancestors bartered goods only to replace half of the exchange with money (which was itself perhaps the first virtual entity in business). We still trade in raw materials and other physical commodities, but this business is dwarfed by the amount transacted in terms of stocks, shares and a whole host of increasingly complex financial instruments and their derivatives. Trading in virtual 'goods' makes good commercial sense – there are fewer transaction costs, and there is greater flexibility (the range of ways to hedge a particular risk is constantly increasing).

At the moment, the priority of anyone trying to sell the virtual aspects of their business should be to analyse their potential portfolio, their markets and the worth of what they are selling to these markets in the way in which we have outlined above. Armed with this thinking, you will be able to achieve a better price in your negotiations with potential purchasers. That is present reality. However, as more and more deals are done, it seems likely that more and more 'standard' prices will emerge. Perhaps the traders of the 21st century will be dealing in intellectual rather than financial capital.

Summary

❑ Virtual assets are difficult to value because they are flexible and fast moving, and their worth may fluctuate wildly, even over comparatively short periods of time.

❑ Little progress has been made in coming up with commonly accepted standards of measuring intangible assets, although a variety of methods exist for doing so. Furthermore, the weakness of many of these methods lies in the fact that they are grounded in traditional (physical) accounting, which takes no account of the very different nature of virtual assets.

❑ Yet, as the balance sheet of major corporations increasingly tilts towards intangible assets, the need to resolve this problem is becoming more urgent.

❑ The best, and most practical, way in the short term to estimate and ultimately realise the value of your intangible assets is through negotiations with other companies. Virtual assets are often more valuable to those who do not possess them.

❑ There are three questions which need to be answered before you start negotiating 'virtual' deals:

- What are you selling?
- Who is going to be the ultimate purchaser of it?
- How much is it worth to potential purchasers, in terms of:
  - the costs that they would have to bear if they replicated it;
  - the opportunity costs of not having it now;
  - the certainty, or otherwise, of the benefits of the asset;
  - the extent to which the asset can be used to manage risk.

Notes

1. Annie Brooking and Enrico Motta, 'A Taxonomy of Intellectual Capital and a Methodology for Auditing It'. Paper presented to the 17th Annual National Business Conference, McMaster University, Hamilton, Ontario, Canada, 24–26 January, 1996.
2. John Perry Barlow, 'Everything you know about Intellectual Capital is Wrong', *Wired*, March, 1994.
3. Peter Martin, *Financial Times*, 13 November, 1997.

18 Final Thoughts

Organisations are undergoing a fundamental change, greater than any since the Industrial Revolution. In many areas, the full extent of this change – and the opportunities and threats it poses – is only just starting to become clear. We are like Galileo, holding up our telescope to the sky for the first time and suddenly realising that the universe we are looking at is very different from the one we thought it was.

We have been brought up to think about business as a physical entity, with products we can touch, offices we can visit and people we can talk to. Everything we learn – from life, from business school – teaches us how to manage this physical business. However, the world we are living in now is different. It is a world that is made up of information, a virtual world, in which the information we have on our customers may be more valuable than the physical products we sell to them. It is a world where the knowledge our organisations have gathered about a particular subject, perhaps over many decades of operation, can now be translated into a virtual 'good' that can be bought and sold.

But even more fundamentally, it is a world in which many of the constraints that we habitually accept in business no longer apply. We have gone from a world in which we need a network of geographically dispersed agents in order to sell our goods, or where product development is an expensive and time-consuming process, involving physical prototypes, retooling assembly lines and constant reworking, to a world in which a small company can sell its products to anyone in the world just as easily as a large one, and where changing a product design takes a matter of seconds and costs nothing. We have gone to a new world where new laws are required.

In the first section of this book, we suggested three laws that underpin business in this new world:

- *Information is the currency of this new way of doing business.* While computer technology became commonplace almost a decade ago, the value of the information we have been collecting has only recently started to become apparent, as the costs of holding and processing the information itself have fallen dramatically.
- *Information is an asset in its own right, not a substitute for an asset.* Key to understanding the value of information is the recognition that information is an asset in its own right rather than just a representation of another object. This asset has its own significant benefits: once produced it costs nothing to replicate; it can be sent, literally at the speed of light, around the world to wherever it is required; and, by combining different pieces of information, you can get far more than the value of the individual bits.
- *Information underpins the law of increasing returns.* Converting assets and processes from the physical world to the virtual world enables their value to be multiplied many times. It is the effective exploitation of the virtual within an organisation that enables increasing returns to be made. Leaving assets and processes within the physical world leaves them subject to the law of diminishing returns, a law we know and understand but which can now be overturned. Organisations that recognise the value of the virtual can change the rules of the game, overturn the orthodoxy and become the revolutionaries that will succeed in the 21st century.

The world is full of companies that are beginning to recognise that new laws apply. The virtual world is full of new opportunities – new markets, new ways of marketing, new types of product, new channels to customers, new ways to succeed. However, especially for those companies which do not come to terms with this new environment, this world is also full of new threats. This is a world in which small companies will be able to enter mature markets and, by exploiting the latent virtual potential of these markets, change the rules of engagement. It is a world in which, for example, you could find yourself 'locked out' of certain core markets because one of your rivals has used its intellectual capital to provide a customised service to clients that you cannot better.

The message emerging from this section a simple one: if you do not come to terms with these changes and find ways to exploit the new opportunities they bring, your business will fail. Whatever industry you are in, however big you are, if you are still relying on your physical business, your future is at best uncertain. Your physical business is expensive to run and difficult to change; your physical products are costly to make and sell. The virtual business may be expensive to set up, but its unit costs are tiny, and its products can be changed at the push of a button. A virtual business can use the information it has on its customers to carry out a very precisely targeted mail-shot that will get a high response rate; a physical business sticks a large poster on an advertising hoarding. There is – there will be – no competition.

In Part II, we highlighted four areas in which we perceive the opportunities and threats to be greatest:

- *Research and development.* Many companies continue to perform R&D and design in the physical world with drawings, models and test beds. Many have been converted to computer-aided design and think that is the end of it. The visionaries, however, realise that the whole process can be taken further, that everything can be done in the virtual world and that the laws of the virtual world can be exploited to make it even quicker, cheaper and more effective.
- *Manufacturing.* The old way of improving your manufacturing was to concentrate on improving the physical, reduce the number of processes required, reduce the raw material input and provide a more successful physical object. The visionaries, however, realise that a cheaper, more effective way of improving their manufacturing is to start to think about how to add information to their products. Once the process has been set up, the laws of the virtual world again take over. That intelligence can be replicated again and again at virtually no cost.
- *Distribution.* The 20th-century process for the distribution of goods has, so far, relied on a geographically distributed network of agents. This has been inconvenient for both the organisations wanting to distribute goods and the consumers who wanted to receive them. The visionaries have realised that this has changed. Many goods do not require such a network; moreover, by removing the network, everyone (except the now redundant intermediaries) can benefit.
- *Marketing.* Most of the 20th century has been about mass-marketing to mass-consumers, but we have not had the ability to

develop individual products and to identify which individual consumers would want them. The visionaries have realised that this has changed. It is possible to develop individual products, especially if they reside mainly in the virtual world. Furthermore, it is also possible, given the vast volumes of information that are now captured, to identify who wants what and then to develop individual marketing programs to persuade them to buy.

The pace of change is phenomenal. In the 9 months since we started this book, we have seen automated ticket sales introduced into our local cinemas, on-line broking in stocks and shares taking a significant market share of the USA and our estate agents offering services over the Internet. We have even seen the trustees of Princess Diana's funds considering patenting Princess Diana's likeness. The business battles of the future are moving more and more decisively towards battles in the virtual world. Organisations are rewriting the rule books and changing the rules of their industry at an ever-increasing pace. So how will you compete?

There are no accepted weapons for fighting in this virtual world. There are no formulaic methods for identifying visionaries in your organisation who can spot opportunities and ruthlessly exploit them. The third part of the book discusses some of the methods that are emerging for identifying opportunities, evaluating their potential and exploiting them:

- *Zero-based physical budgeting.* This adapts the principles of zero-based budgeting to identifying opportunities for moving assets and processes from the physical world to the virtual world of information by forcing organisations to think about the minimum of physical processes needed within their industry.
- *Electronic commerce.* This area looks at what is perhaps the most common way in which organisations move a process from the physical to the virtual, by using the Internet for selling their goods and services. Just as with other aspects of the virtual world, the traditional, physically based techniques of sales and marketing will not work, and companies that have simply tried to apply their current processes on the Internet are not succeeding. This chapter describes some of the new techniques that are required to make a success of this new medium.

- *Complexity and computer modelling.* Throughout this book, there has been an emphasis on making use of the wealth of detailed information now available to most of us so that we can take more factors into account when making a decision. This chapter describes some of the tools that can be used to make sense of all this information and its interrelationships.
- *Work–Learn–Share.* Although many organisations acknowledge that the knowledge within their organisation is of immense importance, few have any idea of how to make best use of it. This chapter explains the basic principles of knowledge management and how to maximise the value of the knowledge created within your organisation.
- *Getting the foundations right.* Even a virtual world must have some contact with the physical. At a minimum, the information must reside on a computer-based system. Most organisations, however, approach the task of creating this computer system from the wrong end. Rather than worrying about the aspects of what they want to keep in the virtual world, they worry first about the physical aspects of their computer system and only then about the information they want to store on it. Reversing this approach can bring significant dividends to those organisations that recognise that the key is information, and that by first understanding what is to be stored and manipulated should dictate the physical structures that underpin it rather than vice versa.
- *Selling your virtual assets.* Traditional accounting methods seriously undervalue most companies because they are unable to include the value of a company's information and virtual assets. As more and more of a company's value is represented by these assets, traditional accounting methods are increasingly going to fail to represent the truth worth of a company. The final chapter in this section explores how you can value your virtual assets and the potential advantages in including them within your balance sheet.

This book has been about a new world, a new economics, a new order. We are in the throes of a revolution, a revolution that will bring with it a new set of business winners and losers. The old order will be overthrown. We hope that we have opened your eyes to some of the possibilities that this revolution creates and given you at least some of the weapons required to make sure that you too will succeed in this new, virtual world of information.

Appendix:
Questions to Consider –
a Checklist

The purpose of these questions is to assist you in understanding how well your own organisation is equipped to use information in new ways in order to create a virtual and more profitable future.

THE VIRTUAL R&D DEPARTMENT

1. Which function within your organisation has most radically changed the way in which it works as a result of the information revolution?

2. What lessons can be learnt from its successes and failures?

3. How are these lessons being assimilated and communicated to the rest of the organisation?

4. How does your R&D department access information? How long does it take?

5. Do you have a systematic method for identifying and accessing the most useful sources of information?

6. Is information readily available to your researchers?

7. Does information have to pass through a 'gate-keeper', such as a librarian, before being accessed by your researchers?

8. How accessible is information generated from within the company?

9. What proportion of information is now transmitted in the virtual domain? What proportion of information is still transmitted physically? Why?

10. What experiments or R&D processes could you convert to a digital form? What savings might be achieved?

11. What learning from your current processes can be captured and reused so that you can start to exploit the law of increasing returns?

12. Have you considered working three shifts in three continents? What might the savings be? Would it benefit your clients?

13. How much effort do you expend trying to automate the processes by which you carry out R&D? Have you calculated how much you might be able to save by introducing new automated technology?

14. How up to date is your organisation on the latest computer science techniques that can be applied to the R&D process?

15. How and when are the consumers brought into your R&D process? Would there be any advantage if they were brought in earlier?

16. Could your working designs be provided to your consumers any earlier if they were provided electronically?

17. Which organisation has most developed a virtual R&D function in your industry? What competitive advantages do you perceive that they achieve from this?

18. How far are you from the leader in the industry? How long would it take you to catch up?

19. What similar industries might your industry learn from? What could be adapted from their experience?

20. What plans do you have to move your R&D function from the physical to the virtual domain?

21. How are you planning to exploit the learning from the R&D function throughout your organisation?

EXPLOITING THE VIRTUAL IN YOUR PRODUCT

1. Why do customers really buy your goods and services?

2. What information have you got that might be of interest to your customers?

3. How could you make that information available?

4. How could you help your customers if you had better information?

5. How could you increase sales if the customer had provided the information?

6. What mechanisms exist by which that information might be obtained?

7. Why do your customers buy your product?

8. What is it that they really want to achieve with your product?

9. What information would enable them best to achieve their ambitions?

10. What would be the most effective way of changing your products in order to

incorporate the information your customers want into them?

11. Is it cost-effective to incorporate the information?

VIRTUAL DISTRIBUTION

1. What proportion of your customers do you communicate with directly?

2. How often do you communicate with them?

3. What information do you give them?

4. What information do you get from them?

5. What do you do with the information you receive?

6. If you could communicate directly more often, how would it help?

7. What methods of communication do you use in talking with your customers?

8. What other methods are you considering?

9. What are the functions of your intermediaries?

10. Could the functions of your intermediaries be split off?

11. Could some of the functions be handled by the new technologies that are emerging?

12. Why would your customers prefer to use an intermediary rather than come to you directly?

13. If you are an intermediary, how can you add value to the transaction chain to ensure your survival?

14. What could you do to entice your customers away from their reliance on an intermediary and come to you direct? What additional information could you obtain, or disseminate, if they came to you direct?

15. How is your organisation directly monitoring the development of technologies and methods for communicating directly with the consumer?

16. What alliances has your organisation formed, or is it considering relinquishing, in order that communication with the customer is performed as effectively as possible?

THE ECONOMICS OF DIFFERENCE

1. The first step to mass-customisation is to consider where it might possibly be applied. Compare your products with those of your competitors. Which contains the greater degree of difference?

2. What additional degrees of difference could you incorporate within your product?

3. Even at this early stage, it is also worth considering what the customer might want. Which difference in your product do your customers most value?

4. Which difference do they value the least?

5. Can you order the differences in your current product range by their importance to the customer buying decision?

6. What additional differences do customers ask for?

7. Consider what systems your organisation has to handle mass-customisation information.

8. How do you get information from the customer to customise your products?

9. How do you convert it into a product description?

10. How do you convert the information in the product description into a product?

11. What changes would be required to convert your current processes so that a greater level of mass-customisation could be incorporated within your product?

12. Refer to Figure 10.2. Where does your industry lie in this marketing segmentation?

13. What is the smallest segment of the market that you can differentiate?

14. What information can you track at an individual consumer level?

15. What changes could you make to your marketing mix as a result of individual consumer behaviour?

16. What does your company do to identify individual consumer preferences?

17. What does your company do to identify individual customer requirements?

18. How does your company exploit this information?

ELECTRONIC COMMERCE

1. Does your organisation have an Internet presence?

2. If it does, what marketing strategy has been developed to support sales over the medium?

3. How much of the strategy is a translation or reflection of the marketing strategy that you use to achieve sales in the physical domain?

Estimating the size of the market for your product on the Internet

Using the factors referred to in Chapter 13 it is possible to start to get an idea of the size of the possible population to which you might be able to sell your goods or services.

Let us imagine for example that we are trading fine wines from a famous château in France. An example of the numbers that might be filled in are shown below.

Estimate	Example	Your figure
1. Enter your estimate of the total number of people on the Internet. (Use a value of 30 million if you don't have a more up-to-date estimate)	30,000,000	
2. Enter the percentage of your sales that you expect to make to men under the age of 40	20%	
3. Enter the percentage of the Internet population that you can reach without excessive shipping charges (this might be very small for large objects. It might be 100% if you are distributing software over the Internet). Assume that half the Internet population is in the USA if you don't have a better estimate	10%	
4. Enter the percentage who will not be scared off because they don't trust the Internet. (This number will be close to 100% if you are a reputable company with a good brand name. It will be smaller if you are trying to sell to people who do not know you)	90%	
5. Enter the percentage who don't have to feel and touch the object before they buy it	100%	
6. Multiply these numbers together and you have an approximate size of the total market on the Internet for your product or products	540,000	

For our château selling fine wines, these figures suggest that approximately one-tenth of the total Internet population might be interested in purchasing fine wines over the Internet. The figures would, of course, be considerably higher if you were selling computer hardware or software, and considerably lower if you were selling large hand-crafted goods from your own, unknown retail outlet.

4. Most companies do not have a coherent strategy for the achievement of footfall on the Internet. Does yours?

5. What is your firm's strategy for getting people to visit your site?

6. How does it differ from your traditional marketing strategy?

7. How have you estimated the potential increase in visits from your strategy?

Estimating Footfall		
It is possible to estimate the approximate footfall that your site might receive from each of the methods described above, and therefore get an estimate of the total traffic that your site might receive. The example figures are based on our fictitious château selling fine wines.		
Factor	**Example**	**Your estimate**
1. Enter the size of the total target market that has Internet access	540,000	
2. What percentage do you expect to capture using traditional advertising and communications? *The château does not traditionally advertise except at trade fairs and local celebrations*	0%	
3. What percentage do you expect to come via people searching using search engines? (Use 5% of those making a search if you think your site will feature in the top 100 sites shown in a search, 0.5% if you think it will appear lower down the order) *The château does not know enough about the Internet to be able to ensure that its name will appear high on the Internet searches. It expects that 10% of its target market might make a search about wine, and that half of one per cent of those will then click on its site*	0.5%	
4. What percentage will come from advertising on the Internet? (Use 10% of those making a relevant search) *The château is not prepared to make such an investment at this time*	0%	

Estimating Footfall (cont'd)		
Factor	**Example**	**Your estimate**
5. What percentage (or number) will come from having sites with similar links? *The château was introduced to this concept by a leading French wine publication, which has offered complementary links. This site receives approximately 30,000 visits a year. The château has assumed that 10% of those visits might also visit the château's site*	10%	
6. Multiply the target market by the total of the percentages and/or add together the number of visits that you have calculated	2,700	

Based on these calculations, the château can expect approximately 2,700 visits in a year. An examination of the visitor counters shown on many sites suggests that this figure is slightly above average for a poorly promoted site.

COMPUTER MODELLING AND COMPLEXITY

1. What is it that your company is optimally designed to output? (You can be reasonably confident that it will not be conventional products or services.)

2. How do you make decisions?

3. How often have things turned out differently from the way you expect?

4. How far into the future can you really see? Next year? Next month? Tomorrow?

5. How complex is your pricing structure?

6. How often do you vary prices, and on what basis do you vary them?

7. Do you look at the prices of groups of products across your customer base as a whole? Or do you price individual products for individual customers?

8. How much more money would you make if you used differential pricing?

9. How non-linear is your organisation? Where do these non-linearities reside?

10. Does it take a lot to make your organisational systems change the performance of your business? Can your particular camel's back be broken by just a small straw?

11. Can you predict the impact of even the smallest changes? How much time did you give over in your last planning cycle to following through the complex implications of your actions?

WORK–LEARN–SHARE

---

1. What is the ratio of your company's market value to its physical assets?

2. How does this compare with that of your competitors in the same industry?

3. Can you explain the differences?

4. Before going on to explore what we mean by knowledge and knowledge management, can you specify what techniques your organisation uses to acquire, share and act upon knowledge?

5. What data are collected by your organisation?

6. How are those data converted into information?

7. How is knowledge extracted from that information?

8. Who is the most insightful in your organisation?

9. Most organisations have some form of customer support function. How does yours work? Does it implement any form of knowledge management?

10. What other functions within your organisation would benefit from implementing this sort of model?

11. Do they implement this model of knowledge management or some similar model?

12. What are the main methods of learning that are employed in your organisation?

13. How have these been changed by the information revolution?

14. What steps is your organisation taking to incorporate new methods of learning within the organisation?

15. Who is responsible for managing the learning within your organisation?

16. What access do you have to learning within your organisation?

17. How do you contribute your learning to your organisation? Could it be improved?

To illustrate the difficulty of implementing the 'ownership' strategy of information management, consider, together with a colleague, the following questions.

18. What are the top five pieces of information or knowledge that your organisation possesses? Where are they kept? How are they disseminated?

19. What are the top five pieces of information or knowledge that your organisation should acquire? Who should be given them?

GETTING THE FOUNDATIONS RIGHT

1. What are the major difficulties that you face in your organisation when developing a strategy for the introduction, organisation and exploitation of your information?

2. Does your organisation have an information strategy? If yes, what proportion of the strategy is about information? What proportion should be about information?

3. Does your organisation have information policies? Should it?

4. How much information is used by your organisation each day? How much is lost and wasted?

5. What are the key items of information that your organisation requires? Why?

6. How many of your key information requirements could be met if you better used the information already within your organisation?

7. What method do you use for specifying the requirements for your applications?

8. Does it divide the tasks appropriately between the various skill groups within your organisation?

9. Would the use of the 'ability to' language help to clarify requirements and how they were delivered?

10. What principles do you use for application selection? Do they meet the criteria that are described above?

11. What hardware strategy does your organisation have?

12. What organisational policies does your organisation adopt for information-related matters? On what principles are they based?

13. If your information technology functions are outsourced, how are your competencies in this area being maintained?

Index